A CENTURY OF
MODERN CHINESE
POETRY

Edited by Michelle Yeh,
Zhangbin Li, and Frank Stewart

A CENTURY OF

Modern Chinese Poetry

AN ANTHOLOGY

University of Washington Press *Seattle*

A Century of Modern Chinese Poetry was made possible in part by a grant
from the Nanjing University School of Literature.

Funding was also provided by the Robert B. Heilman Endowment for Books
in the Humanities, established through a generous bequest from the distinguished
scholar who served as chair of the University of Washington English Department
from 1948 to 1971.

Design by Mindy Basinger Hill / Composed in Garamond Premier Pro

UNIVERSITY OF WASHINGTON PRESS
uwapress.uw.edu

LIBRARY OF CONGRESS CATALOGING-IN-PUBLICATION DATA

Names: Yeh, Michelle, 1955– editor. | Li, Zhangbin, 1983– editor. |
    Stewart, Frank, 1946– editor.
Title: A century of modern Chinese poetry : an anthology / edited by Michelle Yeh,
    Zhangbin Li, and Frank Stewart.
Description: Seattle : University of Washington Press, [2023] | Includes bibliographical
    references and index.
Identifiers: LCCN 2022040226 | ISBN 9780295751146 (hardcover ; alk. paper) |
    ISBN 9780295751160 (paperback ; alk. paper) | ISBN 9780295751153 (ebook)
Subjects: LCSH: Chinese poetry—20th century—Translations into English. |
    Chinese poetry—21st century—Translations into English. | LCGFT: Poetry.
Classification: LCC PL2658.E3 C43 2023 | DDC 895.11/508—dc23/eng/20220826
LC record available at https://lccn.loc.gov/2022040226

Contents

The First Flowering of Modern Poetry

The Modernist Movement and Surrealism

The Anti-Sublime and Multiculturalism

New Lyricism and Postmodernist Experiments
The New Millennium 253

Acknowledgments

A work of this nature and this size requires an enormous amount of organization and coordination. We are lucky that throughout the process of putting together the anthology, we have received a great deal of support, cooperation, and goodwill from the poets, the translators, and colleagues.

As the initiator and chief editor of the project, I am extremely grateful to my fellow editors, Zhangbin Li and Frank Stewart. A brilliant scholar, Zhangbin has contributed his expertise on modern Chinese poetry, and his communications with the poets in China have made including their works a smooth process. Over the years, I have had the honor of working with Frank, a wonderful poet and a great editor and translator. Throughout this project, I have sought his advice and learned so much from him not only about translation but also about people skills.

I am also very grateful to all the poets who agreed to have their works represented in this volume. Many of them took the time to provide the texts, translations, and biographical information; answer inquiries; and obtain permissions from publishers or record companies. Without their generosity, this anthology could not exist in its present form. The same must be said of all the translators, who graciously contributed their labor of love, sometimes at short notice, and patiently worked with me throughout the editing process.

I have benefited from many conversations with my former graduate student Kevin Zhichen Dong about the selections. His perspectives helped me come to decisions when I struggled with the pros and cons of possible choices. I am acutely aware that other poets or poems could have been included, but time, space, and obtaining permissions pose unavoidable limits. I hope readers will appreciate what we are able to offer in this volume.

On behalf of all the editors, I'd like to express our profound appreciation to Lorri Hagman, executive director of the University of Washington Press, for her leadership and support from the beginning, and to our copyeditors Elizabeth Gratch and Joeth Zucco for their meticulous work and their patience. It has been a pleasure and honor to work with them and other colleagues at the press.

Finally, I am extremely lucky to focus my career on poetry. Since my high school days, poetry has been my passion, and through all these years, I have never wavered. Of course, I could not have done it without the love and support of my family—my husband, Kwang; my son, Jonathan; and my grandson, Charlie Ocean. I am grateful for all the joy and steadiness they bring into my life.

Michelle Yeh

We thank the following for their permission to reprint these translations:

Joe Allen:
> "One Generation," "Fiction," and "Ghosts Enter the City" by Gu Cheng, from *Sea of Dreams: The Selected Writings of Gu Cheng*, published by New Directions. Reprinted by permission of Joe Allen.

Shiu-Pang Almberg:
> "Mistake" by Zheng Chouyu, from *Frontier Taiwan: An Anthology of Modern Chinese Poetry*, edited by Michelle Yeh and N. G. D. Malmqvist. © Columbia University Press.

John Balcom:
> "Song of Everlasting Sorrow" and "Because of the Wind" by Luo Fu, from *Frontier Taiwan: An Anthology of Modern Chinese Poetry*, edited by Michelle Yeh and N. G. D. Malmqvist. © Columbia University Press.

Steve Bradbury:
> "A Hymn to Hualian" by Hong Hong, from *Frontier Taiwan: An Anthology of Modern Chinese Poetry*, edited by Michelle Yeh and N. G. D. Malmqvist. © Columbia University Press.

Eleanor Goodman:
> "The Flying Coffin" and "Days When I Hide My Corpse in a Box" by Luo Feng, from *Days When I Hide My Corpse in a Cardboard Box: Poems by Lok Fung* (Hong Kong Atlas Series, Zephyr Press, 2018).
>
> "Train," "Drama," and "Middle-Aged Prostitutes" by Zheng Xiaoqiong, from *In the Roar of the Machines: Selected Poems of Zheng Xiaoqiong* (Giramondo Press, 2022).
>
> "Ashes Primer" by Zang Di, from the *Bennington Review* (December 2019).

Eleanor Goodman and Wang Ao:
> "Light the Lamp" by Chen Dongdong, in *Cha: An Asian Literary Journal* issue 14 (July 2011).
>
> "Spinach" by Zang Di, in *PN Review 187* 35, no. 5 (Winter 2009), and reprinted in the Greenmarket Poetry Series (September 2015).

Lloyd Haft:

"On the Ferry" by Zhou Mengdie, from *Frontier Taiwan: An Anthology of Modern Chinese Poetry*, edited by Michelle Yeh and N. G. D. Malmqvist. © Columbia University Press.

"Aloneland" and "Under the Wisdom Tree" by Zhou Mengdie, from *Zhou Mengdie: 41 Poems*, selected and translated by Lloyd Haft, © Azoth Booths Company, Ltd.

Lucas Klein:

"Organization of Distance" and "Untitled 4" from *The Organization of Distance* by Lucas Klein, © Brill.

"Stargazing on Haergai," "Rereading Borges's Poetry," and "Notes on the Mosquito" by Xi Chuan, from *Notes on the Mosquito: Selected Poems by Xi Chuan*, © New Directions Publishing.

Lucas Klein and Clayton Eshleman:

"Landscape above Zero Degrees," from *Endure: Poems of Bei Dao*, © Black Widow Press.

Andrea Lingenfelter:

"Hope" and "Tropical Rain Forest" by Liu Kexiang, from *Frontier Taiwan: An Anthology of Modern Chinese Poetry*, edited by Michelle Yeh and N. G. D. Malmqvist. © Columbia University Press.

"The Submarine's Lament," "New Swan Lake," and "Report on a Child Prostitute" by Zhai Yongming, from *The Changing Room: Selected Poems of Zhai Yongming*, © Chinese University of Hong Kong.

"Thinking about a Czech Film, but I Can't Remember the Title," "Gifts from On High," and "The Evening of My Life Has Come Too Late," from *Ghosts City Sea* by Wang Yin, © Seaweed Salad Editions.

Denis Mair:

"City in Flames," "Dog Barking at the Moon," "Painter's Studio," and "Type B Blood" by Ji Xian, and "Diva" by Ya Xian, from *Frontier Taiwan: An Anthology of Modern Chinese Poetry*, edited by Michelle Yeh and N. G. D. Malmqvist. © Columbia University Press.

Dan Murphy:

"Motherland (or dreams as horses)," "Facing the Ocean, Spring Warms Flowers Open," and "Spring, Ten Haizis" by Haizi, from *Over Autumn Rooftops: Poems by Haizi*. © Host Publications.

Mike O'Connor:

"Spring 1985" by Sun Weimin, from *Frontier Taiwan: An Anthology of*

Modern Chinese Poetry, edited by Michelle Yeh and N. G. D. Malmqvist. © Columbia University Press.

Arthur Sze:

Wen Yiduo, "Perhaps" and "Dead Water," translated by Arthur Sze from *The Silk Dragon: Translations from the Chinese*. © 2001 by Arthur Sze. Reprinted with the permission of The Permissions Company, LLC, on behalf of Copper Canyon Press, coppercanyonpress.org.

Michelle Yeh:

"Jizi of Yanling Hangs Up His Sword" and "Let the Wind Recite" by Yang Mu, from *Frontier Taiwan: An Anthology of Modern Chinese Poetry*, edited by Michelle Yeh and N. G. D. Malmqvist. © Columbia University Press.

MICHELLE YEH

Introduction

Why Modern Chinese Poetry?

The creator of the new composition in the arts
is an outlaw until he is a classic.
GERTRUDE STEIN, *"Composition as Explanation" (1926)*

Why is it necessary to distinguish "modern" from "classical" when it comes to
Chinese poetry? More than a term of periodization, it is an indicator of linguistic
and formal differences. The history of classical Chinese poetry—hereafter Classi-
cal Poetry—goes back to the *Shijing* (also called *Book of Songs*, *Book of Odes*, and
Classic of Poetry), which contains three hundred poems from the eleventh to the
sixth century BCE. With an unbroken history of more than three thousand years,
Classical Poetry has evolved in various forms, each of which dictates specific tonal
and structural patterns. The medium of Classical Poetry is Classical Chinese, a
written language that requires a high level of education and is characterized by
remarkable economy and concision. Although Classical Poetry may appropriate
some vernacular, it is by and large a literary language distinct from spoken Chinese.

Modern Chinese poetry—hereafter Modern Poetry—differs in both aspects.[1]
Modern Poetry does not conform to traditional Chinese poetic forms and is
mostly written in free verse. Occasionally, some structural regularity exists in a
modern poem, such as a fixed number of characters in each line or use of rhymes,
or a poem bears the name of a classical Chinese form, such as *jueju* (quatrain) or
the tune of a *ci* (song lyrics). However, even in these cases, there is no mistake that
the poems are modern because they do not conform to the formal restrictions
of Classical Poetry and the language of the poems is modern vernacular Chinese
rather than Classical Chinese.

Indeed, Modern Poetry in Chinese, in its beginning, is defined by what it is *not*.
A self-proclaimed iconoclast against Classical Poetry, it celebrates its "liberation"

from the shackles of tradition and asserts the freedom to convey individual experiences in the modern world with a living language.[2] We can better appreciate the modernity of Modern Poetry when we understand the significance of poetry in Chinese civilization.

The word *poetry* (*shi*) was originally the abbreviation for the *Shijing*, first referred to as "Three Hundred Poems" (Shi sanbai), attributed to Confucius (551–479 BCE) as the editor. As Chinese poetry evolved, *shi* became a generic term for all rhymed verses as well as the collective name of some poetic subgenres, such as *jueju* and *lüshi* (a poem of eight lines known as Regulated Verse), in distinction from other genres, such as *fu* (rhymed prose) and *ci*. Besides its continuity—arguably the longest in the world—poetry enjoys an especially privileged position in traditional China.

Poetry Matters

Confucius regarded poetry as essential at multiple levels. *The Analects* contains several passages on the subject. For example, the Master says: "Poetry allows one to be stimulated, to observe [the world], to interact with others, and to express discontent. Close at home, it serves one's father; from a distance, it serves the ruler; it broadens one's knowledge of the names of birds and beasts, flora and fauna."[3] For Confucius, poetry was the cornerstone of moral education, a source of knowledge of the natural world, a guide for proper speech and interpersonal relationships, and an appropriate form of expressing negative emotions. Poetry was never treated as belles lettres; it was highly valued as the foundation of the ideal society.

In the second century BCE, Confucianism was adopted as the state ideology under Emperor Wu (156–87 BCE) of the Han dynasty, which lasted from 202 BCE to 220 CE, and the *Shijing* topped the list of canonical texts. The Confucian classics formed the core curriculum at the first academy in China, established in 124 BCE under Emperor Wu. The political role of poetry became prominent when it was incorporated in varying degrees into the civil service examination system from the seventh to the early twentieth centuries.[4] Success on the exams depended on how well one had mastered the Confucian classics and was the only way for men to become officials in the government.

Paradoxically, notwithstanding the fact that poetry was mostly written by and for members of the elite, from princes to scholar-officials, it was also a form of popular art for two reasons. First, despite the low literacy rate among the general population, poetry was widely circulated and transmitted through the ages. Poems were chanted or sung on various occasions, from rituals to entertainment; certain subgenres of Classical Poetry were in fact ballads and popular songs in their times.

Second, poetry was conspicuous in public spaces. It was written in calligraphy, a highly regarded art in its own right, and was often seen on Chinese paintings. The combination of the three sister arts—poetry, calligraphy, and painting—is a tradition that is still strong today. Moreover, verses appeared in many media and forms: written on folding fans and brush holders, inscribed on columns and panels, engraved on rocks and metals, embroidered on items of clothing and accessories, and the list goes on.

In summary, poetry was never a rarefied art or a private pursuit in traditional China. For three thousand years, it was interwoven into the fabric of Chinese society, playing important roles in multiple domains. On the one hand, it was the epitome of high culture created and revered by the literati—elegant, refined, and learned. On the other hand, it was a multimedia form of both public and applied art that was easily accessible and commonly visible in everyday life.

Historical Challenges

MARGINALIZATION OF POETRY

The role and function of poetry changed dramatically as China entered the twentieth century. In the political arena, the Qing dynasty was overthrown in 1911 and replaced by the Republic of China, the first republic in Chinese history. Even before the demise of monarchy, the Qing court abolished the civil service examination system in 1905 in response to the growing demand for political reform. In the educational sphere, as part of the national project of modernization, China adopted the Western model of education, which meant a new system of categorizing, producing, and disseminating knowledge. In the cultural realm, the May Fourth Movement of 1919—often dubbed the Chinese Age of Enlightenment, or Chinese Renaissance—represented a wholesale reform movement to rid China of its "feudal" concepts and practices derived from the Confucian orthodoxy and folk traditions. In their place, such Western ideas as democracy, scientism, and nationalism were introduced and circulated by the modern mass media. Finally, alongside the structural and epistemological transformations, the everyday life of Chinese people changed too, ranging from print culture to entertainment industry, from Western fashion to modern means of transportation, from city-scapes to consumption goods. By the time Modern Poetry arrived on the scene in 1917, China had been undergoing seismic shifts in almost every respect.

As a result of these structural changes, poetry lost its traditional roles and functions. Concomitantly, the prestige it enjoyed in Confucian China was diminished. Poetry was undergoing marginalization.[5] Even within the literary domain, late Qing reformers turned to fiction as an effective tool for social reform and nation building. Whether as a vehicle of education and enlightenment or as a form of entertainment, fiction has replaced poetry as the privileged genre, and its popularity has continued to this day because of its adaptability to cinema and television.

This does not mean Modern Poetry has never taken on a broader, more public role in modern times. During the Sino-Japanese War of 1937–45, poets joined other writers in creating uplifting works to unify Chinese people against the invaders. Patriotic poetry was recited and performed at street corners or posted on billboards and city walls. Another example of its public role is the folk song campaign during the Great Leap Forward in China in the late 1950s, which produced millions of poems by the masses across the country. It was Chairman Mao Zedong who called an end to the movement. A more recent example is the Wenchuan earthquake in May 2008. National mourning of the devastating loss of lives spurred an outpouring of grief and consolation in poetry in both classical and modern styles. However, these examples are all related to specific historical moments and sociopolitical events. The public role of poetry in these instances is the exception rather than the rule. Moreover, few of the populist poems have stood the test of time.

In "The Motive of the Magazine" in the inaugural issue of *Poetry: A Magazine of Verse*, Harriet Monroe, the American poet who founded the avant-garde magazine in Chicago in 1912, makes this plea in defense of poetry:

> Painting, sculpture, music are housed in palaces in the great cities of the world; and every week or two a new periodical is born to speak for one or the other of them, and tenderly nursed at some guardian's expense. Architecture, responding to commercial and social demands, is whipped into shape by the rough and tumble of life and fostered, willy-nilly, by men's material needs. Poetry alone, of all the fine arts, has been left to shift for herself in a world unaware of its immediate and desperate need of her, a world whose great deeds, whose triumphs over matter, over the

wilderness, over racial enmities and distances, require her eve-living voice
to give them glory and glamour.

Poetry has been left to herself and blamed for inefficiency, a process
as unreasonable as blaming the desert for barrenness. This art, like every
other, is not a miracle of direct creation, but a reciprocal relation between
the artist and his public. The people must do their part if the poet is to
tell their story to the future; they must cultivate and irrigate the soil if the
desert is to blossom as the rose.[6]

I have quoted the passage at length because it is equally applicable to Chinese
Modern Poetry. Clearly, the marginalization of poetry was not unique to China.
In the United States in the 1910s, poetry also experienced declining public respect
and support because it was perceived as unpractical and ineffective in meeting
social and economic needs. The Chinese case was even more daunting because
poetry's "fall from grace" was more precipitous than its American counterpart,
given its prestige and importance in traditional China. Monroe's image of cul-
tivating the desert so flowers can grow also applies to the historical conditions
of Chinese Modern Poetry as it faces a twofold challenge: besides the structural
changes that resulted in the marginalization of poetry, Modern Poetry must build
a community of readers who were—and probably still are—better educated in,
and more familiar with, Classical Poetry, to which we now turn.

"FETISHIZATION" OF CLASSICAL POETRY

Chinese people rightly take pride in their poetic tradition. With its impressive
longevity and beauty, Classical Poetry is at the core of the identity of cultural
China. Not only has it been influential in East Asia, where, traditionally, Classical
Chinese was the lingua franca, but, through translation in modern times, it has
become well-known to the world and has inspired generations of Western poets,
such as the Imagists and the Beat Generation.

At a deeper level, Classical Poetry has helped shape the Chinese language;
an analogous case would be the relation between Shakespeare and modern-day
English. Famous verses from Classical Poetry have become idiomatic expressions
and are extensively and deeply "sedimented" in the Chinese language. Native
speakers use such expressions liberally in formal and informal speech and writing
even if they may not be aware of their origins. To give two examples, most Chinese
people today would have difficulty understanding the ancient *Shijing* without

modern annotations, but they can readily quote the first lines of the opening poem "A demure girl is a good mate for a gentleman" or these verses expressing longing from Poem number 72 of the same collection: "One day not seeing you / feels like three autumns."

A profound ramification of the sedimentation of Classical Poetry in the Chinese language is that the aesthetic paradigm embodied therein is ingrained in Chinese people's perception and expectations of poetry. When it comes to poetry, native speakers, whether they are highly educated or not, knowingly or unwittingly, tend to apply Classical Poetry as the standard-bearer or the sole criterion for the art. One consequence is that Modern Poetry is found wanting in aesthetic pleasure, especially with regard to musicality. Indeed, rhymes and tonal patterns are two of the most recognizable features of Classical Poetry; they make it easier to memorize a poem and give it singsong qualities. As the old Chinese saying goes: "No rhyme, no poetry." Even for Lu Xun (1881–1936), who is best known for his modern stories and essays but is also the author of the first collection of Chinese prose poems, the biggest disadvantage of Modern Poetry was its lack of rhythmic patterns: "Without rhythm and rhyme, it cannot be sung. Unsingable, it cannot be remembered. Hard to remember, it cannot squeeze out old poetry from people's minds and take its place."[7]

Thus, we can imagine the puzzlement Chinese readers must have felt when they first encountered Modern Poetry because it was incongruous with the long-established norm of poetry in almost every way. Since its inception, the "foreignness" of Modern Poetry has generated much skepticism. Is it poetry when it sounds like plain speech? Is it poetry when it looks no different from prose? Is it poetry when it doesn't rhyme? Is it poetry when it doesn't have traditionally "poetic" images? These questions all stem from the self-identity of Modern Poetry as defiantly different from Classical Poetry, and they express doubt about the raison d'être of Modern Poetry: Is it poetry? Is it *Chinese* poetry? These doubts have underscored many critiques, debates, and controversies in the century-long history of Modern Poetry. Ironically, even as it has become more familiarized and naturalized for general readers, often it is scholars with expert knowledge of Classical Poetry who have a harder time accepting and appreciating Modern Poetry.

THE PARADOX OF READERSHIP

Since the early twentieth century, literacy among the general population has risen markedly as education becomes more widespread. In theory, the readership of

Modern Poetry should grow exponentially since anyone with a basic education can read modern vernacular Chinese. Paradoxically, the expansion of the reading population also means a "dilution" of readership for Modern Poetry. Unlike Classical Poetry in traditional China, which enjoyed a community of well-educated readers with the same cultural competency and hermeneutic horizons grounded in Chinese classics, Modern Poetry no longer has that luxury. The situation is compounded by the reverence for, or "fetishization" of, Classical Poetry, on the one hand, and the highly experimental nature of Modern Poetry, on the other. In Taiwan the legitimacy of Modern Poetry was questioned well into the 1960s. In mainland China, for decades the most widely read poetry was that of Chairman Mao, who, despite his effort to encourage poets to write Modern Poetry, only wrote in classical forms. How to cultivate a new community of readers has been another challenge facing modern poets.

Cultural Contributions of Modern Poetry

Having lost its traditional roles and prestige, in what sense does Modern Poetry still matter? In my view, the contribution of Modern Poetry is twofold: cultural and literary. The first speaks to its role as a cultural vanguard; the second is demonstrated by the renewal of the Chinese poetic tradition that it has brought about.

MODERN POETRY AS VANGUARD

Modern Poetry not only responded but also contributed to the epochal changes it faced by challenging the most revered form of writing in Chinese civilization. Born in 1917, Modern Poetry was a harbinger of the May Fourth Movement of 1919. The call for revolutionizing Chinese poetry and its uncompromising emphasis on modernity were consistent with, and an integral part of, the wholesale reform represented by the cultural movement. Modern Poetry also played a key role in introducing world literature—authors, works, and movements—into China in the 1910s–1930s, ranging from poets such as Baudelaire, Walt Whitman, Paul Valéry, Rabindranath Tagore, and T. S. Eliot and movements such as Romanticism, Symbolism, and Imagism, to give just a few examples.

In Taiwan from the early 1950s to the mid-1960s, it was the poets who led the Modernist movement before fiction writers and dramatists embraced it. In the conservative and repressive atmosphere under the Nationalist Party (Kuomintang;

KMT) regime, it was the poets—often creating alongside avant-garde painters—who carved out a space with their ingenuity in which they engaged in a wide range of experiments and ushered in a golden age in the history of Modern Poetry in Taiwan.

Yet another example of poetry's role as a vanguard is the underground poetry in mainland China. During the Cultural Revolution (1966–76), underground poetry popped up in many parts of China. Even under extremely dangerous conditions, many young men and women, who were dislocated from their homes in urban areas and "sent down" to the countryside as "educated youth," turned to poetry as an outlet for their creativity and angst, aspirations and disillusionment. Compared to other genres of writing, poetry was typically short and therefore easy to memorize and transmit. Much of the underground poetry was hand copied and circulated widely among the uprooted youths. When China reopened its doors and witnessed a "thaw" on the cultural scene in the late 1970s and early 1980s, it was underground poetry that led the way in rejecting the orthodoxy and creating a renaissance that went beyond literature to include fine art, film, philosophy, historiography, and other fields.

TRANSLATED MODERNITY

Shocked and humiliated by a series of military defeats by Western powers, the Qing court recognized early on the importance of translation as a means to modernize and strengthen China by bringing in new knowledge. The first modern translation bureau was established in 1862. In the early 1870s, China started sending groups of youngsters overseas to study. The numbers went up dramatically in the period from 1909 to 1929, when the Boxer Indemnity Scholarship Program, in the wake of the disastrous Boxer Rebellion against foreign powers in China in 1900, sponsored approximately thirteen hundred Chinese students to Britain, France, Germany, Japan, and the United States. Many returned to China to become leaders in various fields.

Similarly for Modern Poetry, the impact of translation has been profound and lasting. To quote Ezra Pound: "Translation is likewise good training, if you find that your original matter 'wobbles' when you try to rewrite it. The meaning of the poem to be translated cannot 'wobble.'"[8] These words aptly describe the fertile symbiosis between translation and creative writing throughout the history of Chinese Modern Poetry. In reading and translating foreign texts, poets not only have benefited from new images and ideas but also have been inspired to coin new words and expressions, craft new images and figures of speech, and create new syntactic structures in Chinese.

An early example of the importance of translation is Hu Shi (1891–1962), the "father of modern Chinese poetry." While studying in the United States, he took classes in English poetry and was especially drawn to Shakespeare and Robert Browning. According to Hu's own account, his growth as a poet came from the experience of translating English poetry into Chinese. He singled out one poem as particularly formative: "Over the Roofs" by the American poet Sarah Teasdale (1884–1933), which appeared in *Poetry* in March 1914:

I said, "I have shut my heart
As one shuts an open door,
That Love may starve therein
And trouble me no more."

But over the roofs there came
The wet new wind of May,
And a tune blew up from the curb
Where the street-pianos play.

My room was white with the sun
And Love cried out to me,
"I am strong, I will break your heart
Unless you set me free."[9]

Neither the original poem nor Hu's translation comes across as remarkable today. In its time, however, "Over the Roofs" was well received. It may have inspired the Chinese poet in several ways. First, the colloquial language reinforces the last of Hu's "Eight Don'ts" for Modern Poetry: "Do not avoid colloquial words and expressions."[10] Although personification and dramatization are not uncommon in Classical Poetry, the dialogue between the speaker and personified Love as impatient and eager to break out of the heart is novel. The bold and explicit description clearly distinguishes the poem from Chinese Classical Poetry, in which longing for love is typically expressed in a wistful tone and veiled in such familiar tropes as spring breeze and mandarin ducks.

Finally, and perhaps most important, the syntax of the original poem is preserved in Hu's translation. Each stanza is in fact a complete sentence; the conjunctions *as*, *and*, and *but* are repeatedly used to move the sentences along. In contrast to Classical Poetry, the syntactic expansiveness and complexity seen here was to become a common feature of Modern Poetry as it developed over the next hundred years.

In retrospect, Hu Shi had the foresight in crediting the translation of "Over the Rooftops" as ushering in a "new epoch in New Poetry." Before 1917 Western poetry was usually translated into Classical Chinese. With the rise of Modern Poetry, translators began to adopt modern vernacular Chinese, which has been the norm ever since. A translator of many genres of literature, Xu Zhimo (1897–1931) emphasized the importance of translation when he posted a call in 1924 for submissions of translated poetry in the *Fiction Monthly*, which he edited. For him, translation was a means of exploring "new possibilities of refined thoughts and measured cadence," the "elasticity and resilience" of the "newly discovered tool of expression" after the liberation of the Chinese language.[11] In scope and impact, the translations of world literature into modern Chinese may be compared to the translations of Buddhist sutras in medieval China; both have played a transformative role in the evolution of Chinese.

In sum, Modern Poetry draws on a wide range of literary and cultural resources. In addition to those indigenous to the Chinese tradition, countless ideas, approaches, and styles have come from abroad. As the biographical notes in this anthology show, many poets have studied or lived abroad for extended periods of time; more have studied foreign languages and have varying degrees of proficiency. Unlike classical poets, many modern poets are also prolific translators.

REMAKING TRADITION

Poetic Form

Liberation is a word that has often been used by proponents to describe Modern Poetry. Hu Shi spoke of the "great liberation" in poetic form, Xu Zhimo of the liberation of language. The spirit of freedom has led to countless innovations and successes. Without the restrictions of traditional forms, modern poets have expressed themselves in free verse, prose poetry, concrete poetry, forms borrowed from other traditions such as the sonnet and haiku, and forms of their own creation.

The organic relation between form and content is a modern concept that many poets advocate and practice. To give a few examples: the opening stanza of Bai Qiu's poem "The Wanderer" uses the sharp decrease in the length of the line to suggest the solitude of a small tree standing on the horizon, which is then juxtaposed with the wanderer in the next two stanzas. The tree's gaze at distant clouds and the wanderer's gaze toward the east connote hope and longing. Yang Mu's "Tale (in the meter of *Metamorphosis II* by Philip Glass)" recounts an unforgettable love through such devices as imagistic and syntactic repetitions, circular structure (of beginning and concluding the poem with the same words), and open ending. The meandering syntax and haunting rhythm create the same effect as the minimalist piano composition in the poem's subtitle. Finally, Chen Li's "War Symphony" gives a portrait of war from glory to fierce fighting on the battlefield to silent graves. The poem is a unique Concrete poem, but it goes beyond typical Concrete Poetry in its ingenious combination of visual effects (of the four Chinese characters and the typography) with aural suggestiveness (derived from the sounds of the characters and the tripartite structure of a symphony). At the opposite end of formal experiments, prose poetry is deceptively simple, with its narrative frame, subdued tone, and prosaic language, whether it is the silent tribute to courage and sacrifice in Lu Xun's "Autumn Night," the alienation of a middle-aged city dweller in Shang Qin's "Electric Lock," or the self-deprecating reflection on desire and vanity in Yinni's "Earth God and Poetry."

Modern Poetry displays all modes of writing: lyrical, narrative, and dramatic. Dramatic monologue stands out as a distinct achievement, with personae that range from historical figures and fictional characters to animate and inanimate things. The great conqueror and unifier of China, the first emperor of the Qin dynasty is destroyed in Wen Yiduo's eponymous poem by his ambition and finds himself in the company of a hedgehog and a python in his afterlife. The contrast between the abject scene and his well-known pursuit of eternal life is ironic and poignant. In "Jizi of Yanling Hangs Up His Sword" by Yang Mu, Prince Jizi fulfills his unspoken promise by leaving his precious sword by the grave of the Lord of Xu, but his sorrow comes from a deeper source: the degeneration of Confucianism into empty rhetoric and obsequiousness to power. In Zhu Zhu's "South-of-Yangzi, a Republic," Liu Rushi, the legendary courtesan and loyalist at the end of the Ming dynasty, dons a scarlet coat with a white fur collar to review the troops guarding the city against the invading Manchus. Among other personae appearing in this anthology are a defiant old crow, a heavenly dog that devours the cosmos, an abandoned woman, an old and carefree tree, and a potted plant.

Poetic Language

It is a myth that because Modern Poetry is written in the vernacular and adopts new models from other traditions, it has little to do with Classical Poetry and Chinese classics. Nothing could be farther from the truth. As noted, Classical Poetry is deeply "sedimented" in spoken and written Chinese. The modern language contains numerous idioms and expressions not only from Classical Poetry but also from ancient philosophical texts, classic novels and prose, and historical records. Despite its iconoclastic claim and avant-garde aspirations, Modern Poetry is inextricable from traditional Chinese literature and culture. Intertextuality associated with countless classical images, allusions, motifs, and expressions resonates and adds nuance and depth to Modern Poetry. For example, Chang Yao's "A Field of Fragrant Grass" opens with these lines: "We have agreed not to touch on the past that hurts, / We will only do small talks, only view the fragrant grass."

The scenario is the reunion of two friends, who agree that they won't talk about the past. The juxtaposition of these lines highlights a pair of contrasts: one in time (the emotionally charged memory versus the present moment), another in significance (the past that still weighs on their hearts versus the pleasant sight of green grass and the small talks). In agreeing to focus on the grass to avoid talking about past hurts, the poem implies just how deep the pain is. The idea is reinforced with the echoes of two classical poems: Du Fu's (712–70) "Presented to Retired Gentleman Wei the Eighth," probably written in the spring of 759, and Wang Wei's (701–61) "Seeing a Friend Off in the Mountains," written in retirement. Du's poem is also about a reunion of friends. The two men have not seen each other for twenty years. Remembering mutual friends, they are shocked and saddened that half of them are no longer alive. In the other poem, Wang Wei asks the departing friend if he will return when green grass grows again next spring. The image of spring grass is itself an allusion to an older poem, "Summoning the Recluse" in the *Chuci* (*Songs of the South*), dated the second century BCE. Illustrating the above-mentioned "sedimentation" of Classical Poetry in modern Chinese, the multiple layers of intertextuality make "A Field of Fragrant Grass" more affective and powerful but no less modern and innovative.

Besides drawing on the classical legacy, Modern Poetry also uses numerous loanwords, transliterated foreign words, and even words in foreign languages, as a result of extensive exposure to other cultures, whether directly or as mediated by translation. Thus, Modern Poetry displays a wide spectrum of linguistic registers, ranging from the classically flavored to the exotic, from the formal to the colloquial and slangy. Generally speaking, the language of Modern Poetry in mainland China tends to be more colloquial, while that in Taiwan comes across as more literary, sometimes with a classical flair. This is the result of historical development under different social, political, and cultural conditions. What is important is that a century of continuous effort has developed a language that is natural, expressive, and malleable.

By the same token, Modern Poetry also boasts an enlarged repertoire of images, symbols, and allusions because of the combined resources that are traditional and modern, native and foreign. Modern poets are as comfortable citing Rilke, T. S. Eliot, and Tsvetaeva as Tao Yuanming (365–421), Li Shangyin (ca. 813–ca. 858), and Su Shi (1037–1101). While classical Chinese images are often used, Modern Poetry does not shy away from those that are traditionally considered "unpoetic"—the ugly, the absurd, and the grotesque. To cite a few examples from this anthology: the poet is compared to a fly crawling in a garbage can in Wen Yiduo's "Confession"; the poet's long skinny body evokes that of the crucified Jesus in Ji Xian's "Type B Blood"; the cat that visits the speaker every night after his girlfriend has left him turns out to be invisible in Shang Qin's "The Cat That Enters through the Wall"; the "nameless umbilical cord" hangs over a gravestone in Ying Peian's "On the Operating Table"; the crowded bus that races on Hong Kong highways in Luo Feng's poem is a "flying coffin"; ghosts go for a swim and blow on "weeping bottles of wine" in Gu Cheng's "Ghosts Enter the City." These images are used not for novelty's sake; they represent new experiences in the modern world and new conceptualizations of poetry.

Modern Poetry and Song

The *Shijing* is a collection of songs in three categories: folk songs from various states, songs composed by aristocrats, and songs performed at sacrificial rituals honoring royal ancestors. Throughout its long history, Classical Poetry was chanted or sung. Even when the original music is lost, such as in the case of *ci*, classical poems have singsong qualities because of their use of rhymes and other sound patterns. In contrast, Modern Poetry for the most part does not use rhymes but relies on the inherent rhythm and cadence of natural speech to convey a mood or enhance an idea. In theory, every modern poem has its own musicality, its own rhythm and intonation.

However, this does not mean the connection between poetry and song in Classical Poetry is completely lost in modern times. As mentioned earlier, Classical Poetry is either chanted or sung even though most of the music has not been preserved. Poems that are originally songs include all the works in the *Shijing*, ancient ballads known as Music Bureau (Yuefu), the *ci* lyrics, and the *qu* (aria) in Yuan drama. Some poems in the other subgenres are also singable. In general, Classical Poetry is set either to existing tunes or to new tunes.

In contrast, the vast majority of modern poets do not think of their works as songs. In fact, there is some tension between poetry and song. This is most evident in Modern Poetry that subscribes to the Modernist ethos, which dwells on the alienation and absurdity of the human condition and sees the individual as pitted against the world. If poetry is the art of the few, song is entertainment for the masses. If poetry is upheld as a spiritual pursuit to dedicate oneself to, song is closely associated with commercialism and economic gain. Ji Xian (1913–2013), who led the Modernist movement in Taiwan in the 1950s, was adamant about decoupling poetry from song. For him the modern poem should be intellectual and free of sentimentality, qualities uncharacteristic of song lyrics. Practically speaking, the dense imagery, syntactical complexity, and semantic ambiguity of many modern poems are diametrically opposed to song lyrics, which, as a rule, use a regular structure, end rhymes, and words that are intelligible upon hearing.

The distinction between elite art and popular art, between transcendence and accessibility, is found not only in Modernism. It is the attitude of many poets throughout the century-long history of Modern Poetry. However, modern poems have, in fact, been set to music; they can be divided into two types: art songs (based on the model of German *Kunstlieder*) and popular songs (including contemporary folk songs). One of the earliest examples is "How Can I Not Miss Her," a poem written by Liu Bannong (1891–1934) in 1920 while he was studying in London. It became a classic art song composed by the linguist Yuen Ren Chao (1892–1992) in 1926.

In the mid- and late 1970s, the Campus Folk Song movement (Xiaoyuan Minge yundong) created a cultural phenomenon in Taiwan, and it spread to mainland China in the 1980s and 1990s. Born on college campuses, the movement sought to create folk songs that would be both contemporary and "Chinese." It coincided with the critique of the excessive Westernization of Modern Poetry and the effort to reflect native reality at the time. Strumming a guitar, those young singer-songwriters were inspired by the folk revival in the United States in the 1960s. For the lyrics, they often turned to the works of contemporary poets, such as Yu Guangzhong (1928–2017) and Zheng Chouyu (b. 1933). In addition, works from the May Fourth era were rediscovered. The poem "Hope" by Hu Shi was set to music under a new title, "Orchid Leaves." Many poems by Xu Zhimo were also turned into songs. Hu's "Orchid Leaves" and Xu Zhimo's "By Chance" and "Second Farewell to Cambridge" have become beloved classics.

The collaboration between poetry and song popularized by the Campus Folk Song movement has remained strong to this day. While songwriters frequently adapt modern poems to music, some poets also write song lyrics. Most notably, Xia Yu (Hsia Yü, b. 1956) writes lyrics under the penname Li Gedi. One of her biggest hits is "I am ugly, but I am gentle," sung by Zhao Chuan (b. 1961). Chen Kehua (b. 1961) is another prolific lyricist. "The Sky of Taipei," his best-known work, has been used as the signature song of the cosmopolitan city. It is interesting that earlier in her career, Xia Yu made a clear distinction between her poetry and her song lyrics in the Modernist mode: she wrote lyrics to make a living. However, in recent years, she has published a collection of her song lyrics as a companion to her book of poetry.

In the tradition of folk songs as social commentaries, Zhou Yunpeng (b. 1970), a poet, songwriter, singer, and writer of prose and fiction from mainland China, is best known for his "Children of China," which was released in 2007. The folk song mourns the suffering of children in a society that fails to protect them from natural disasters, parents' drug addiction, AIDS that their parents contracted from selling blood plasma, and a corrupt bureaucracy behind the social ills. It ends with these heartrending lines:

> Don't become the children of Chinese people
> When driven by hunger, they will eat you
> They aren't even like sheep in the wild
> Whose eyes grow fierce to protect their lambs[12]

Music is an effective way to introduce the public to Modern Poetry. Through art songs, pop songs, and new folk songs, many people who are unfamiliar with or not interested in Modern Poetry become readers and develop an appreciation for it. Another example of song as a good way to popularize poetry is "Slowness of the Past" by Mu Xin (1927–2011). Liu Huyi, a pop singer, songwriter, and keyboardist, turned the poem into a song and performed it for the first time on January 16, 2015. The song was well received and won an award on the TV show "Sing My Song." A month later, the song appeared in the annual national Spring Festival Gala, the most coveted show to be invited to for singers in China. It was sung by the famous singer-songwriter Liu Huan and accompanied by the internationally acclaimed pianist Lang Lang. Although Mu Xin's poetry had been published in China and Taiwan earlier, it was through these and subsequent performances of

"Slowness of the Past" that Mu Xin has become known to millions of people. His complete works in sixteen volumes, including poetry, fiction, and literary memoirs, were published in Shanghai in 2020.

While poetry and song are two cultural products whose originary impulse, intent, and creative process may be quite different, history has shown occasional crossovers and blurring of the line between songwriters and poets. Two shining examples familiar to Chinese poets and songwriters are Leonard Cohen, the Canadian poet, singer, and songwriter, and Bob Dylan, the American singer-songwriter and Nobel laureate of 2016. The Nobel Prize Committee identified the influence of "modernism and the beatnik generation" on Dylan and praised him "for having created new poetic expressions within the great American song tradition."[13]

It is not surprising that some Chinese songwriters have been lauded as poets for lyrics they've written that are profound, moving, and beautiful. I agree. This anthology is graced by three talented and influential lyricists. Luo Dayou (b. 1954) writes in a wide range of styles: folk, rock, and pop. His lyrics span the spectrum from nostalgic ballads ("Childhood") to moving love songs ("Roiling Red Dust") to social and political critiques ("The Orphan of Asia"). If Luo pioneered rock and roll in Taiwan in the 1970s, then Cui Jian (b. 1961) is the "father of rock and roll" in mainland China in the 1980s. In the liberal atmosphere of the post-Mao era, he burst on the scene with the song "Nothing to My Name" in 1986. With defiant and satiric lyrics, he has remained the most powerful voice of the "Angry Generation." Cui's third album, *Eggs under the Red Flag*, was released in August 1994; it was mysteriously pulled out of circulation a month later. At the other end of the spectrum, Fang Wenshan (b. 1969) has almost single-handedly created the phenomenon of "Chinese style" (Zhongguo feng) in pop music by writing lyrics that are—in language, imagery, and mood—evocative of the elegance, subtlety, and beauty of Classical Poetry, especially the *ci*. "Blue-and-White Porcelain" remains the iconic example. Set to the original music of Jay Chow (b. 1979), Fang's lyrics have received numerous accolades in the Chinese-speaking world.

Modern Poetry is a monumental milestone in the Chinese poetic tradition. It has created something that is truly new and unprecedented. Over the course of a century, it has overcome historical, aesthetic, and linguistic challenges; risen above criticisms and controversies; endured wars, massive exodus, and social upheavals; and survived censorship and political persecutions. It has produced many talented poets and fine works and rightly takes its place in the ranks of world literature.

While Modern Poetry started out in opposition to Classical Poetry, freedom from tradition does not mean severance from it. It is a false dichotomy to define tradition and modernity as diametrically opposed because it is based on the misconception that tradition is static and does not change over time. To describe the dynamic nature of the living tradition of Chinese poetry, I prefer to use the word *transplantation*.

I am fully aware of the controversy surrounding the word. Ji Xian, who founded the *Modern Poetry Quarterly* in 1953 and the Modernist School in 1956, announced in his manifesto that Modern Poetry was the outcome of "horizontal transplantation" rather than "vertical inheritance."[14] Namely, Modern Poetry looked to avant-garde poetry in the West, not to the native tradition, as the model. Like the pioneers in the 1910s and 1920s, Ji Xian exaggerated the difference between tradition and modernity as total and absolute in order to make a case for bold experimentation. However, *transplantation* does provide an apt metaphor for the continuous, "organic" remaking of tradition with new elements.

This brief overview shows that Modern Poetry has enriched and expanded the Chinese tradition with abundant energy and imagination. Taken as a whole, Modern Poetry represents Chinese experiences in the modern world and embodies ideas, affects, and worldviews derived from those experiences. As a young transplant, it has taken a century to be acclimated and naturalized in Chinese soil.

In my view, the cycle of foreignization and naturalization defines the logic of literary history. Literature, like language, never stands still. When something new appears to challenge the mainstream or status quo, it is often met with skepticism and rejection. Over time it is naturalized, maybe even canonized, and, in turn, challenged by the next new thing that comes along. We can see this in the succession of movements and styles throughout history, not only in literature but in art as well, whether it is Romanticism followed by Symbolism and Modernism in poetry or Impressionism by Fauvism and Expressionism in painting.

Naturalization and canonization are achieved through education and other forms of institutionalization. Modern Poetry in Chinese has found its way into textbooks for elementary and secondary schools since the 1980s. Although relatively small in number, the poems expose young people to the genre at an early age. Besides its inclusion in the curricula, Modern Poetry has established itself as an academic discipline and an area of scholarly research in mainland China, Hong Kong, and Taiwan. Courses and writing workshops are offered in colleges and graduate schools; numerous book-length studies, anthologies, and journal articles on the subject are published; national awards are handed out and international poetry festivals organized.

Modern Poetry is becoming more and more visible in public space in multimedia. It is published in newspapers and magazines. It is adapted not only to music but also to other art forms, such as dance, drama, video, and film. Like Classical Poetry, Modern Poetry is inscribed in scenic spots and posted on buses; it is quoted on paintings, bookmarks, throw pillows, and other items in everyday life. Last but not least, poetry has gone digital. From Bulletin Board System (BBS) and blog in the 1990s to Facebook, Instagram, Line, WeChat, and TikTok today, these platforms have facilitated the writing, reading, performance, and appreciation of poetry. They have also enabled poets to engage in new modes of creation, such as interactive poetry, hypertexts, and video poems. Available 24/7 and transcending geographical boundaries, the internet provides a fertile ground and has played a key role in bringing about a golden age in the history of Modern Poetry.

Liberated from the restrictions and conventions of Classical Poetry, Modern Poetry started out with a clean slate, a blank canvas, on which to freely create. Besides countless innovations in what and how to write, it has advanced discussions of the fundamentals of poetry: "What is poetry?" "To whom does poetry speak?" "Why poetry?" After a century of theory and practice, the new paradigm that is Modern Poetry has won its place in history alongside Classical Poetry. Just as Classical Poetry has shaped how Chinese people speak and write, Modern Poetry is gradually finding its way into the spoken and written language. Today no one would question its validity as a major genre of Chinese literature and a legitimate representative of Chinese poetry in the twenty-first century. Neither competing with nor imitating Classical Poetry, Modern Poetry is always already part of tradition.[15]

Notes

1. In this introduction, I use the English terms *Classical Poetry* and *Modern Poetry* for economy's sake. When Modern Poetry first appeared, it was called New Poetry (Xinshi), or Vernacular Poetry (Baihuashi), in contradistinction from Classical Poetry (Gudianshi), or Old Poetry (Jiushi). Since the 1960s, it has been customary in Taiwan and Hong Kong to use *Modern Poetry* (Xiandaishi), while *New Poetry* continues to be the standard term in mainland China.

2. For a discussion of the differences between Classical and Modern Poetry, see my book *Modern Chinese Poetry: Theory and Practice since 1917* (New Haven, CT: Yale University Press, 1991), esp. chap. 1, "A New Orientation to Poetry: The Transition from Traditional to Modern," 5–28.

3. From "Yang Huo Chapter" in *The Analects*. Another key passage is from the chapter on "Annotating Canonical Texts" in the *Book of Rites*, also a Confucian classic: "Gentleness and kindness, [such is] poetry as edification." All translations are mine unless otherwise noted.

4. The system varied somewhat in contents from dynasty to dynasty. For example, poetry was removed from the exams in 1370 until 1756, when it was reintroduced. See Benjamin A. Elman, *Civil Examinations and Meritocracy in Late Imperial China* (Cambridge: Harvard University Press, 2013), 3. However, this does not change the fact that poetry was a crucial part of foundational education for all scholars; moreover, it was fully integrated into their political, social, and cultural praxis.

5. Classical Poetry in the early twentieth century did not escape the fate of marginalization either. Shengqing Wu analyzes the cognitive and representational crisis faced by poets in classical styles and how they held on to poetry as a way to preserve order and harmony. See *Modern Archaics: Continuity and Innovation in the Chinese Lyric Tradition, 1900–1937* (Cambridge: Harvard University Asia Center, 2013), 113, 116.

6. *Poetry: A Magazine of Verse* 1, no. 1 (October 1921): 26–27.

7. "Letter to Dou Yinfu," dated November 1, 1934. See Lu Xun, *Complete Works of Lu Xun*, 12 vols. (Beijing: Renmin wenxue, 1981), 12:556.

8. Ezra Pound, "A Retrospect," in *Prose Keys to Modern Poetry*, ed. Karl Shapiro (New York: Harper & Row, 1962), 108.

9. *Poetry: A Magazine of Verse* 3, no. 6 (March 1914): 200.

10. Originally published in *New Youth* (*Xin qingnian*) 2, no. 5 (January 1917), collected in *Poetic Commentaries by Hu Shi* (*Hu Shi shihua*), ed. Wu Benxing and Li Xinghua (Chengdu, Sichuan: Sichuan wenyi chubanshe, 1991), 145.

11. *Fiction Monthly* 15, no. 3 (March 1924).

12. Wikipedia, https://zh.m.wikipedia.org/zh-hans / 中国孩子, accessed on May 22, 2021.

13. "Bob Dylan: Facts," Nobel Prize website, https://www.nobelprize.org/prizes /literature/2016/dylan/facts, accessed November 30, 2021.

14. *Modern Poetry Quarterly*, no. 13, February 1, 1956, 4.

15. Poetry in classical forms—which some scholars call "classicist poetry"—continues to be written by many in the Chinese-speaking world and circulated in conventional and digital media.

Notes on Selections, Translations, and Terminology

Compiling an anthology is an explicit act of inclusion and exclusion as well as an implicit act of canonization. As editors, we take the responsibility seriously. The first and foremost consideration is the artistic quality of the original poems in Chinese, complemented by the secondary consideration of their historical significance. A third consideration is whether the translations are as accurate as possible while doing justice to the originals as English-language poems. Aesthetic judgment is inevitably based on individual background, training, and taste; therefore, we don't expect every reader to agree with all the choices we have made. It is our hope that the poets and poems included in this anthology will stand the test of time.

The Hanyu Pinyin system of phonetic transliteration of Chinese names and terms is used throughout the book, except for the names of people who have chosen to represent their names with another romanization system or according to non-standard-Chinese (Mandarin) pronunciation (e.g., Chiang Kai-shek, Sun Yat-sen), institutions that use alternate romanization (e.g., Peking University), and place names outside of the People's Republic of China (e.g., Taipei). Poets' names are romanized according to standard Chinese pronunciation; where applicable, some also reflect Cantonese pronunciation or are romanized from other languages.

Chinese characters for personal names, poem titles, and other terms are provided in the glossary-index.

Italicization is used in two situations: when an English word is used within an original Chinese poem or title (such as the poem "*Rhapsody*" by Xin Di) and for subtitles and epigraphs.

Whenever available, the precise date of composition of a poem is given, followed by the name of the translator. If this date is not available, we do our best to provide the year of the poem's initial publication.

A CENTURY OF
MODERN CHINESE
POETRY

The Formative Period

The Wuchang Uprising on October 10, 1911, spearheaded the Xinhai Revolution led by the Nationalists that overthrew the Qing dynasty, thus ending five millennia of monarchy and ushering in the first republic in Chinese history. The new modern state immediately faced serious challenges. The continued presence of imperialist powers in China—most notably, Britain, France, Germany, Japan, Russia, and the United States—not only encroached on the autonomy but even posed a threat to the very existence of the young nation. Contentions among various domestic factions—from the Qing loyalists and military leaders to the Nationalists—led Dr. Sun Yat-sen (1866–1925), the founding father of the Republic of China, to step down and Yuan Shikai (1859–1916) to grab power; he became the president in 1912 but then installed himself as the emperor in 1915–16. After his reign was defeated and the Republic restored, China fell into the hands of warlords who ruled different regions. Fragmentation lasted until 1926, when Chiang Kai-shek (1887–1975), Sun Yat-sen's protégé, led a military campaign, the Northern Expedition, that reunified the nation in 1928.

However, peace remained elusive. The Nationalists soon launched a campaign against the Chinese Communist Party, which had increasingly appealed to young intellectuals since its founding on July 23, 1921. The purge forced Communist leaders to retreat from the base in Jiangxi, embark on the Long March in 1934–35, and eventually settle down in Shaanxi in the northwest. In the meantime, the crisis of national survival was exacerbated with the Japanese attack of Manchuria on September 18, 1931, and the establishment of the puppet regime Manchukuo, headed by Pu Yi (1906–67), the last emperor of Qing who abdicated in 1912.

In the midst of political crises and social turmoil, the cultural sphere underwent dramatic transformation as well. The May Fourth Movement started out as a political demonstration in Beijing in 1919 but quickly turned into a cultural reform that sought to replace traditional ideas and practices associated with Confucianism, Daoism, and Buddhism with new concepts of science and democracy introduced from the West. Going beyond technological and material progress, the May Fourth Movement was compared to the Age of Enlightenment on the one hand but critiqued for its radical anti-traditionalism on the other.

It is against this background that Modern Poetry burst onto the scene in January 1917, when Hu Shi, then a graduate student in the United States, published "A Preliminary Proposal for Literary Reform" in the progressive journal *New Youth*; in the February issue of the same journal, Hu published eight poems based on his vision of a new poetry. Despite the skepticism of and attacks from conservatives, Modern Poetry had a broad appeal to young people, including the abdicated emperor Pu Yi. Similar reforms took place in fiction and drama.

Lu Xun (1881–1936)

Lu Xun, the pen name of Zhou Shuren, was born into a declining family of scholar-officials in Shaoxing, Zhejiang. After graduating from the School of Mines and Railways in Nanjing in 1902, he went to Japan to study Western medicine. The circumstances surrounding his decision to quit medicine and become a writer have become the stuff of legend. Lu Xun published his first short story, "A Madman's Diary," in 1918; it was one of the first modern works of Chinese fiction and borrowed its name from a tale by the Russian writer Nikolai Gogol, whom Lu Xun admired and translated. He went on to publish the novella *True Story of Ah Q* and two collections of short stories, many of which mounted scathing criticism of Chinese tradition and society, consolidating his position as the "founder of modern Chinese literature." Aside from fiction, Lu Xun was influential as an essayist, translator, literary scholar, editor, poet in both classical and modern styles, as well as a patron, promulgator, and collector of woodblock prints. Nobel laureate Ōe Kenzaburō (b. 1935) called Lu Xun "the greatest writer Asia produced in the twentieth century."

Of the selections here, "Boer" is from a series of prose poems titled "Talking to Oneself," published in 1919; the other two are from *Wild Grass*, a collection of twenty-four prose poems published in 1927.

BOER

Boer ran off angrily.

This child Boer is already as tall as a low hut, but he's still naughty, I do not know where he learned all these bad things, but now he wants to grow flowers.

I do not know where he went to get these roses he planted in dry ground, watering them in the morning, then in mid-morning and again at noon.

At noon he watered them and was overjoyed at a speck of green on the soil. In the afternoon he watered them, but the speck of green had disappeared, perhaps eaten by insects.

Boer went to get the watering pot, angrily running to the riverside, where he saw a girl crying.

"Why are you here crying?" he asked.

The girl replied: "Have you tasted the river water?"

Boer tasted the water and said: "There's nothing special about the flavor."

The girl told him: "I shed a tear into it, yet it is still tasteless, so how could I not cry?"

Boer replied: "You are a foolish girl!"

Angrily, he ran to the ocean shore, where he saw a boy crying.

Boer asked: "Why are you here crying?"

The boy asked: "What color do you think the water in the ocean is?"

Having looked at the water in the ocean, Boer replied: "It is green."

The boy told him: "I shed a drop of blood into it, yet it is still green. How could I not cry?"

Boer responded: "You are a foolish boy!"

Yet it is Boer who is the fool. How in the world can there be roses that put forth buds in half a day, when they are still seeds in the ground?

Even if they never come forth, it's not as though there won't be other roses on the earth.

published September 7, 1919
translated by Jon Eugene von Kowallis

AUTUMN NIGHT

In my backyard one can see, beyond the wall, that there are two trees—one is a date tree, and there is yet another, also a date tree.

The night sky above them is strange and high—I have never in my life seen so strange and high a sky. It is as if it intends to leave this mortal world, so that when humans raise their faces upward, it will no longer be visible to them. Yet now it is uncommonly blue, and dozens of star-filled eyes twinkle brightly from it—blinking cold eyes. From the corners of its mouth appears a slight smile, as though it were in possession of some deep truth, and it showers the wildflowers and grasses in my garden with a heavy frost.

I do not know the true names for those flowers and grasses or what people commonly call them. I remember there was one species that bloomed with a delicate, tiny pink flower—which in fact is still in bloom but has become even tinier and more delicate. In the cold night air, she shivers in dream, dreaming of the arrival of spring, of the coming of autumn, of an emaciated poet who wipes his tears on her last petals, telling her autumn will come and winter will come, yet spring will follow again, when butterflies flutter and bees begin humming songs of spring. Thereupon, she will smile, though her color has frozen into a mournful crimson and she must remain curled up, shivering.

The date trees have shed their every leaf. There used to be one or two children who would come to shake down the dates left behind by others, but now not a one remains and the leaves have all fallen. They know the tiny pink flower's dream of spring after autumn, and they know the dream of the fallen leaves that autumn will come again after spring. They have lost their leaves completely and have only branches left, but these, no longer bent under the weight of a whole tree's worth of fruit and leaves, are stretching out their limbs in comfort. A few boughs, though, are still hanging low, nursing the wounds made in their bark by the poles that were used to shake down the dates, while, rigid as iron, the straightest and longest branches have already silently pierced the strange, high sky, causing it to blink eerily. They pierce even the round, full moon up in the stratosphere making it feel so ill at ease that it turns a pale white.

Blinking ghostly eyes, the restless sky takes on a hue of even deeper blue, as if it wants to depart this mortal world, dodging the date trees and leaving only the moon behind. Yet the moon has secreted itself away in the east; while the starkly bare branches still silently pierce, like iron, this strange, high sky, determined to inflict a mortal wound upon it, regardless of the various ways it goes about winking with so many enticing eyes.

Waah!!—with a shriek, a fierce night bird flies by.

Suddenly I hear the sound of midnight laughter coming forth muffled, as if unwilling to startle those asleep; and yet, from all sides, the air resounds with this laughter. It being the middle of the night with no one else around, I recognize the sound as coming from my own mouth and am immediately driven by the resounding laughter back into my room, where I at once turn up the wick on my kerosene lamp.

On the glass pane of my back window a *ding-ding* sound begins, as a bevy of tiny insects dash themselves helter-skelter upon it. In a short time, several get in, perhaps through holes in the paper-covered window. As soon as they gain entry, they again begin to dash themselves *ding-ding* on the glass chimney of the lamp. One dashes in through the open top of the chimney, thereupon meeting with the flame, which I take to be for real. Two or three rest on the paper shade of the lamp, panting. The shade is a new one I put on last night, of snow-white paper that has been pleated into a wavelike pattern on its surface, with a scarlet Cape jasmine flower painted at one corner.

When the scarlet Cape jasmine blossoms, the date trees will again dream the dream of the tiny pink flower and bend under the weight of their verdant foliage. . . . I again hear the sound of laughter at midnight; quickly, I sever this train of thought and look at those tiny green insects that have remained on the white lamp shade—their heads large and tails small, like sunflower seeds, but only half the size of a grain of wheat, their entire bodies a lovely, delicate emerald green.

I break into a yawn, light a cigarette, and blow out a stream of smoke; facing the lamp, I silently pay my respects to these exquisite, emerald-green heroes.

September 15, 1924
translated by Jon Eugene von Kowallis

BEGGARS

I'm walking beside a tall, decaying wall, treading the loose dust. A few other people are walking along by themselves. Above the wall, a breeze rustles unwithered leaves on the trees overhead.

A breeze stirs, dust is all around.

A child approaches me, begging. He is wearing a warm jacket and doesn't look all that miserable, but he kowtows in front of me, blocking my way, then wails along behind me.

I detest the sound of his voice, his posturing; I despise that he isn't really all that miserable, almost as if it's a game; I can't stand the way he wails.

I keep walking. A few other people are walking along by themselves. A breeze stirs, dust is all around.

Another child approaches, begging. He, too, is wearing a warm jacket and doesn't look all that miserable, but he's mute. He stretches out his hands theatrically.

I really despise his mock hand gestures. It's possible he isn't even mute, that it's just another begging tactic.

I give them nothing, I'm not generous at heart, charity is beneath me, instead I dole out annoyance, suspicion, and revulsion.

I'm walking beside a collapsed mud wall; broken bricks are piled in the gaps, walling in nothing. A breeze stirs, autumn's chill pierces my warm jacket; dust is all around.

If I were to beg, I wonder what technique I'd use. Crying out—but in what pitch? Playing mute—but with what hand gestures? . . .

A few other people are walking along by themselves.

I'd get no handouts, encounter no generosity, only the annoyance, suspicion, and revulsion of those who consider charity beneath them.

I'd use indifference and silence to beg! . . .

At the very least I'd get some nothingness.

A breeze stirs, dust is all around. A few other people are walking along by themselves.

Dust, dust, . . .

. . . .

Dust . . .

September 24, 1924
translated by Nick Kaldis

Hu Shi (1891–1962)

A leading thinker, historian, literary critic, educator, and diplomat of modern China, Hu was born in Shanghai into a wealthy family from Jixi County in Anhui. In 1893–95 he lived in Taiwan while his father served as an official in Tainan. After attending middle school and college in Shanghai, in 1910 Hu left for the United States to study agriculture as an undergraduate at Cornell University. In 1914 he became a doctoral student in philosophy at Columbia University, where he studied with John Dewey. He rose to national prominence in 1917, when he published an essay calling for a new poetry by replacing classical Chinese with the modern vernacular and abandoning traditional forms and conventions. He also published the first collection of modern Chinese poetry, titled *Experiments*, in 1920. For these reasons, Hu is rightly called the "father of modern poetry." "Old Crow" is a response to his critics, whereas "Dreams and Poetry" is, according to the poet, his manifesto of "poetic empiricism."

Through writings and actions, Hu was a vocal and consistent advocate of democracy, liberalism, individualism, and human rights. He played a leading role in many spheres—literature, culture, education, and politics—having served in a number of important positions from the 1930s to the end of his life, including dean of the Faculty of the Arts at Peking University (1931–37), Chinese ambassador to the United States (1938–42), president of Peking University (1946–48), and president of Academia Sinica in Taiwan (1957–62). Hu received close to three dozen honorary doctorates from international universities, including Harvard, Oxford, Princeton, and Yale.

OLD CROW (1 of 2)

I.

Up early, I stand on a rooftop cawing and cackling.
People say I'm a nuisance, that I bring nothing but bad luck;
But why should I tweet and chirp to please them!

December 11, 1917
translated by Michelle Yeh

DREAMS AND POETRY

All are ordinary experiences,
All are ordinary images;
By chance they surge into a dream,
Turning out many an original pattern!

All are ordinary feelings,
All are ordinary words;
By chance they encounter a poet,
Turning out many an original verse!

Only one who has been drunk knows the strength of wine;
Only one who has been in love knows the power of love.
You cannot write my poems
Just as I cannot dream your dreams.

October 10, 1920
translated by Michelle Yeh

Guo Moruo (1892–1978)

Guo Moruo is the pen name of Guo Kaizhen, who was born in Leshan, Sichuan. In 1914 he went to Japan to study and in 1918 entered the medical school of Kyushu Imperial University. In 1921 he cofounded the Creation Society in Tokyo with Yu Dafu (1896–1945), Cheng Fangwu (1897–1984), and others; he also published his first book of poetry, *Goddesses*. Guo joined the Chinese Communist Party in 1927, taking refuge from the Nationalists by relocating to Japan, where he devoted himself to the study of Chinese ancient history and archaeology. In 1937 he returned to China and during the war composed historical plays. After the founding of the People's Republic of China in 1949, he served in many national leadership posts, including the vice premier of the State Council, president of the Chinese Academy of Social Sciences, and chair of the China Federation of Literary and Art Circles.

In Chinese mythology, Heavenly Dog swallowed the sun and the moon, causing the phenomena of solar and lunar eclipses. Fudetate Yama is a mountain west of the city of Moji, Japan. The peak offers a panorama of the ocean, the land, ships, and shipyards. In all three poems, italicized words in the originals also appear in the English translations.

HEAVENLY DOG

I am a heavenly dog!
I have swallowed the moon,
I have swallowed the sun,
I have swallowed all the stars,
I have swallowed the entire universe.
Now I have become me!

I am moonlight, I am sunlight,
I am the lights of all the stars,
I am X Ray beams,
I am the sum of all *Energy* in the universe!

I run like the wind, I shout wildly, I am on fire,
I burn like an inferno!
I shout wildly like the ocean!
I run like electricity!
I run, I run, I run,
I peel my skin, I eat my flesh,
I suck my blood, I gnaw on my guts,
I race on my nerves, I race on my spine,
I race on my brains.
I am I! My I is about to explode!

February 1920
translated by Michelle Yeh

ON TOP OF FUDETATE YAMA

The throbbing veins of the metropolis!
Thumping life!
Beating, trumpeting, roaring,
Gushing, soaring, vaulting,
The sky and suburbs all around are dim in the smoky haze!
My heart is about to leap out of my mouth!
O, the rolling peaks and hills, the waving tiles and rooftops,
Swell, heave, surge, rush!
All sounds in the universe resonate in *Symphony*,
A wedding of nature and human life!
The coast curves like *Cupid*'s bow!
Our life is an arrow, shooting over the ocean!
In the darkening bay, anchored steamships, sailing steamships,
    countless steamships,
Out of the chimneys black peonies blossom!

O, famous flower of the twentieth century!
Stern mother of modern civilization!

June 1920
translated by Yi Zheng

SHANGHAI IMPRESSIONS

I woke up from my dream with a start!
The sadness of *Disillusion*!
The aimless walking dead,
Lecherous flesh,
Men in long robes,
Women in short skirts,
All around I see skeletons,
The streets crowded with hearses
Rushing,
Halting.
My tears are flowing,
I am sick at heart.
I woke up from my dream with a start.
The sadness of *Disillusion*!

April 4, 1921
translated by Yi Zheng

Xu Zhimo (1897–1931)

Born into a wealthy family in Haining, Zhejiang, Xu graduated from Peking University in 1918. Encouraged by his teacher Liang Qichao (1873–1929), he went to the United States, where he studied history at Clark University in Massachusetts and received an MA degree in political science from Columbia University in 1920. He continued his studies at the London School of Economics and Political Science, but his interest shifted as he befriended the philosopher Goldsworthy Lowes Dickinson, the writer E. M. Forster, and through them the art critic Roger

Fry and other members of the Bloomsbury Group. In March 1922 he moved to Cambridge in the hope of studying with Bertrand Russell, not knowing that the philosopher had left Trinity College four years earlier. It was in Cambridge that Xu developed a strong interest in Romanticism and started writing modern poetry in Chinese. In October 1922 he returned to China and, within a few years, became a prominent writer, editor, professor, and founding member of the Crescent Society. Nationally known for his poetry and prose, Xu was equally famous for his unrequited love for Lin Huiyin (1904–55) and for his affair with Lu Xiaoman (1903–65), who became his second wife in 1926. On November 19, 1931, en route from Nanjing to Beijing, Xu was killed in a plane crash near Jinan, Shandong.

Both "By Chance" and "Second Farewell to Cambridge" have been set to music and are among the most popular modern poems in the Chinese-speaking world.

BY CHANCE

I am a cloud that by chance casts a shadow
On the rippling waves of your heart.
Don't be surprised,
Or, even less, rejoice,
For I will move on in the blink of an eye.

We met on the sea of night;
You traveling on your way and I on mine
Remember our meeting if you wish
Or perhaps it's better to forget
The fireworks in that moment!

1926
translated by Michelle Yeh and Frank Stewart

SEA MELODY

I.

"Young woman, solitary woman,
Why are you lingering
On the twilight shore?
Young woman, why don't you go home?"
"Oh no, I don't want to go home,
I love the evening breeze!"
On the sandy beach, in the twilight breeze,
A young woman with her hair down—
    Roams and roams.

2.

"Young woman, woman with your hair down,
Why are you wandering
By the cold sea?
Young woman, why don't you go home?"
"Oh no, listen to my song,
Ocean, I will sing and you will harmonize."
Under the moonlight, in the cold wind,
The young woman's clear voice vibrates—
    High and low.

3.

"Young woman, fearless woman,
The edge of the sky draws a dark curtain,
A sudden storm is on the way—
Young woman, why don't you go home?"
"Oh no, watch me dance in the air,
Like a seagull weaving through the waves"—
In the nightfall, on the sandy shore,
A slender shape twirls so fast—
    Whirls and whirls.

4.

"Listen, how the ocean roars.
Young woman, why don't you go home?"
Look, the waves charge like wild beasts,
Young woman, why don't you go home?"
"Oh no, the waves won't swallow me,
I love the tumbling sea!"
In the ocean's roar, in the gleaming waves,
Oh, a young woman panicking in the foam
      Falters and falters.

5.

"Young woman, where are you?
Where is your vibrant voice?
Where is your slender form?
Where, oh, is the brave young woman?"
The dark night has swallowed the starlight,
There is no more light by the sea;
The waves have washed over the sandy beach,
The woman is no longer on the shore—
      The young woman is no more!

1927
translated by Michelle Yeh and Frank Stewart

SECOND FAREWELL TO CAMBRIDGE

I am leaving
      as quietly as I came;
I gently wave farewell
      to the rose-colored clouds in the west.

The willow on the riverbank
      is like a bride standing in the sunset;
Her golden reflection on the water
      shimmers in my heart.

Water poppies in the soft mud
　　　sway and wave;
How I'd rather be that reedy sweet-grass
　　　in the lapping waves of the River Cam!

The pool of water in the elm shade
　　　is not a clear spring but a rainbow in the sky.
The ruffling colors among the duckweed
　　　sink into a rainbow dream.

Searching for a dream? Push with a long pole
　　　to guide your punt upstream for greener banks;
Overflowing with starlight, your small boat
　　　will sing a carefree song in the radiant night.

But for me, I cannot sing without cares,
　　　as the song of my farewell is the silence;
Even summer insects have hushed for me,
　　　silent is the Cambridge night.

I am leaving,
　　　as quietly as I came.
Raising my sleeve, I wave farewell,
　　　taking with me not even a wisp of cloud.

November 6, 1928
translated by Michelle Yeh and Frank Stewart

THE TRAIN GRIPS THE TRACKS

The train grips the tracks as it charges through the dark night,
across rivers and hills, beside graveyards where the dead are sleeping.

Thundering over bridges, its iron bones screech like an enraged bull,
across wilderness and past temples with broken windows and doors,

Across dark ponds where frogs thump like bass drums,
through hushed villages where not a single candle is burning,

Passing frozen platforms where no passengers come or go
and stations with their bloated bellies like vices.

A few stars are startled awake by the train's roar
and peek out from behind the clouds:

What's going on here, they seem to ask;
instead of a peaceful night, there's this havoc!

Like a long serpent, the train breathes fire
and plunges recklessly into the darkness.

Supported by only thin, narrow rails,
it hauls its burden like a heavy dream.

Weighed down! Inside, the strange and gentle folk
lie back and peacefully sleep.

For good or bad, they entrust their fate to the train—
whether it's scaling mountains or plunging into valleys,

Whether uncanny birds in deep woods are cursing or
the glorious celestial bodies are careening toward the abyss.

Yawning, the travelers care only about the present;
tomorrow at their destinations, they'll grab their bags and rush on!

This is not a bad attitude after all, as there is no end to suffering;
we stars must shine without respite.

Eyes always open, we see through it all;
but can even we control our fate?

Don't speak anymore of light, wisdom, and eternal beauty;
we all suffer and we all travel on the same track; the only

Difference is that stars live longer than humans;
in either case, life is but a game without meaning.

July 19, 1931
translated by Michelle Yeh and Frank Stewart

Wen Yiduo (1899–1946)

A native of Huanggang in Hubei, Wen attended Tsinghua School, a preparatory
academy founded with the Boxer Indemnity Scholarship and the predecessor
of Tsinghua University. From July 1922 to May 1925, he studied painting at the
School of Art Institute of Chicago, Colorado College, and School of Visual Arts
in New York. Wen published his first poem in 1920 and stopped writing poetry
after 1931. Despite his brief tenure as a poet, his poetry and poetic theory were
immensely influential. For the rest of his life, Wen was devoted to scholarship
on Chinese classics, such as the *Shijing* and *Songs of the South* (*Chuci*). During
the Sino–Japanese War, he ended up in Kunming, Yunnan, where he taught at
National Southwestern Associated University, the conglomerate of Peking, Tsing-
hua, and Nankai Universities. On July 15, 1946, for his outspoken criticism of the
Nationalist regime, he was assassinated on his way home after giving a speech con-
demning the assassination of his friend Li Gongpu (1902–46) three days earlier.

In "First Emperor of the Qin Dynasty" Jing Ke (?–227 BCE) and Zhang Liang
(?–189 BCE) each made a failed attempt on the emperor's life, respectively in 227
and 218 BCE. Julu was the site of the decisive battle that toppled the Qin Empire.
Xianyang, the capital city, was destroyed by the rebels in a fire that allegedly lasted
three months. It is widely believed that the "you" in "Perhaps (an elegy)" is the
poet's daughter, Liying, who passed away in 1926, at the age of four, while he was
working out of town.

FIRST EMPEROR OF THE QIN DYNASTY

Jing Ke's assassin's dagger, Zhang Liang's iron hammer
Flashed like bees before my eyes
In my rib cage I harbored a black wolf,
which would murder me in the end.

I swallowed six kingdoms to feed the wolf;
Fattened up on them, he nevertheless devoured me.
I built the Efang Palace to entertain the black wolf;
And when he grew bored, we lay down together and slept.

Now nothing can startle or awaken us,
Even the uprising at Julu and the conflagration in Xianyang . . .
A loving hedgehog holds my skull in its arms, and
A ten-meter blue python coils around my feet.

published 1925
translated by Michelle Yeh and Frank Stewart

DEAD WATER

Here is a ditch of hopelessly dead water.
A cool breeze would not raise the slightest ripple on it.
You might throw in some scraps of copper and rusty tins,
or dump in as well the remains of your meal.

Perhaps the green on copper will turn into emeralds,
or the rust on tin will sprout a few peach blossoms.
Let grease weave a layer of fine silk-gauze, and
mold steam out a few red-glowing clouds.

Let the dead water ferment into a ditch of green wine,
floating with pearls of white foam;
but the laughter of small pearls turning into large pearls
is broken by spotted mosquitoes stealing the wine.

Thus a ditch of hopelessly dead water
can yet claim a bit of something bright.
And if the frogs can't endure the utter solitude,
let the dead water burst into song.

Here is a ditch of hopelessly dead water.
Here beauty can never reside.
You might as well let ugliness come and cultivate it,
and see what kind of world comes out.

1925
translated by Arthur Sze

PERHAPS (AN ELEGY)

Perhaps you have wept and wept, and can weep no more.
Perhaps. Perhaps you ought to sleep a bit;
then don't let the night hawk cough, the frogs
croak, or the bats fly.

Don't let the sunlight open the curtain onto your eyes.
Don't let a cool breeze brush your eyebrows.
Ah, no one will be able to startle you awake:
I will open an umbrella of dark pines to shelter your sleep.

Perhaps you hear earthworms digging in the mud,
or listen to the root hairs of small grasses sucking up water.
Perhaps this music you are listening to is lovelier
than the swearing and cursing noises of men.

Then close your eyelids, and shut them tight.
I will let you sleep, I will let you sleep.
I will cover you lightly, lightly with yellow earth.
I will slowly, slowly let the ashes of paper money fly.

1926
translated by Arthur Sze

CONFESSION

I am not trying to deceive you—I confess I am not a poet
though I love the strength and loyalty of white boulders,
blue pines and ocean, sunsets carried on the backs of crows,
a tapestry woven with bats' wings in the twilight sky.
And you know how much I admire heroes and mountains
and love my country's flag unfurling in the wind
and chrysanthemums from pale yellow to bronze.
Also remember, I live on no more than a pot of bitter tea!

But then there is another me, are you scared?—
With thoughts like flies, I crawl about in a garbage can.

1927
translated by Michelle Yeh and Frank Stewart

Li Jinfa (1900–1976)

Li Jinfa, the pen name of Li Shuliang, was born in Mei County, Guangdong, into a Hakka family. In 1919–24 he studied in France, first at the Dijon Fine Arts School and later at École des Beaux-Arts in Paris. He was the first Chinese student to study sculpture in France. After returning to China, he worked as a professor, editor, and diplomat in Vietnam, Iran, and Iraq. In 1951 he moved to the United States, where he ran a chicken farm in New Jersey. He passed away from a heart attack in Long Island.

While in France, Li started writing poetry under the influence of Charles Baudelaire and Paul Verlaine. His pen name, Jinfa, means "golden hair," which, according to the poet, came from a dream in which a blonde-haired woman appeared to him. He published three books of poetry in 1925–27 and shocked the poetry scene in China with his grotesque imagery and mix of classical and modern Chinese. Li is widely considered the first symbolist poet in China.

THE ABANDONED WOMAN

My thick tresses hang down,
blocking out the shaming glares,
the cataracts of blood, and corpses in deep slumber.
Night sneaks up buzzing with mosquitoes.
It climbs the corner of the wall just yonder
and circles around to shout in my chaste ear,
raging like the wind on the steppe
that terrorizes countless nomadic hearts.

Riding a blade of grass, I roam with God's soul through the deep valley.
Only the brain of the rambling bee can fully register my sorrow;
sometimes I plummet with the alpine waterfall,
and then vanish with the crimson leaves.

The abandoned woman's secret pain overlies her every gesture.
The fire of the setting sun cannot reduce time's woes
 to ashes that fly up through chimneys
and forever stain the feathers of crows
so that they might roost side-by-side on shoreline boulders
and heed the boatman's song.

Her aging skirt moans
as she lingers by the tomb,
never letting a hot tear
drop into the grass
to magnify the world's splendor.

1922
translated by Randy Trumbull

WORDS WRITTEN ON MY SELF-PORTRAIT

The moon, though slumbering in the river's bed,
still manages a smile for the purple forest.
The Protestant soul is too ardent.

I thank these hands and feet,
for, although they are yet young,
they suit me well enough.

The mighty warrior of old
donned his armor to slay tigers.
As for me, I prefer humble tasks.

As hot as the white sun,
as gray as the cloud-bedded moon.
My grass sandals carry me to only one corner of the world.
Why grow wings and fly, when that asks so much?

1923
translated by Randy Trumbull

Fei Ming (1901–1967)

A native of Huangmei in Hubei, Fei Ming, the pen name of Feng Wenbing, entered Hubei First Normal School in 1917; there he was exposed to modern literature and developed a strong interest in poetry. In 1922 he was admitted into the preparatory program of Peking University, where two years later he majored in English literature. In June 1926 he changed his name to Fei Ming, which literally means "abolishing names." Upon graduation in 1929, he taught at his alma mater as a lecturer. During the war against Japan, he refused to stay in Beijing under Japanese occupation and went back to his hometown, where he taught at a junior high school. In 1946 he returned to Peking University as an associate professor in the Chinese Department. In 1952 he was transferred to Jilin University in northeastern China and worked there till he passed away from cancer. As early as 1921, Fei Ming had corresponded with Zhou Zuoren (1885–1967), who became a lifelong mentor and friend. In addition to poetry, Fei Ming published fiction, literary criticism, and a treatise on Buddhist philosophy.

VANITY TABLE

Because I dreamed I was a mirror,
I would be a mirror if I sank into the sea.
A young woman would find me
and put me on her vanity table.
And because it was a vanity table,
no sadness would ever be allowed.

1931
translated by Michelle Yeh and Frank Stewart

DREAM

In a woman's dream, I write the word Good
In a man's dream
I write Beauty
For a world-weary poet, I paint a pleasant landscape
For a child, I paint the world

1931
translated by Michelle Yeh and Frank Stewart

STREET CORNER

I walk to the street corner
and a car drives by—
thus, the loneliness of the mailbox
thus, the loneliness of the license plate number X
thus, the loneliness of numbers
the loneliness of the car
the loneliness of the street
the loneliness of humankind

1937
translated by Michelle Yeh and Frank Stewart

The First Flowering
of Modern Poetry

1930S–1940S

On July 7, 1937, under the pretext of searching for a missing soldier during a drill at the Marco Polo Bridge near Beijing, the Japanese army exchanged fire with the Nationalist army, which led to an all-out war known to the Chinese as the eight-year War of Resistance against Japan, or the Second Sino-Japanese War in modern history, the first being the war in 1894–95, in which the Qing empire was defeated and ceded Taiwan.

The devastation to China was massive. As Japan advanced from the north to the Yangzi region and the south, public and private institutions had to be relocated across thousands of miles, millions of people were uprooted and on the run, and countless lives and properties were lost. The United States entered World War II after Japan bombed Pearl Harbor on December 7, 1941, and the Allies came to China's aid. On August 6, 1945, the United States dropped an atomic bomb on Hiroshima; three days later, a second bomb was dropped on Nagasaki. On August 15 Japanese emperor Hirohito announced surrender, thus ending World War II in the Pacific region. After the hard-won victory, peace and stability was nevertheless short-lived. Taiwan was retroceded to China. However, the return to the motherland was fraught with challenges as a result of the differences in language and culture after fifty years of Japanese occupation. The February 28 Incident of 1947, in which the Nationalist government crushed local protests, created deep distrust. On the mainland the tension between the Nationalists and the Communists escalated and culminated in a civil war.

Despite these dire circumstances, literature and art thrived in the 1930s and 1940s, best represented by occupied Shanghai, the "orphaned island"; Kunming, in the southwest, where eminent scholars and writers gathered at Southwestern Associated University; Yan'an, in the northwest, the Communist base; and Hong Kong, where many writers from the mainland found shelter. While established poets created new milestones, a new generation of young poets burst onto the scene and made history.

Dai Wangshu (1905–1950)

A native of Hangzhou, Zhejiang, Dai attended Shanghai University in 1923–25 before he transferred to Aurora University, where he majored in French. In 1932–35 he studied in Lyons and Paris. In the 1920s–30s he cofounded several literary journals with fellow writers Shi Zhecun (1905–2003) and Du Heng (1907–64), including *Les Contemporains* in Shanghai in 1932. After the Sino–Japanese War broke out, Dai moved to Hong Kong, where he edited newspapers and literary journals. After Hong Kong fell to the Japanese at the end of 1941, he was imprisoned and tortured. He returned to China in 1949 and worked as a translator before he died of asthma. Dai published his first book of poetry in 1929 and was also a prolific translator of French, Russian, and Spanish literature.

Xiao Hong (1911–42), in the poem "Improvised by Xiao Hong's Tomb," is a major prose and fiction writer. A native of Heilongjiang Province in Manchuria, she moved to Hong Kong in January 1940. She was misdiagnosed with a throat tumor, underwent surgery to remove it, and passed away on January 22, 1942.

MY MEMORY

My memory remains forever true to me.
Its loyalty puts the best friend to shame.

It smolders on cigarette butts.
It lives on lilies carved on a penholder,
in a shabby compact of face powder,
and on brambles climbing a ruined wall.
It survives in a half-drunk bottle,
on the torn bits of an aborted poem, on a pressed flower,
on the gloom of a dim lantern, on a mirror of water.
On all things, whether or not they possess a soul,
my memory carves a toehold,
just as I do while clinging to this world.

My memory is timid and shrinks from clamor,
but when loneliness strikes it pays a kind visit.
Its voice turns low
but its words flow on forever
as it dispenses fragments and refuses to stop;
its ancient voice always tells the same story,
and while singing in key it shuns new tunes.
Sometimes it affects the whining of a young coquette
as its voice weakens
and it interjects sobs and sighs.

My memory visits on no schedule,
arriving at all times and places,
often when I'm in bed, drowsy and about to drift off,
or else at the crack of dawn.
Outsiders think it rude,
but as old friends we don't stand on ceremony.

My memory never falls silent
unless I cry in grief or plunge into deepest sleep;
but I could never fault it
because it remains forever true to me.

1927
translated by Randy Trumbull

I THINK

I think, therefore I am a butterfly . . .
Ten thousand years from now, a little flower's gentle call—
Through misty clouds of no dreams and no awakenings—
Will flutter my splendid colorful wings.

March 14, 1937
translated by Michelle Yeh

IMPROVISED BY XIAO HONG'S TOMB

A lonely walk of six hours
To lay a bouquet of red camellias by your head,
Here I wait, through the long night,
While you lie there listening to the tide's chitchat.

1942
translated by Michelle Yeh

I RUN MY MANGLED PALM

I run my mangled palm
across the face of our wide land;
in this corner I touch ashes,
in that corner, only blood and dirt;
My home ought to have stood by this lake
where springtime unfurled tapestries of flowers on the shore,
and willow twigs, when snapped, once breathed perfume.
I feel the cold of algae and water
and the bone-deep chill of snowy peaks in the north.
I feel the muddy water of the Yellow River slide through my fingers.
Now weeds replace the supple green shoots
that waved over rice paddies of the heartland;
The flowering lychee trees of the south stand unattended and withering.
My palm stretches farther, into bitter seas where fishermen no longer sail . . .
My hand glides over every invisible river and mountain.
Blood and ashes soil my fingers; my palm picks up wet darkness.
But one faraway corner in this land remains inviolate,
warm and bright, secure and vibrant.
I stroke the spot with my mangled palm
as tenderly as a lover might his beloved's hair,
or as an infant might, suckling at mother's breast.
I gather my strength on this ruined palm
and press it to the spot with all of my love and longing,

because there one may still find sunlight and springtime
enough to banish shade and restore life,
because there one need not live like a dog
or die like an ant . . .
There, in eternal China!

July 3, 1942
translated by Randy Trumbull

Feng Zhi (1905–1993)

Feng Zhi, the pen name of Feng Chengzhi, was a native of Zhuo County in
Hebei. In 1921 he entered the Department of Foreign Languages and Literatures
at Peking University, where he majored in German and started writing poetry.
He published two books of poems in 1927 and 1929. In June 1930 Feng went to
Germany to study literature and philosophy in Berlin and Heidelberg. Among
German poets, Novalis and Rainer Maria Rilke exerted a formative influence on
him. After receiving a doctorate in 1935, he returned to China to teach at several
universities and eventually to serve as the director of the Institute of Foreign
Literatures of the Chinese Social Science Academy.

In 1941, after a hiatus of ten years, Feng wrote a series of twenty-seven sonnets
in Kunming in the midst of the Sino-Japanese War. At that time he was teaching
at Southwestern Associated University.

SNAKE

My loneliness is a snake,
Long, icy cold, and silent—
My dear, if you ever dream of it,
Promise me you won't be afraid.
It is my intimate companion
Burning with homesickness for the lush grasslands—
The silky lushness of your black hair.

Gentle as the moonlight,
It swims noiselessly toward you
And brings me your dream
Like a scarlet flower.

1926
translated by Michelle Yeh and Frank Stewart

SONNETS (4 of 27)

I.

We are preparing wholeheartedly to receive
unimaginable miracles: into the seemingly endless
march of time, there'll come
a comet in the sky, a sudden gale

and in that moment our life
with all the joys and sorrows of the past
as in a first embrace suddenly congeals
into a lasting form before our eyes.

We praise the insects:
after a single mating
or braving a single danger

they terminate the wonder of their lives.
We spend a lifetime taking upon ourselves
a sudden gale, a comet in the sky.

19.

We wave for a moment, part
and our world splits into two;
we feel a cold beside us, vastness before us,
like two babies just born.

Ah, a parting, a birth . . .
We take up the hardship of work,
making the cold warm, the strange familiar,
each tilling our separate world

for the sake of a future reunion. So, at a first encounter
we remember the past with gratitude;
so, at a first meeting, we suddenly sense a previous lifetime.

How many springs, how many winters in a life?
We can feel only the ordered change of seasons,
not our allotted span in each other's world.

22.

Deep in the mountains:
listen to the night rain pound.
The village ten miles farther,
the market twenty—

do they still exist?
Mountains and rivers of ten years past,
dreams and visions of twenty
are sunken beneath the rain.

Such narrow surroundings—
like being back in the womb.
God, deep in the night, I pray

like a man out of ancient ages:
"Give my narrow heart
a big universe!"

27.

From a formless mass of ever-spreading water
the water-bearer fills an oval flask,
and so this bit of water takes on form.
Look at the windsock waving in the autumn wind—

how it grasps certain things that can't be held—
the distant light, the distant dark of night,
the blooming and fading foliage of distant places,
aspirations racing toward infinity,

and keeps a bit of all of them on one pennant.
In vain we listened all night to the wind,
watched all day while grass turned brown and leaves red.

Where can we find a place for our thoughts, our longings?
May these poems be like a windsock
grasping certain things that can't be held.

1941
translated by Lloyd Haft

Ai Qing (1910–1996)

Born into a landlord's family in rural Jinhua, Zhejiang, Ai Qing, the pen name of Jiang Haicheng, enrolled in Hangzhou National Art Academy in 1928, went to France to study painting the next year, and returned to China in January 1932. He joined the Chinese Leftist Artists' League in Shanghai and was arrested that summer for attempting to undermine the government. He was incarcerated for two years. In 1941 he went to Yan'an and joined the Communist Party. After the founding of People's Republic of China, in 1949, he held several important posts in the cultural establishment until 1957, when, during the Anti-Rightist Campaign, he was exiled to Heilongjiang in the northeast. Persecution continued through the Cultural Revolution (1966–76). In 1979 he was "rehabilitated" and served as vice president of the Chinese Writers Association.

"Dayanhe, My Wet Nurse" was written during the poet's imprisonment and was also the title of his first book of poetry, published in 1934. *Dayanhe*, "Great Yan River," is the poet's transliteration of the woman's real name, "Broad-Leaf Lotus," as a child. At age one the poet was sent to live with her because his superstitious parents believed that he would bring misfortune if he were raised at home.

DAYANHE, MY WET NURSE

Dayanhe, my wet nurse:
Her name was the name of the village that gave her birth;
She was a child-bride:
My wet nurse, Dayanhe.

I am the son of a landlord,
But I have been brought up on Dayanhe's milk:
The son of Dayanhe.
Raising me, Dayanhe raised her own family;
I am one who was raised on your milk,
Oh Dayanhe, my wet nurse.

Dayanhe, today, looking at the snow falling makes me think of you:
Your grass-covered, snow-laden grave,
The withered weeds on the tiled caves of your shut-up house,
Your garden-plot, ten-foot square, and mortgaged,
Your stone seat just outside the gate, overgrown with moss.
Dayanhe, today, looking at the snow makes me think of you.

With your great big hands, you called me to your breast, soothing me;
After you had stoked the fire in the oven,
After you had brushed off the coal ashes from your apron,
After you had tasted for yourself whether the rice was cooked,
After you had set the bowls of black beans on the black table,
After you had mended your sons' clothes, torn by thorns on the mountain ridge,
After you had bandaged the hand of your little son, nicked with a cleaver,
After you had squeezed to death, one by one, the lice on your children's shirts,
After you had collected the first egg of the day
With your great big hands, you cradled me on your breast, soothing me.

I am the son of a landlord,
After I had taken all the milk you had to offer,
I was taken back to my home by the parents who gave me birth.
Ah, Dayanhe, why are you crying?

I was a stranger to the parents who gave me birth!
I touched the red-lacquered, floral-carved furniture,
I touched the ornate brocade on my parents' bed,
I looked dumbly at the "Bless This House" sign above the door—which
    I couldn't read,
I touched the buttons of my new clothes, made of silk and mother-of-pearl,
I saw in my mother's arms a sister whom I scarcely knew,
I sat on a lacquered stool with a small brazier underneath,
I ate white rice that had been milled three times.
Still, I was bashful and shy! Because I,
I was a stranger to the parents who gave me birth.

Dayanhe, in order to survive,
After her milk had gone dry,
She began to put those arms, arms that had cradled me, to work,
Smiling, she washed our clothes,
Smiling, she carried the vegetables, and rinsed them in the icy pond
    by the village,
Smiling, she sliced the turnips frozen through and through,
Smiling, she stirred the swill in the pigs' trough,
Smiling, she fanned the flames under the stove with the broiling meat,
Smiling, she carried the baling baskets of beans and grain to the open square
    where they baked in the sun,
Dayanhe, in order to survive,
After the milk in her had run dry,
She put those arms, arms that had cradled me, to work.

Dayanhe was so devoted to her foster child, whom she suckled:
At New Year's, she'd busy herself cutting winter rice candy for him,
For him, who would steal off to her house by the village,
For him, who would walk up to her and call her "Mama,"
Dayanhe, she would stick his drawing of Guan Yu, the war god, bright green
    and bright red, on the wall by the stove,
Dayanhe, how she would boast and brag to her neighbors about her
    foster child.
Dayanhe, once she dreamt a dream she could tell no one,
In her dream, she was drinking a wedding toast to her foster child,

Sitting in a resplendent hall decked with silk,
And the beautiful young bride called her affectionately "Mother."
. . . . . .

Dayanhe, she was so devoted to her foster child. Dayanhe, in a dream
　　from which she has not awakened, has died.
When she died, her foster child was not at her side,
When she died, the husband who often beat her shed tears for her.
Her five sons each cried bitter tears,
When she died, feebly, she called out the name of her foster child,
Dayanhe is dead:
When she died, her foster child was not at her side.

Dayanhe, she went with tears in her eyes!
Along with forty-nine years, a lifetime of humiliation at the hands of the world,
Along with the innumerable sufferings of a slave,
Along with a two-bit casket and some bundles of rice straw,
Along with a plot of ground to bury a casket in a few square feet,
Along with a handful of ashes, from paper money burned,
Dayanhe, she went with tears in her eyes.

But these are the things that Dayanhe would not know:
That her drunkard husband is dead,
That her eldest son became a bandit,
That her second died in the smoke of war,
That her third, her fourth, her fifth,
Live on, vilified by their teachers and their landlords,
And I—I write condemnations of this unjust world.
When I, after drifting for a long time, went home
On the mountain ridge, in the wilds,
When I saw my brothers, we were closer than six or seven years ago,
This, this is what you, Dayanhe, calmly sleeping in repose,
This is what you do not know!

Dayanhe, today, your foster child is in jail,
Writing a poem of praise, dedicated to you,
Dedicated to your spirit, purple shade under the brown soil,

Dedicated to your outstretched arms that embraced me,
Dedicated to your lips that kissed me,
Dedicated to your face, warm and soft, the color of earth,
Dedicated to your breasts that suckled me,
Dedicated to your sons, my brothers,
Dedicated to all of them on earth,
The wet nurses like my Dayanhe, and all their sons,
Dedicated to Dayanhe, who loved me as she loved her own sons.

Dayanhe—My Wet Nurse
I am one who grew up suckling at your breasts,
Your son.
I pay tribute to you,
With all my love.

On a snowy morning
January 14, 1933
translated by Eugene Chen Eoyang

SNOW IS FALLING ON THE LAND OF CHINA

Snow is falling on the land of China,
A frigid season has imprisoned it in ice . . .

The wind
Wails like a grieving old woman
Who trails close behind
And stretches out a frozen hand
To seize the lapel of a passerby,
As she babbles in phrases as old as the Earth
On and on without stopping . . .

Emerging from the forest
On a horse-drawn cart,
You, China's farmer,
Wearing a fur hat

Braving the heavy snowfall,
Where are you going?
Listen to me,
I too am the son of farmers—
In the deep wrinkles
Carved in your face
I recognize the hardships
Endured by people like you
Who live
On the grassland

But I
Am not happier than you are
Floating on the river of time—
Again and again the tides of suffering
Have drowned me then tossed me on shore—
My wandering and imprisonment
Have cost me the priceless days
Of my youth
My life
Is as careworn
As yours.

Snow is falling on the land of China,
A frigid season has imprisoned it in ice . . .

In the night on the snowy river
A small lamp is swaying;
In an old decaying boat
Under the dim light,
Who is sitting there with lowered head?

—You, young woman
with a soiled face and unkempt hair,
Is it true
That your home,
The center of happiness and warmth,

Was burned to the ground
By the remorseless enemy?
Is it true
That on a night like this one
Having lost your husband's protection
And threatened with death
You were repeatedly assaulted with enemy bayonets?

On a cold night like this one
Is it true
Countless
Old mothers like ours
Are trembling without homes or shelter
Wandering like strangers
Not knowing which road
They'll travel down tomorrow . . .
And the roads of China
Are so rugged
And so muddy.

Snow is falling on the land of China,
A frigid season has imprisoned it in ice . . .

From the snowy grassland of the night
To fields dark with the thick smoke of battle
Countless farmers,
—Having lost their livestock
And their fertile fields,
—Are crowded
Into life's filthy alleys in despair:
The famished earth
Stretches its trembling arms
Toward the desperate sky
Begging for help.

The sufferings and misfortunes of China
Are as vast and endless as this snowy night!

Snow is falling on the land of China,
A frigid season has imprisoned it in ice . . .

China,
On this night without a lamp
Can my humble lines
Bring you even a little warmth?

December 28, 1937
translated by Michelle Yeh and Frank Stewart

Bian Zhilin (1910–2000)

Born in Nantong, Jiangsu, Bian graduated from middle school in Shanghai and entered Peking University in 1929, where he studied with Hu Shi and Xu Zhimo. In 1936 he published *Han Garden*, a jointly authored book of poetry with his friends Li Guangtian (1906–68) and He Qifang (1912–77). In 1938 Bian and He went to Yan'an, the wartime base of the Communist Party, and after 1940 he taught at Southwestern Associated University in Kunming. He spent 1947–49 at University of Oxford as a research fellow and, after returning to China, taught at his alma mater for two years. For most of his career, Bian worked at the Literature Institute of Chinese Academy of Social Sciences as a scholar and translator of Shakespeare and English poetry.

According to the poet's notes to "The Organization of Distance," "I can't discern the soil in the lamplight" (line 7) alludes to a contemporary newspaper account of a man who got lost and picked up a handful of soil to find out where he was. "Did nobody play with my basin boat?" (line 9) comes from the classic *Strange Tales from the Make-Do Studio* by Pu Songling (1640–1715) about a master of the White Lotus cult. Before he left on a trip, he told his disciples not to peek inside the covered basin of water. Curious, they lifted the cover and were surprised to see a blade of grass with a little mast and sail on the water. Shortly after, the master came home and scolded them for disobeying his order. When they denied it, he revealed that by tipping the blade of grass in the basin, they had caused his boat to capsize and almost drown him.

THE ORGANIZATION OF DISTANCE

As I am about to ascend a tower alone to read *The Decline and Fall of the
    Roman Empire,*
Suddenly the star portending Rome's fall appears in the paper.
The newspaper drops. The atlas opens, reminiscent of a far-off friend's
    exhortations.
In that postcard scene the dusk was growing vaster too.
("Waking as the sky doth darken"—bored—going to visit a friend.)
Gray skies. Gray seas. Gray roads.
But where? I can't discern the soil in the lamplight.
Suddenly I hear my own name from outside a thousand double doors.
So tired! Did nobody play with my basin boat?
A friend brings over five o'clock and a sense of snow.

January 9, 1935
translated by Lucas Klein

THE ROUND JEWEL BOX

I imagine snatching from someplace (the Milky Way?)
a round jewel box
containing several pearls:
one translucent mercury
concealing the sensual spectrum of the world,
one golden illumination
enshrouding a glorious banquet,
one fresh raindrop
containing your sighs last night . . .
Don't go to watch shops
to hear your youth getting eaten up by silkworms,
and don't go to antique stores
to buy your grandfather's old knickknacks.
Look at my round jewel box
flowing with my boat
downstream, even though everyone in the cabin

is in the eternal embrace of the sky,
even though your handshakes
are bridges—bridges! But bridges
too are built inside my round jewel box,
and perhaps for you, or them,
it is something to wear on the ear,
a pearl—a jewel—a star?

July 8, 1935
translated by Lucas Klein

FRAGMENT

You stand on the bridge overlooking the landscape,
and upstairs someone looking at the landscape looks at you.

The moon adorns your window,
and you adorn somebody's dream.

October 1935
translated by Lucas Klein

UNTITLED (1 of 5)

4.

Clay flown past the river onto your rafters,
Fountains yoked past the courtyard into your cup,
Overseas luxuries shipped upon your breast:
I want to study the history of communications.
Last night a light sigh was paid,
This morning two smiles have been received,
Paid: flowers in the mirror; received: the moon in the water . . .
For you I keep a running tab.

1937
translated by Lucas Klein

He Qifang (1912–1977)

A native of Wan County in Sichuan, He Qifang, whose original name was He Yongfang, grew up in a conservative family and received a traditional education. It wasn't until he attended middle school that he was first exposed to, and became interested in, modern Chinese literature and foreign literature. In 1931–35 he was a philosophy major at Peking University and expressed a passion for late-Tang poetry and French Symbolism. His first book of poems, *Han Garden*, was jointly published with fellow poets Bian Zhilin and Li Guangtian. After the Sino-Japanese War broke out, in July 1937, He returned to Sichuan to teach while continuing to write. In the summer of 1938, he moved to Yan'an, where he joined the Communist Party and taught at Lu Xun Art Academy. After 1949 he occupied several important posts, including director of the Literature Institute of Chinese Social Science Academy. During the Cultural Revolution, from 1966 to 1976, he was persecuted as a "Capitalist roader," but he continued to devote himself to translating German poetry. He passed away in Beijing.

PROPHECY

The miraculous day of your arrival has finally come!
Your approaching footsteps sigh like the night.
Neither like the whisper of leaves in the dark wind
Nor the quiet steps of deer in the mossy forest!
Tell me, in your voice like silver bells,
Are you the young god that was prophesized?

You must have come from the warm south!
Tell me about the moonlight and sunshine there.
Tell me how spring breezes beget new blossoms
And swallows fall in love with green willows.
My eyes will close as your singing fills my ears—
Bringing to mind memories of things long forgotten.

Please stop a while and rest from your long journey!
Come in and recline on the tiger skins.
Let me burn the leaves I gather every autumn
And hum my own song for you to hear.
I will sing like the flames that rise and fall,
The flames that are the story of my life.

Please don't go! Ahead of you is an endless forest
With ancient trees stripped and scarred by wild beasts,
And strangled in a death grip by vines like pythons;
Starlight can't penetrate the dense canopy.
When you hear the mournful echo of your first step
You will be too frightened to take another.

Must you go? Then please wait a moment for me.
My feet know every safe path to follow,
My untiring song will ease your weariness,
And my warm hand in yours will comfort you.
In the blackness of night, when we cannot see,
You can be guided by the light in my eyes.

But you are oblivious to my pleading!
Despite my anguish, your steps have not paused.
Like a somber breeze that fades at twilight,
You have moved on in your glorious passage.
Did you really arrive and depart without speaking?
Gone without a word for me, my young god?

1931
translated by Michelle Yeh and Frank Stewart

JOY

Tell me, what is the color of joy?
White like a dove's wings, red like a parrot's beak?
What's the sound of joy? Like a reed pipe?
Like the rustling pine trees, the murmur of flowing water?

Can it be held like a warm hand?
Can it be seen like a bright, loving look?
Does it make the heart lightly tremble
And spill quiet tears of sorrow?

How does joy arrive, and from where?
Like a firefly sparkling in the dusk?
Like the fragrance of rose petals?
Does it arrive wearing bells on its ankles?

When it comes to joy, my heart is bewildered,
Can joy be as beautiful as my melancholy?

1932
translated by Michelle Yeh and Frank Stewart

AUTUMN

Resounding in the dewy morning,
The woodcutters' axes echo from the valley.
The scythe is laid aside, sated with fragrant rice;
Baskets carrying ripened melons are unloaded.
Autumn has come to reside in a farmer's home.

A round net cast into the misty stream
Catches blue bream flickering like cypress leaves.
The reed boat, loaded down with frost,
Is gently rowed by homeward oars.
Autumn is delighting in a fisherman's boat.

The crickets' chirping makes the meadow seem even broader.
The streambed reveals itself in the dry season.
Where is the melody of the ox herder's bamboo flute
Overflowing with the summer nights' warm fragrance?
Autumn is dreaming in the eyes of a shepherdess.

1932
translated by Michelle Yeh and Frank Stewart

CYPRESS FOREST

Sunlight on the glossy leaves of the castor bean plant,
Orange jasmine beehives in the Earth god's shrine.
Racing the lengthening shadows, I have returned
Full circle to my beginning
Where I realize that time has stood still.

But in the green meadow, where are
The chubby-armed kids who chased crickets?
Where are my childhood pals whose excited cries
Rose over the treetops into the blue sky?
The once-vast kingdom of my childhood
Looks pitifully small under my feet, now
Muddied with the soil of foreign lands.

In the desert, travelers cherish a cup of water.
On the sea, sailors dread the white waves swelling over their oars.
Once I thought I was sovereign in a kingdom of joy
Whose happiness I kept in the deepest corner of my memory.
Since then, I have tasted the loneliness of adulthood,
And now I prefer the winding paths of dreams.

1933
translated by Michelle Yeh and Frank Stewart

Xin Di (1912–2004)

Xin Di, the pen name of Wang Xindi, was born in Tianjin to parents who hailed from Jiangsu. He began studying English at the age of ten. At seventeen he became interested in Baudelaire and translated *Les Fleurs du mal* (in English translation) into Chinese. In 1935 Xin Di graduated from the Department of Foreign Languages and Literatures at Tsinghua University and spent the next four years at Edinburgh University, where he majored in English literature. He was especially drawn to Gerard Manley Hopkins, W. H. Auden, and T. S. Eliot, whose lectures he attended. After returning to China, he became a professor at Jinan and Guanghua Universities, where he taught Shakespeare and English poetry. After 1949 he worked in the tobacco and food industries. Until 1980, Xin Di's poetry was only known to some poets in Taiwan and Hong Kong. It was in 1981—when a collection of nine young poets active in the 1940s, including Mu Dan, Chen Jingrong, and Zheng Min, was published under the title *Nine Leaves*—that Xin Di gained recognition in mainland China.

RHAPSODY

The multi-storied building is like a ship
It really is like a ship
Feet of countless people
Windblown rain attacks the windows
But the roaring is just an alternate loneliness
I try to think of the coolness of early summer
Cool lotus leaves in cool arms
I want to use a lotus leaf as an umbrella
As a fan
But why is it so cold beneath the umbrella
I twist a burning orange torch
I'm in a dark place
I'm far away
I quietly espy
A pair of sea eyes
A pair of eyes hiding a beaded lamp

And a name
Tonight the sea roars
Oh, the ever-changing sea
Tonight, I no longer see the glow of the serpent's belly
Its long white tail
But why can I still hear that broken flute
I know not tonight, last night, tomorrow night
Night after night
On a windy night
On a rainy night
On a foggy night
A black sailing vessel on black water
Is it departing or arriving
And "who" is it carrying
I want to call
I want to call the distant territory of the nation
Sounds of wind and rain
The storied building is like a ship
The storied building is really like a ship
Sounds of footsteps, noise, and laughter
The sound of doors opening and closing
Someone has returned to the neighboring house
"It's me, it's me"
I want to ask
I want to call
I want to tell him: Anton Chekhov
I want to tell him:
He is a Khitan
He is sick
He has a pale heart
He reads poems on fans
He has lost the flowers of spring and the swallows of autumn
He has forever lost the night . . .

May 1937
translated by John Balcom

THE SOURCE OF LONELINESS

Two towering walls block our way
People walk between them as if through a valley
A ribbon of blue sky spans the distance between birth and death
If the argument for freedom is stirred by the wind
The electrified air will echo back at any moment
Where you meet with trouble today is a myriad colored sea of garbage
Fetid odors of the city and death are the only things that shock
Time scolds the darkness as it walks toward dawn
The universe is a giant gray elephant
If you don't step back you'll never see it clearly or touch it all
Cries fall in the empty desert
Just like you striking yourself with a bare fist.

1946
translated by John Balcom

SCENERY

The train rolls over China's ribs
One social problem after another
Our neighbors are the graves between thatched houses and fields
The destination of the living is just that close
The land in summer is so green, rich and fertile nature
The new khaki uniforms of the soldiers fade the old misery
Used to thinking of the places I have passed through
I can't say it's unfamiliar but just a general bleakness
The scrawny oxen and the scrawnier people
All is sickness, not scenery!

Summer 1948
Translated by John Balcom

Ji Xian (1913–2013)

Ji Xian is the pen name of Lu Yu, who was born in Hebei into a family that had come from Qin County in Shaanxi. He graduated from Suzhou Arts Academy, where he majored in Western-style painting. In 1929 he started writing poetry under the pen name Louis and published his first book of poems four years later. He befriended Dai Wangshu and contributed to *Les Contemporains* and other journals. He moved to Taiwan in 1948 and taught for many years at Chenggong Middle School in Taipei. In 1953 Ji Xian launched the *Modern Poetry Quarterly* and advocated the "second revolution of new poetry." The journal became a magnet for young poets in postwar Taiwan and Hong Kong. He founded the Modernist School in 1956 and published the controversial manifesto "Six Tenets." The first tenet states that modern Chinese poetry is the fruit of "horizontal transplantation" rather than "vertical inheritance." In 1976 he moved to California, where he lived in Millbrae till he passed away.

CITY IN FLAMES

Looking through the window of your soul,
Into its darkest recesses,
I see a city in flames, no one coming to the rescue
Only a tide of naked madmen.

I hear a sound pierce through the boundless maelstrom
Of my name, name of the lover, name of the enemy,
Names of the dead and living unnumbered.

When I answer in hushed voice
"Yes, I am here,"
I too become a fearsome city in flames.

1936
translated by Denis Mair

DOG BARKING AT THE MOON

A train carrying a dog that howls at the moon rolls by and out of sight.
The tracks heave a sigh of relief.
Then songs with personality sung by naked girls astride giant thorny cacti
Arise from all sides:
A chorus with no consistent meaning,
Discordant sounds.
Dark shadows of cacti recline on the flatland.
The flatland is a suspended disc.
The fallen train no longer crawls back from the curved horizon,
But forlorn howls have struck the gong of the nickel moon and now bounce back
To swallow the voices of girls singing.

1942
translated by Denis Mair

PAINTER'S STUDIO

I have a studio that is closed and cut off from everyone. Inside of it, I can face
the mirror and paint my naked body on canvas. My naked body is skinny, pale,
and riddled with wounds: blue, purple, old and new, never fully healing, just
like my hatred, never fading away.

As to who struck me with a whip, I do not know; who hacked at me with an axe,
I do not know; who tightened a rope around me, I do not know; who branded
me with hot iron, I do not know; who splashed acid on me, I do not know.

I only know the wish for vengeance burns fiercely in my heart.

But my only means of vengeance, which I have already adopted, is to draw my
wounds over and over, to paint them over and over, in perfect likeness, then
take them somewhere, to show at an exhibition, to let everyone look at them,
let them also shudder in disgust, let them also know pain, and most of all fill
them also with undying hatred like my own. And that is all, that is all.

1946
translated by Denis Mair

TYPE B BLOOD

Bath finished on a summer afternoon
Stretched out for a moment's rest
Suddenly my long lean body strikes me
With its resemblance to Christ
It too could be betrayed
Could be pierced with nails
And my type B blood
Would also be pure and holy
It must not flow in vain
How can I let it flow in vain?
So let it flow!

1961
translated by Denis Mair

Chen Jingrong (1917–1989)

Chen Jingrong, the pen name of Chen Yifan, was a native of Leshan, Sichuan. In 1932, while she was still in middle school, she met her substitute teacher, the poet Cao Baohua (1906–78), and ran away from home with him. They were caught, and she had to return home. But in 1935 she ran away again and met up with Cao in Beijing. While there, she met many writers, including He Qifang (1912–77) and Ba Jin (1904–2005), and started publishing poetry. In 1946 she settled down in Shanghai and edited two poetry journals. Ten years later she became the editor of *World Literature*. Besides poetry, she wrote prose and translated the tales of Hans Christian Andersen and the poetry of Charles Baudelaire and Rainer Maria Rilke, among others. Her work was rediscovered in 1981, along with that of eight other poets who were active in the 1940s; the group is collectively known as the Nine Leaves.

SPRING OF THE LOGIC-CRAZED

1.

Fast-flowing water
Seems not to flow,
A turning wheel
Seems to stand still
A big smile can
Seem like a grimace
Light too bright in the eyes
Is just like being in the dark
Unable to see.

Complete equals incomplete,
Full equals empty,
The biggest equals the tiniest,
Zero equals infinity.

Old beyond old, this world
Seems eternally fresh
Empty Grandma's trunk
And you can open a boutique

2.

How many forms, gestures, symbols and voices
Wearied us ages ago; but
You, blue sky, never age!
A warm spring morning
A bomber circles in the sunlight.

Nature is a huge hospital,
Spring is the physician, sunlight the medicine,
Reviving weary souls,
Calling the withered vegetation back to life.

We have a thousand worries, a thousand woes,
The days pile them up mercilessly on our backs,
But spring is here, and we feel like
Stretching and yawning.

We can imagine all we want a boundless stretch of green
But water, water
As usual we embrace
Unending thirst.

3.

Living life,
Eat and drink, work, sleep,
Smile for some reason, cry for some reason,
Nothing is unexpected.

The turtle dove cries in clear skies,
Calling wind and rain—
Pitiful, pitiful, most pitiful hope
Sometimes dies of despair.

Erect a wall of the will,
Then pace in hesitation,
Forgiving yet
Hating yourself.

4.

In your dream a strong wind suddenly blows,
Carrying a dog's barking,
After the wind stops, whose
Heavy door closes with a thud
As if I
Were locked out of sleep,
To listen alone to the sound of
A distant speeding train.
Ah, a cold front from
Siberia has already passed—

Then is this really
Spring? Yes. Don't you see
The sunlight has softened,
Down hang the willow catkins,
Green hair sprouts from the earth,
Is even the wind drunk too?

We wait for thunder.
Thunder, the first thunder of spring,
It will awaken sleeping insects;
That will be real thunder,
And not just a cough
of the sky sick with a cold.

5.

Children's Day! Several lucky children
Brightly attired for the event,
Salute, recite speeches, and receive awards
While many others labor in factories
Their health ruined by eight
Ten or more hours of work per day.

Deceit and falsehood are one family,
Oh spring, we know you have
So many short-lived flowers!
A mournful horn plays at a funeral,
We are alive but have no time
To weep.

In this big modern city
We are little sardines,
Lacking clothes, food, housing, and transportation,
Crowded together because there's no room for us.

Birds, beasts, bugs, and fish
Are not our concern
Our own sorrow and happiness, parting and togetherness

Are all so common,
Everything squeezed out
Leaving a blank.

Last night's dream arouses no sadness this morning,
Mountains and rivers, the bridge of dreams lost;
Tomb-Sweeping Festival or Mid-Autumn Festival,
The rain and the moon are always hard to control.

There's always something to say, something to do,
At every end there is a beginning;
If one day you suddenly stop,
Willing or not, that will be death.

April 1–5, 1947
translated by John Balcom

Mu Dan (1918–1977)

Mu Dan, the pen name of Zha Liangzheng, was born in Tianjin into a family that hailed from Haining in Zhejiang. In 1935 he entered Tsinghua University and two years later, after the Sino-Japanese War broke out, moved to Kunming as a student at Southwestern Associated University. After he graduated, in 1940, he stayed at his alma mater as a teaching assistant before volunteering for the expeditionary army against Japan in Burma (today's Myanmar) as an English interpreter. In 1949–53 he studied in the English Department at the University of Chicago. After returning to China, he became an associate professor in the Department of Foreign Languages at Nankai University in Tianjin and engaged in translations of English and Russian literature. He was persecuted during the Anti-Rightist Campaign in 1958 and was deprived of his position and his right to publish poetry. It was not until after the Cultural Revolution that he was "rehabilitated." The poems he wrote in his last years were published posthumously.

"I" and "Eight Poems" were both inspired by Plato's *Symposium*, in which a person in love is viewed as longing for his or her other half and love is the pursuit of wholeness.

SPRING

A green flame flickers over the grass,
He longs to embrace you, a flower.
Resisting the soil, the flower stretches
As a warm breeze blows with sorrow or pleasure.
If you are awake, push open the window,
See how beautiful the desires filling the garden are.

Under the blue sky, our tightly clasped,
Twenty-year-old bodies are bewitched by that eternal mystery,
Identical to that birdsong made of clay,
You've been set aflame but with nowhere to find refuge,
Oh, light, shadow, sound, and color, all are stripped bare,
Suffering, waiting to be recombined anew.

February 1940
translated by John Balcom

I

Severed from the womb, warmth lost,
I am a part longing to be rescued,
Forever alone, locked in a wasteland,

I am parted from the whole in a static dream,
Painfully I feel the flow of time, with nothing to cling to,
Memories won't bring my self back,

Meeting another part, we cry together,
It's the joy of first love, I try to break free from my cage,
Reaching out to embrace myself

Form is illusory, a greater disappointment,
Forever alone, locked in a wasteland,
Hating mother for parting me from the land of dreams.

November 1940
translated by John Balcom

EIGHT POEMS (3 of 8)

1.

Your eyes see a conflagration,
You don't see me, though I kindled you;
Oh, it is just maturity that burns.
Yours and mine. As if mountains stood between us.

In this natural process of transformation,
I love but a transient you.
Even if I weep, become ash, become ash and am born again,
Young girl, it is but God toying with himself.

4.

Silently, we embrace in
A world illuminated by words,
But that formless darkness frightens,
Possibility and impossibility perplex us.

Those sweet words, suffocating us,
Died before birth,
Their shrouded specters set us adrift,
Drifting into the freedom and beauty of a mad love.

8.

There's no getting any closer,
All coincidences are fixed between us;
Only the sunlight shines through the riot of leaves
Shines on two willing hearts, alike.

With the change in season, we each fall
But the huge tree that gave us life is evergreen,
Its cruel mockery of our heartlessness
(and tears) will turn to peace united among old roots.

1942
translated by John Balcom

MEDITATION

1.

Why, as the soul of all things, is
Our lot no better than a small tree's?
Today you shake it, laughing with superiority,
Tomorrow you'll become the soil under its roots.
Why are handwritten words
More lasting than this hand, and more robust?
They can cast aside a rotting hand,
And exist silently on a tattered sheet of paper.
And so, proudly I live for a few decades,
Seemingly as the director of all things,
But under that long lasting order,
I'm actually just an actor with a bit part.

2.

I carry the spring of life in both hands,
I feel its freshness,
It is strong wine, refreshing foam,
Flowing into my rushing about, my labor, and my adventure.
As if a garden never seen by those in the past
Is about to appear before me.
But nowadays, suddenly finding myself facing the grave,
With a backward glance, detached
I only see the entwined joys and sorrows it has watered
Disappearing entirely into a desert from time immemorial
Only then do I know that all my efforts
Have gone into living merely an ordinary life.

May 1976
translated by John Balcom

Zheng Min (1920–2022)

Zheng was born in Beijing into a family that had come from Fujian. In 1939–43 she attended Southwestern Associated University, where she majored in philosophy. She studied German and started writing poetry under the mentorship of Feng Zhi, whose *Sonnets* exerted a significant influence on her. In 1948 she went to Brown University for an MA degree in English literature. In 1951 she attended Illinois State University for her doctorate. There she met her future husband, Tong Shibai (1920–2005), who was also a graduate of Southwestern Associated University. They married later that year and moved to New York. In 1955 they returned to China, where Zheng worked at the Foreign Literature Institute of the Chinese Social Science Academy and later at Beijing Normal University. During this time she did not write any poetry, and it wasn't until 1979 that she resumed writing. Zheng published her first book of poetry in Shanghai in 1949; her early work was rediscovered in *Nine Leaves*.

MEETING IN THE EVENING

I'm reluctant to raise my hand and knock on the door,
Afraid lest it sound too harsh
A little boat just returned,
No oar dips into the water
It simply waits for the evening sea breeze,
If you sit by the lamp,
And hear soft breathing outside,
Feel someone quietly nearby . . .
Put down your cigarette,
Open the door in silence,
You'll find me there. Waiting by your door.

1943
translated by John Balcom

SHE AND THE EARTH

She spoke to the earth
        Be silent
                Silent in thought

Be firm
        Firm enough to support angry footsteps
                Of a racing army

Be soft
        Softly bury
                The nobility drenched in blood

Be not forgetful
        Never forget that awful humiliation
                The tramped dignity
                        The slave's honored skull

Be branded
    With the imprints of shackles

Be vigilant
    Against the smell of blood

1989
translated by John Balcom

The Modernist Movement and Surrealism

As the civil war raged on, it was clear that the Communists were winning. On October 1, 1949, Mao Zedong (1893–1976) stood in Tiananmen Square in Beijing and proclaimed the founding of the People's Republic of China. The same year, Chiang Kai-shek and approximately one million followers retreated from the mainland to Taiwan. In June 1950 war broke out on the Korean Peninsula, with the Soviet Union and China aiding North Korea, and the United States supporting South Korea. The conflict marked the beginning of the Cold War between the Communist bloc and the "Free World" led by democratic countries in North America and Europe.

After the Korean War ended, in July 1953, the United States sent the Seventh Fleet to the Pacific to contain the spread of communism in the region and signed the Sino-American Mutual Defense Treaty with the Republic of China in Taiwan in December 1954. To "liberate" Taiwan, in 1954–55 the People's Republic unleashed heavy artillery bombardments of Kinmen (Quemoy) and Matsu Islands off the southeastern coast of the mainland. This is known as the First Taiwan Strait Crisis. The Second Taiwan Strait Crisis refers to intermittent bombings on the islands from 1958 to the beginning of 1979, when the United States established diplomatic relations with the People's Republic of China.

Internally, the People's Republic was embroiled in a series of political campaigns initiated by Chairman Mao Zedong, such as the Three-Anti and Five-Anti Campaigns of 1951–52 and the Anti-Rightist Campaign of 1957–59. The objectives were to consolidate the power of the Communists by purging the so-called counterrevolutionaries—capitalists, landlords, intellectuals, and those formerly associated with the Nationalists. Numbering in the millions, those who were thus labeled were persecuted, sent to prisons or labor camps, or executed. The Great Leap Forward, the economic plan that spanned the years 1958 to 1962, sought to increase industrial and agricultural production through the commune system, but it turned out to be a disaster and led to the Great Famine, during which it is estimated that tens of millions died from starvation. Another consequence was wide criticism of Chairman Mao and a shift of power within the Communist Party. To combat dissent, he turned to young people and started the Great Proletarian Cultural Revolution in 1966.

In postwar Taiwan, the fear of Communist infiltration and the chasm between the ruling Nationalist government and the native Taiwanese people underscored the oppressive policies of what is known as the White Terror (1949–87). Culturally, in contrast to the destruction of the Chinese tradition and attack on anything associated with the capitalist West on the mainland, the Nationalists promoted Confucianism and classicism on the one hand and welcomed Western—especially American—cultural products on the other. Situated between the mainland and Taiwan, Hong Kong was the "buffer zone" where contending ideologies coexisted. A British colony, Hong Kong enjoyed a higher degree of freedom and had relatively easy access to information from the world.

Despite the conservative and repressive atmosphere in Taiwan, a golden age in modern poetry evolved. Senior émigré poets, such as Ji Xian (1913–2013) and Qin Zihao (1912–63), inspired and mentored a new generation of young poets, who engaged in bold experiments in language and form. Although surrealism had been introduced into mainland China and Taiwan as early as the 1930s, it was not until the 1950s that it took root and blossomed in Taiwan. Exploring the unconscious and the alienation of modern man, Surrealism, as part of the Modernist movement, represented a bold rejection of the anti-Communist literature promoted by the government.

Zhou Mengdie (1921–2014)

A native of Xichuan County in Henan, Zhou Mengdie is the pen name of Zhou Qishu. *Mengdie* literally means "dreaming of butterfly," an allusion to the Daoist parable in *Zhuangzi* in which the philosopher Zhuang Zhou (third century BCE) dreamed of being a butterfly and, upon waking, wondered whether he was dreaming or awake. Zhou attended Kaifeng Normal College before he joined the Nationalist army, moved to Taiwan in 1948, and was honorably discharged in 1955. From 1959 to 1980, Zhou ran a bookstand on Wuchang Street outside Café Astoria, the first Western-style bakery in Taiwan and a popular hangout for writers and artists. Zhou started writing poetry in 1952 and joined the Blue Stars

Poetry Society when it was founded, in 1955, by Qin Zihao and Yu Guangzhong. In 1962 he became a Buddhist and would practice meditation while running his bookstand in the midst of the clamor of downtown Taipei.

The wisdom tree in the third poem is the Bodhi tree, which refers to the sacred fig tree in India, under which Gautama Buddha meditated and reached enlightenment. It is also called the "tree of awakening."

ALONELAND

Last night, again in dream I saw myself
sitting naked, cross-legged on a snowy mountain peak.

The climate here is stuck where spring grafts onto winter.
(The snow here is gentle as swan's down.)
Here there are no importunate cries from the marketplace,
only the faint sound of time chewing time's cud.
No cobras here, no owls, no beasts with human faces,
only thorn apples, olive trees, and jade butterflies.
Here no text, no coordinates, no Buddha with a thousand hands and eyes,
but at every turn the unspoken power of a nebulous teeming silence.
Here, day has the quiet and seclusion of night,
night is more enchanting, richer, more brilliant than day
and this cold is like strong drink, rich in poetry and beauty.
Even the Void knows how to play *go*; it invites a skyful
of stars that need no words to understand . . .

The past stays standing; what's to come doesn't come.
I'm the servant of Now. and its Sage Emperor.

July 1958
translated by Lloyd Haft

ON THE FERRY

Boat—carrying the many, many shoes,
carrying the many, many
three-cornered dreams
facing each other and facing away.

Rolling, rolling—in the deeps,
flowing, flowing—in the unseen:
man on the boat, boat on the water, water on Endlessness.
Endlessness is, Endlessness is upon
my pleasures and pains,
    born in a moment
    and gone in a moment.

Is it the water that's going, carrying the boat and me?

Or am I going, carrying boat and water? Dusk fascinates.
Einstein's smile is a mystery, comfortless.

June 1960
translated by Lloyd Haft

UNDER THE WISDOM TREE

Who is the one whose heart conceals a mirror?
Who would be willing to trudge through a lifetime barefoot?
All eyes are clouded over with eyes.
Who could sift fire out of snow, forge fire back to snow?
Under the Wisdom Tree, a man with but half a face
raises his eyes to the sky, sighs in answer to the azure
that's poised for the fathomless bow from its heights toward him.

Yes! Someone has sat here!
The grass is lush green. Even if it's winter,
though the meditator's footfalls have long since passed away,
pillowed on the harmonies of nature, you can still enjoy
a tête-à-tête with the back of the moon, of the wind.

How many springs have you sat through till they snapped?
How many summers matured through your sitting?
When you came, the snow was snow and you were you.
Overnight, the snow was snow no longer, and you weren't you—
till tonight, ten years below zero,
when in a flash the first falling star again lights up

and you're amazed to see:
the snow is still snow, you're still you,
and though the meditator's footfalls have long since passed away,
the grass is lush green.

June 1961
translated by Lloyd Haft

Mu Xin (1927–2011)

Mu Xin, literally "wooden heart," was a painter, poet, fiction and prose writer, and literary and art critic. Born Sun Pu into a wealthy family in Wu Town, Zhejiang, he attended Hangzhou Art Academy at the age of sixteen and two years later transferred to Shanghai Art Academy, where he studied with Lin Fengmian (1900–91). His education was interrupted when he was expelled for his role in a student movement. Wanted by the Nationalist authorities, he escaped to Taiwan but later returned to Shanghai and graduated in 1948. After 1949, Mu Xin held a number of positions as editor and professor; he was incarcerated three times for political reasons, including for eighteen months during the Cultural Revolution, when twenty volumes of his writings were destroyed. In 1982 he left China to attend The Art Students League of New York. Between 1989 and 1994, he gave eighty-five lectures on the history of world literature to a group of Chinese writers and artists at his home. In 2006 he returned to China, where he passed away from pneumonia complications. Mu's paintings are collected by the British Museum, Harvard University, and Yale University, among other places. His complete works were published in thirteen volumes in Taiwan in 2013 and in sixteen volumes in Shanghai in 2020.

"After the Sleigh Incident" alludes to two events in the life of the nineteenth-century Russian writer Alexander Pushkin. In 1820–23 Pushkin was in exile in Bessarabia, in southern Russia. In the summer of 1830, he was confined to the village Boldino in southeastern Russia due to a cholera outbreak. His wedding to Natalia Goncharova was delayed, he was under financial strain, and his relationship with the czar was untenable. Although he was experiencing considerable anguish, the three months in Boldino turned out to be the most productive period in Pushkin's life; he wrote dozens of short stories, plays, lyrics, and narrative poems.

FROTH

There are many kinds of love
Most end as soon as they begin
Venus, O my goddess Aphrodite
Born at dawn out of the sea foam!
Foam and froth, spraying everywhere—
All the assignations and partings in my life,
All the lovers I've held and kissed are froth too
I wish I had embraced and kissed even more—
They are the effervescence of even briefer moments
I've grown tired and jaded
But lying back in my warm, nutmeg-scented bath
The gleaming lather of the soap brings back memories
As though love were cleansing my skin, and the cool pure water
Was washing away the froth all over my body

1996
translated by Michelle Yeh and Frank Stewart

SLOWNESS OF THE PAST

I remember in my youth long ago
people were honest and sincere
every word they said could be trusted

I would set out at dawn for the train station
not a soul was walking on the dark streets
alive with the aroma of soy milk being heated in small cafés

In the old days the sun took a long time to set
bikes, horses, and mail delivery were slow too
a lifetime was long enough to love only one person

In the old days the locks were beautiful
and the keys were exquisitely made
When you turned the key, everyone understood

published in 2008
translated by Michelle Yeh and Frank Stewart

AFTER THE SLEIGH INCIDENT

If you love someone
the two of you will have endless things to talk about
But if that's really the truth of love
then no such person exists
I remember sitting in a restaurant with my uncle
it was probably after the sleigh incident
The couple at the next table weren't talking
the entire dining room was silent
We waited for the food as if waiting for a savior
If you love someone
you will have endless things to talk about
The diners, the sleigh that toppled into the Congo River—
In the winter of 1821
Pushkin was on his way to Bessarabia
And at the coach station he rested
As he waited for breakfast

he took a scrap of paper from his pocket—
Poets don't need a desk to write on
In the summer of 1836, Boldino Village
such beautiful wild places
with seemingly endless prairies!
He galloped his horse across them and returned refreshed
He leaned over the pool table or reclined on the long sofa
and wrote about water, ice cubes, jam in earthen jars
If you love a world
you will have endless poems to write
If that's really the truth of the world
then no such world exists

published in 2008
translated by Michelle Yeh and Frank Stewart

Luo Fu (1928–2018)

Born in Hengyang, Hunan, Luo Fu, whose family name was Mo, started writing poetry at the age of eighteen. In 1949 he followed the Nationalists to Taiwan and, two years later, entered Fu Hsing Kang Academy (today's National Defense University). In 1959 he was stationed on Kinmen as a news correspondent. In November 1965 he was assigned to Vietnam as the English secretary in the military advisory corps. "Poems of Saigon" were written during this period. In 1973 he graduated from Tamkang University with a major in English. The same year he was honorably discharged from the navy and devoted himself to writing and calligraphy. He moved to Vancouver, Canada, in 1996, and lived there for twenty years, then moved back to Taiwan. In July 1954 Luo Fu cofounded the *Epoch Poetry Quarterly* with Zhang Mo (b. 1931) and Ya Xian (b. 1932). Beginning in its eleventh issue, the journal changed the format and embraced surrealism. The trio continued to serve as editors until 1985; the journal is still publishing today.

The title of "Song of Everlasting Sorrow" refers to the classical poem by Bai Juyi (772–846), which narrates the love story of Emperor Xuanzong (685–762) of the Tang dynasty and Yang Yuhuan (719–52), or Lady Yang. The emperor was so infatuated with her beauty that he neglected to govern. A rebellion broke out, and the emperor fled the capital. During the journey, the imperial guards demanded that Yang be executed, and the emperor acquiesced. At the end of the poem, the grief-stricken emperor and Yang are reunited and vow eternal love in a dream.

SONGS OF SAIGON (2 of 11)

1. After the Coup
The motorcycle belongs to the Texan
Dust belongs to me
The stick belongs to the gang of unruly kids
Blood belongs to me
The sun belongs to the fasting Buddhist monks and nuns at the roadside
Hunger belongs to me
Saigon River belongs to the sky
The void that can be neither grasped nor tasted, is neither graspable nor bitable, neither pain nor itch, neither luck nor bad luck, neither Buddha nor Zen belongs to me

2. Tomb-Sweeping Day
It is really inappropriate for us to say anything
On the face of April
Teardrops shine like flowers
On the lawn, the dandelion is a child flying a kite
Frolicking while suspended from a cloud

The cloud hangs a child
The airplane hangs a bomb
Children and bombs are both something you can't lose your temper over
It is really inappropriate of us to say anything

We are all accustomed to this game
It's not crying
It's weeping

April 1968
translated by Michelle Yeh and Frank Stewart

SONG OF EVERLASTING SORROW

That rose, like all roses, blossoms
only for a single morning.
—*Balzac*

1.

Tang Emperor Xuanzong
Plucked black-haired grief
From the sound of water

2.

She is the
White flesh
On the first page
Of the Yang genealogy
A rose in a mirror
Blossoming under the most tender caresses
Heaven-sent beauty
Bubbles
On the Flower Pure Pool
Waiting to be raised up
In two hands
Music of the immortals
Drifts from Li Palace
Mingled with wine and bodily perfume
After imbibing, the lips
Just moan
And the bodies on the ivory bed
Are mountains
And rivers
One river sleeping soundly in another
The subterranean flow
Rolls
Across ten thousand miles
Till a white song
Sprouts, breaking the soil

3.

He raises his burning hand
And shouts:
I make love
Because I want to make love
Because
I am the emperor
Because
We are accustomed to meeting in the flesh

4.

He began reading the paper in bed, eating breakfast in bed, watching
Her hair being combed in bed, handling the affairs of state in bed
     affix the seal
     affix the seal
     affix the seal
     affix the seal

From that time
The emperor quit attending court in the morning

5.

He was emperor
But war is a stain
A sticky fluid
That cannot be wiped off
The satin sheets
The fighting far away

Heaven was mute
As the war drums beat to a stunning coiffure
Faraway, signal fires rose like snakes and licked the earth
With fiery red tongues

6.

Rivers
Still burn between two thighs
War must be fought
It was a national affair
Wife, the blood of woman can only flow in one direction
If the Sixth Army fails to set out today
It will be all over, on the slopes of Emei Mountain
You are a poplar catkin
Raised on the wind from the square

A chunk of high-priced fat
Will nourish
Another rose
Or
Another terminal disease
In history

7.

Sorrow usually begins in fire
He looks into the distance outside
His head
Turns following the flight of birds
His eyes follow the changing colors of sunset
The name he calls
Is buried in its echo

Pacing round the room all night long
He has stood
In every window of Wei Yang Palace
Cold white fingers pinch the candles
Among faint coughs
All the cherry trees in the Forbidden City
Wither one night
An autumn wind

He ties his beard in knots then unties them after which he puts his hands
Behind his back and paces back and forth, back and forth,
Back and forth, a fragrant lily explodes behind the curtains; later he
Reaches for the Classic of Rivers and hears the flowing water, but
He can't understand why the river weeps instead of roaring when it
Passes through his hands
He throws his clothes over himself and stands up
He burns his own flesh
He awakens from a cold piece of jade

A thousand candles burn in a thousand rooms
The moon beyond the tower shines on the sleepless
A girl walks on top of the wall
Her face indistinct in the emptiness

8.

In a sudden frenzy
He searches for that black hair
But she has handed it on
On a thread of smoke
Water must rise as clouds
Soil must be trampled into thirsting moss
A face hidden among the leaves
Is more despairing than a setting sun
A chrysanthemum on her lips
A black well in her eyes
A war in her flesh
A small, unbrewed storm
In her hands
Her teeth will never ache again
Nor will that Tang rash
Ever flare up again
The face dissolves in water is
Relatively white and absolutely black
She will never offer a dish of salt and cry of thirst
Her supported hand

Trembles
Pointing at the stone road
To Chang'an

9.

Time: July seventh
Place: Palace of Long Life
A tall thin man dressed in blue
A woman with no face
Flames rise without stopping
In the white air
Wings
More
Wings
Fly from the palace toward the moon
The intimate whispers
Slowly fade
Twinkle bitterly

One or two brief echoes return in the wind and rain

August 15, 1972
translated by John Balcom

BECAUSE OF THE WIND

Yesterday, following the riverbank
Strolling slowly
I came upon a place where reeds stooped to drink
In passing, I asked a chimney
To write for me a long letter in the sky
Though carelessly writ
My heart's intent
Shone like the candlelight at your window
Still somewhat obscure
That cannot be helped
    Because of the wind

It matters not if you understand my letter
What matters is
You must, before the daisies wither
Quickly lose your temper, or laugh
Quickly find that thin shirt of mine in the trunk
Quickly face the mirror, combing your soft black charm
Then light a lamp
With a lifetime of love
I am a flame
To be extinguished any moment
  Because of the wind

1981

translated by John Balcom

Yu Guangzhong (Kwang-chung Yu, 1928–2017)

Born in Nanjing, Yu came from Quanzhou, Fujian. After the Sino-Japanese War broke out in 1937, he lived in various cities, including Hong Kong, before settling in Chongqing, the wartime capital of the Republic of China, where he went to school from 1938 to 1945. After the war, he entered the University of Nanking (then known in Chinese as Jinling University, now Nanjing University) but, concerned about the looming civil war between the Nationalists and the Communists, in 1949 he transferred to Xiamen University and then moved to Hong Kong. The next year he went to Taiwan and entered the National Taiwan University as a junior in the Department of Foreign Languages and Literatures. In 1954 he cofounded the Blue Stars Poetry Society with senior poets Qin Zihao (1912-63) and Zhong Dingwen (1914–2012). In 1958 he studied English literature at the University of Iowa; after receiving an MA degree, he returned to Taiwan to teach at the National Taiwan Normal University. He was a visiting professor in the United States in 1965–66 and 1969–70. After teaching at the Chinese University of Hong Kong in 1974–85, he returned to Taiwan to serve as the founding dean of the School of Humanities at the National Sun Yat-sen University in Gaoxiong, from which he retired in 2016. Yu published his first book of poetry in 1952. In addition to being a poet, he was an influential essayist, translator, and literary scholar.

  "Lord, Do Not Cross the River" is an ancient ballad in which the wife of an old man tries to stop him from crossing the turbulent water. Li Bai (701–62) famously rewrote it. Here Yu juxtaposes the original ballad of four lines with the bitter reality that during the Cultural Revolution, some men tried to swim to Hong Kong from the mainland and many were killed or drowned in the desperate attempt.

IF A WAR IS RAGING FAR AWAY

If a war is raging somewhere far away,
Should I cover my ears, or sit up and listen with self-reproach?
Should I cover my nose, or inhale the stench of burning corpses?
Should I listen to your passionate breathing,
Or to the high-pitched whine of bullets insisting on their ultimate truth?
Slogans, medals, sacrifices—
Can they satisfy insatiable Death?
If a war is scorching some nation,
And far away heavy tanks are harrowing the spring soil,
And a baby is wailing
Beside a dead mother, with an unspeakable future—
And if a nun is immolating herself,
Her sorrowing flesh crackling,
Her shriveling limbs reaching toward Nirvana
In an ineffectual gesture of hopefulness—
If we are lying here with each other
While others are lying on some battlefield
Seeking the peace of barbed wire,
Should I feel dread or happiness,
Feel relieved that I am making love to you and that I'm not at war,
That it's your naked body near me, not enemy soldiers?
If a war is raging somewhere far away but we are there,
Then you are an angel with immaculate white wings,
Leaning over a hospital bed to gaze at me
Lying here without hands, feet, eyes, or genitals
In a field hospital that reeks of blood;
If a war is raging somewhere far away,
My love, if we are far away . . .

February 11, 1967
translated by Michelle Yeh and Frank Stewart

HOMESICKNESS

When I was young
Homesickness was as thin as a postage stamp
Me on one side
Mother on the other

When I grew up
Homesickness was as slender as a boat ticket
Me on one side
My bride on the other

Later,
Homesickness was as deep as a grave
Me outside
Mother inside

And now
Homesickness is as wide as a strait
Me on one side
The mainland on the other

1972
translated by Michelle Yeh and Frank Stewart

LORD, DO NOT CROSS THE RIVER

Lord, do not cross the river   a barbed-wire fence is expecting you
Lord, you are crossing the river after all   a pair of binoculars is watching you
Falling into the river and dying   a hail of bullets whistles by
What am I to do with you, Lord   a clump of reeds shakes its head

A searchlight warns: Lord, do not cross the sea
A patrol boat bellows: Lord, you are crossing the sea after all
A frenzy of sharks rushes   You falling into the sea and dying
A surge of bloody water bubbles up   What can a song do in the face of that

November 16, 1976
translated by Michelle Yeh and Frank Stewart

Shang Qin (1930–2010)

Born Luo Xianxing, Shang Qin was a native of Gong County in Sichuan. At the age of fifteen, he was seized by Nationalist soldiers. Although he tried to escape, he was conscripted and traveled with the army through southern and southwestern China. He moved to Taiwan in 1949 and started writing poetry in 1953 under different pen names until he settled on Shang Qin, which means "a bird singing a sad tune." After he was honorably discharged from the army, in 1968, he held various jobs, such as dockworker, gardener, truck driver, and beef noodle restaurateur. In 1969 Shang Qin was invited to the International Writers' Workshop at the University of Iowa. The same year he published his first book of poetry, *Dreams or Dawns*. After staying in the United States for two years, he returned to Taiwan to serve as the chief editor of the *China Times Weekly*. In his last years, he suffered from Parkinson's disease and passed away in Taipei on June 27, 2010.

GIRAFFE

After the young prison guard noticed that, according to their physical exams, the prisoners were getting taller every month because their necks were growing, he reported to the warden: "Sir, the windows are too high!" But the warden replied: "No, they are gazing upward at Time."

The kindhearted, young prison guard could not discern the face of Time, nor did he know where it came from and where it was going, so night after night he went to the zoo and paced back and forth outside the giraffe enclosure.

1959
translated by Michelle Yeh and Frank Stewart

DOVES

Suddenly, I make a fist with my right hand and pound it hard into my left palm, "Smack!" How desolate is the wilderness! And yet a flock of doves flies across the pallid sky: do they fly alone or in pairs?

With my left hand, I hold my right fist tightly as it slowly opens; the fingers begin to relax, but they cannot straighten out fully, and the fist can only twist back and forth. Ah, my innocent hand that has labored and will continue to labor, has killed and will eventually be killed, how you resemble a wounded bird. In the dizzying sky, a flock of doves flies over: do they fly alone or in pairs?

Now, with my left hand I comfort my trembling right hand; but my left hand is trembling too, like a woman grieving for her wounded companion. Ah, a heartbroken bird. Now, with my right hand, I comfort my left hand . . . Maybe it is a hawk flying overhead.

In the pallid sky, there is not a single bird. Comforting each other, trembling, my innocent hands that have labored and will continue to labor, have killed and will eventually be killed—at this moment, let me raise you up high. How I wish that—like freeing a pair of birds whose wounds have healed—I could fling you into the sky!

1966
translated by Michelle Yeh and Frank Stewart

ELECTRIC LOCK

Tonight, as usual, the streetlights near my residence went out at midnight.

Seeing that I was searching for my house key, the kindhearted taxi driver kept his headlights on me while I looked. Their harsh glare projected onto the iron entry gate the inky silhouette of a middle-aged man. It was only after I had found the right key on the chain and inserted it straight into my heart that the good fellow drove away.

I turned the key in my heart with a click, extricated the delicate length of metal, pushed the gate open, and resolutely entered. In no time at all, I grew used to the darkness inside.

1987

translated by Michelle Yeh and Frank Stewart

THE CAT THAT ENTERS THROUGH THE WALL

Ever since she left me, a cat has been coming in and out of my home as it pleases; doors, windows, even walls can't stop it.

When she was here with me, all the sparrows outside the iron gate and window grid envied our life together. She cared for me in every imaginable way—on dark nights when the lights failed, she would bring the crescent moon to me in her hands, and on hot summer nights she would cool me with the refreshing breeze of her body.

One day, despite my usual reticence, I made the mistake of making a comment about happiness. I said, "Happiness is the half of himself that a person cannot have." The next morning, she left without saying goodbye.

She is not the kind of woman who writes a farewell note on the vanity mirror with lipstick. She didn't use a pen either. Instead, she inscribed these words on the wallpaper with her long fingernails: "From now on, I will be your happiness and you mine."

Since the cat started coming in and out of my house as it pleases, I have never seen it, for it always comes to me at midnight and leaves at daybreak.

1987

translated by Michelle Yeh and Frank Stewart

SNOW

I turn the letter over and fold it. The back is blank and perfectly white—it's a good thing that the man has written on only one side. I fold the sheet again and again, then fold it diagonally into a triangle, then I cut it with a small pair of scissors, make more cuts, then spread it open—

I always imagined this is how snowflakes are created. I unfold the origami figure I've made—it's a good thing that the man's handwriting is so light that it does not show through the pure white sheet. When I spread it out, a six-petal snowflake lies in my sallow hand.

High above, three thousand kilometers or more, a host of angels are at their wits' end when they see bodies littering the large city square below, and the temperature of the atmosphere drops precipitously to below zero, as their pleas and sighs crystallize and fall one by one.

1990
translated by Michelle Yeh and Frank Stewart

CHICKEN

Sunday, I sit in a quiet corner of the park on an iron bench that is missing a leg, enjoying my lunch of fried chicken bought at a fast-food restaurant. As I gnaw and suck on the bones, it suddenly occurs to me that it's been decades since I heard a rooster crow.

I try to assemble the chicken bones into a bird that can summon the sun to rise. But I cannot find any vocal cords among them, since crowing is no longer called for. The chickens' job is merely to eat without stopping and to reproduce.

Under the artificial sunlight
There are neither dreams
Nor dawns

1993
translated by Michelle Yeh and Frank Stewart

Ya Xian (b. 1932)

Born in Nanyang, in Henan, Ya Xian, the pen name of Wang Qinglin, joined the armed forces and moved to Taiwan in 1949. In 1954 he graduated from the National Defense University, where he majored in drama. The same year he started publishing poetry and cofounded the Epoch Poetry Society with Luo Fu and Zhang Mo in South Taiwan. In 1966–68 he attended the International Writing Program at the University of Iowa, and in 1976 he received an MA degree in East Asian Studies from the University of Wisconsin–Madison. Ya Xian stopped writing poetry in 1965. From 1977 to 1998 he was the editor-in-chief of the literary supplement to the *United Daily*, one of the largest newspapers in Taiwan. After his retirement, he moved to Canada. He now divides his time between Vancouver and Taipei.

In "Salt" Fyodor Dostoyevsky is considered the greatest Russian novelist whose work expresses humanitarian compassion for the poor and the oppressed. "The Party" refers to the Nationalist Party, or Kuomintang, which led the revolution that overthrew the Qing dynasty (1644–1911) and founded the Republic of China in 1912. Wuchang, in Hubei, was the city where the victorious uprising broke out. In "Paris" the epigraph comes from the 1897 prose poem *Fruits of the Earth* (*Les Nourritures terrestres*) by the French poet André Gide, in which the narrator addresses the young man Nathanaël about casting off the bondage of conventional values and embracing a life of intensity and sensuality.

SALT

Second Granny and Dostoyevsky never met. That spring she cried out, "Salt, salt, give me just a bit of salt!" Angels sang in the tops of the elm tree. Almost none of the sweet peas blossomed that year.

An official from the Ministry of Salt led a camel caravan along the seashore seven hundred miles away. Not a strand of seaweed ever passed before Second Granny's sightless eyes. She cried out, "Salt, salt, give me just a bit of salt!" Angels tittered as they shook snowflakes down on her.

In 1911 the Party came to Wuchang. By then Second Granny was hanging
by a strip of her foot-binding cloth from the limb of an elm tree, swaying to
the panting of wild dogs and the flapping of vultures' wings. Voices whirled
plaintively on the wind: "Salt, salt, give me just a bit of salt!"

Nearly all the sweet peas blossomed with white flowers that year. But
Dostoyevsky and Second Granny never met.

1958
translated by Michelle Yeh and Frank Stewart

PARIS

> *Nathanaël, with regard to bed, what will I say to you?*
> —*André Gide*

The soft velvet slippers of your lips
wander lightly across my eyes. At dusk,
the very first meteor astonishes me, just as Paris plunges into
a degenerate new era, enthralled by pillow talk
Between the evening newspapers and the starry sky
blood splashes on the grass
In the womb between the rooftops and the dew,
rosemary is blossoming
You are a valley
you are a pretty mountain flower
you are a crepe, the color of a sickly mouse
trembling in a timorous mouth

How much truth can a blade of grass bear? God,
when your eyes get accustomed to the midnight poppies
and the silky sky beneath your feet, when tendrils of beggarweed
entangle the South between your knees
does last year's snow remember those heartless footprints? God,
when a baby with muted wailing curses the umbilical cord
when next year he passes through Notre Dame with his face hidden
into this sordid age of pillow talk that can offer him nothing

You are a river
you are a blade of grass
you are last year's snow that no footprint remembers
you are fragrance, the fragrant slippers
between River Seine and inference
who is choosing death
Between despair and Paris
only the Eiffel Tower holds up the sky

July 30, 1958
translated by Michelle Yeh and Frank Stewart

DIVA

At sixteen her name made the rounds in the city
a forlorn but lilting melody

Those almond-colored arms deserved to be guarded by eunuchs
that little topknot would have been ravishing to men from Manchu times

Is that an aria from the opera *Spring in Jade Hall*?
(each night the theater was filled with faces nibbling melon seeds!)

"How I weep ..."
her hands bolted into a cangue

Some people tell
of an affair with a White Russian officer in Jiamusi

A forlorn but lilting melody
all the matrons cursed her in every city

1960
translated by Denis Mair

THE COLONEL

That was simply another kind of rose
Born of flames
In the buckwheat field they fought the biggest battle
And his leg bade farewell to him in 1943

He has heard history and laughter

But what is immortality?
Cough syrup, razor blade, last month's rent, and so on and so forth
In the skirmishes his wife's sewing machine engages in
He feels that the only thing that can take him captive
Is the sun

1960
translated by Michelle Yeh

ANDANTE CANTABILE

The necessity of tenderness
The necessity of affirmation
The necessity of a little wine and sweet Osmanthus flower
The necessity of seriously watching a woman walk by
The necessity of understanding that you are no Hemingway
The necessity of the European War, rain, cannons, weather, and the Red Cross
The necessity of taking a stroll
The necessity of walking the dog
The necessity of peppermint tea
The necessity of rumors drifting in from the far corners of the stock exchange

Like weed at seven o'clock every evening. The necessity
Of revolving doors. The necessity of penicillin. The necessity of assassination.
    The necessity of evening newspapers
The necessity of wearing flannel trousers. The necessity of a horserace
    betting ticket

The necessity of an aunt's inheritance
The necessity of balcony, ocean, and smiles
The necessity of idleness

Perceived to be a river, one has to keep flowing
The world is like this, has always been like this—
Bodhisattva on the distant mountain
Poppies in the poppy field

1964
translated by Michelle Yeh and Frank Stewart

Zheng Chouyu (Wen-tao Cheng, b. 1933)

Born in Jinan, Shandong, into a military family, Zheng Chouyu is the pen name
of Zheng Wentao. With his father, a major general in the Nationalist army, he
traveled to different places in China. In 1949 he moved to Taiwan, where he grad-
uated from Xinzhu Middle School and the National Chung Hsing School of Law
and Business (today's National Taipei University). He worked at the Tax Bureau at
Jilong Port until 1968, when he was invited to the International Writing Program
at the University of Iowa, where he received an MFA degree in creative writing.
From 1973 to 2004 he taught Chinese at Yale University. Since his retirement, he
has held visiting professorships and residences in Taiwan and Hong Kong. Zheng
published his first poem in 1948 and his first book of poetry in 1949 in mainland
China. In 1956 he joined Ji Xian in the Modernist School and the same year joined
the Epoch Poetry Society, founded by Luo Fu and others.

"Mistake" has been included in Chinese textbooks and set to music by Luo
Dayou. The indigenous Atayal Tribe lives on South Lake Mountain in Taroko
National Park in Central Taiwan. "Pure Clarity" (Qingming) is the traditional
Tomb-Sweeping Day on April 4, when families visit graves to pay respect to
ancestors. "Pagoda" in this and the last poem refers to a columbarium.

MISTAKE

I passed through the south of Yangzi
The face waiting at the turn of seasons, like a lotus flower, blooms and wilts

Without the east wind, the willow catkins in March do not flutter
Your heart is like the lonesome small town
Like its streets of cobblestones near nightfall
When footfalls are silent and the bed curtains of March are closed
Your heart is a small window tightly shut

My clattering hooves are a beautiful mistake
I am not a homecoming man but a passing traveler . . .

1954
translated by Shiu-Pang Almberg

PAGODA

Pagoda: spirits sit quietly in the cell without a mattress
When the spring wind jingles the eave bells
Spirits lean over the small arch window to enjoy a temple view

I and my buddies, among the crowd of the fallen,
Are also looking around and recalling what happened in the last battle

Down there, the old leaf-sweeper monk walks by
Then, as usual, there are the three woodcutters
Ah, can it be my son, all grown up, among the tourists today?
He is wearing my old uniform, dyed apparently, gesturing
And arguing with his girlfriend (must be a science student)
About how long a handful of ashes can burn

1957
translated by Ching-hsien Wang

PURE CLARITY

Drunk on wine, I feel the night flowing quietly through me
Let the mystery resonate within as I cover my ears
The scent of fresh flowers wafts from my skin
This moment of supreme beauty, I accept homage
Accept from a thousand families the offerings of soaring kites

Stars stream down, inspirit the overflowing wine in the pagoda
The fog gazes, as still as prayerful eyes
So many eyes, a flowing all at once through my hair
I want to return, to comb the vegetation that completely covers me
I am here now, eternally a supine range of green hills

1959
translated by Michelle Yeh and Frank Stewart

ATAYAL TRIBE

My wife is a tree, so am I.
And my wife is a very nice handloom
With a squirrel for a shuttle, weaving elusive clouds
Up high, she loves weaving those clouds.

But I, how I wish my only job
Was striking the bell at the elementary school
Nestled in my bosom,
For I have reached that age—
That age when woodpeckers perch on my arms.

1962
translated by Michelle Yeh and Frank Stewart

Chang Yao (1936–2000)

Chang Yao, whose family name is Wang, was born in Taoyuan County, Hunan. In 1950 he served in the People's Liberation Army and later volunteered to fight in the Korean War. After being discharged because of his injuries, he enrolled in the college for veterans in Hebei in 1953 and started publishing poetry the following year. In 1957, during the Anti-Rightist Campaign, Chang Yao was labeled a Rightist and sentenced to reform through labor in the northwest for more than twenty years. During this time he was taken in by a Tibetan family and married one of the daughters. In 1979 Chang Yao was "rehabilitated" and worked at the Writers Association in Qinghai. Over the next two decades, he revised his poetry extensively and was considered a leading poet of the "New Frontier Poetry." In 2000, suffering from lung cancer, he died by suicide.

In number 4 of "Lost Manuscripts from the Years of Calamity," Wengzhong is Ruan Wengzhong, who is legendary for his giant stature and valor. Under the First Emperor of the Qin dynasty, he served as a general guarding the frontier against the Huns. After his retirement, a statue of him was placed outside the royal palace. Wengzhong has become a symbol of protection in China. His statues are seen in cemeteries, and his image, carved in jade, is worn as an amulet. "The Hungry Horse Shakes Its Bell," in "A Field of Fragrant Grass," refers to a piece of Cantonese music for the Chinese string instrument pipa; it became popular in the 1920s.

LOST MANUSCRIPTS FROM THE YEARS OF CALAMITY (2 of 9)

I.

I love viewing the mountains.
Seated in their shadows, I gaze up for a long, long time.
Then suddenly my mind is far away.
I love walking along the cliff's edge, hands clasped behind my back,
but suddenly some vague impression or unspeakable thought
plunges me deep into despair.

4.

Yes, in those famine years, we were stupefied by hunger.
I slept in the forest, grass for a bed, bamboo for a pillow,
A Cathay fir leaned fawningly over my young face, as if
To assure me that my motherland was genuinely beautiful.

But when at dusk I crossed the barren shoreline,
I saw the statue of white-bearded Wengzhong standing in the damp graveyard
Making me contemplate again the eternal truth he has been guarding.
I sensed sharp talons approach my threadbare vest.
And yet—whose lips, warm as cherries,
Gently kindled the flame inside my chest?

1961–62
translated by Christopher Lupke

SUCH A MAN

Utter stillness—who sighed?

Just now rain is blowing over the Mississippi, climbs the far bank and bolts.
On the other side of the Earth, someone sits in wordless solitude.

1985
translated by Christopher Lupke

A FIELD OF FRAGRANT GRASS

We agree not to mention the painful past,
to only make small talk, only admire the fragrant grass.
to accept that the rest is empty relics.
Time no longer pollinates the present.
Moths no longer light a weeping candle.
We've no need for a lamp to mull it over.
We still have "The Hungry Horse Shakes Its Bell."
What truly belongs to this moment
is this endless field of fragrant, emerald grass.
The rest is just the ancient, well-worn paths.
The rest is just abandoned, hometown wells.

1990
translated by Michelle Yeh and Frank Stewart

Bai Qiu (1937–2023)

Bai Qiu is the pen name of He Jinrong, who was born in the city of Taizhong in Central Taiwan. As a child, he spoke Japanese before learning Chinese at the age of nine. With a degree from the Taizhong Business School, he has worked in interior design and advertising for years. Bai started writing poetry in 1952 and was active in the modernist movement. In 1964 he cofounded the Bamboo Hat Poetry Society with ten other poets; while modernist in its early phase, the group took a nativist turn and became the first and oldest poetry society in Taiwan to embrace nativism.

THE WANDERER

gazing at the cloud in the distance a silk fir
gazing at the cloud a silk fir
a silk fir
silk fir
on
the
ho
ri
zon
a silk fir
on
the
ho
ri
zon

his shadow, tiny. his shadow, tiny
he has forgotten his name. forgotten his name. he only
stands there.   only stands there. alone
    he stands. stands. stands. stands
                    stands
        facing the east.

          a solitary silk fir.

ca. 1958
translated by Michelle Yeh and Frank Stewart

A THOUSAND ROADS, A THOUSAND ROOTS

In memory of my parents

A thousand roads—each one is calling out to me
A thousand roots—each one is calling out to me

But the roads by which I came
have been buried in dust storms
The roots from which I came
have decayed

In this world of hustle and bustle
I am the only one left

Only one.

ca. 1964
translated by Michelle Yeh and Frank Stewart

PUBLIC SQUARE

The crowd broke up in an uproar
The men went back to bed
To embrace their women who smelled nice

But the bronze statue stands firm on its *ism*
And to the empty square
Signals a call to action with an arm raised high

Only the naughty wind
Kicks the leaves around with chuckles
To erase all the footprints

1970
translated by Michelle Yeh and Frank Stewart

Fang Qi (1937–2021)

Fang Qi, the pen name of Huang Zheyan, was born in Taipei and received his bachelor's degree in physics from the National Taiwan University in 1962. He went on to receive a doctorate in physics from the University of Maryland, where he taught for all of his career. He published two books of poetry, in 1966 and 1972. He also published his first knight-errant novel under the pen name Lu Yu in 1961. It was the first work of the genre to employ stream of consciousness; for this reason, he is considered a pioneer of the New Knight-Errant Fiction, along with Gu Long (1938–85) and Shangguan Ding (b. 1943).

The French poet, fiction writer, and playwright Jules Supervielle appears in "Composition"; he opposed the Surrealist movement and was nominated for the Nobel Prize three times.

LITTLE BOAT

all lonely little boats are moored at a slant
it's the same on all the beaches in the world
like slanting heads
filled with sadness

published in 1966
translated by Michelle Yeh

COMPOSITION

In the bottom of the closet a lock of hair a book of poems a yellowed poetry manuscript a program and a ticket stub and a dimly shining silver coin chaotic like my brain empty like that universe of yours

the music hall resembled the cavernous belly of a giant beast flower baskets and lanterns with writing on them a black piano on the stage a white dress to his right he took out a coin and tossed it to decide if he should walk over a long time later she happened to leaf through *Gravity* and found between the pages the short poem "Flames" only then did she understand the strange look in his eyes that night it was Supervielle who once lent them his eyes of a Frenchman like a telescope so they could look out the same window and watch the flat city in the depth of the sky all this was enough for a story if one added the lock of hair she gave him on the eve of their parting it would be even more complete

is this all there is

why not

seventeen the age of tea and sympathy on the morning of her birthday she cut a lock of black hair as a memento he searched in all the stores and found a volume of *Gravity* for her birthday in the tony used books store but was too timid to send it he could only secretly write a poem in class he found out indirectly that she played piano he took a chance and mailed her a ticket to the concert when music wafted from the depth of the pit he looked at the vacant seat next to him and in that moment refused to accept it after the concert he picked up a public phone nearby yet could not bring himself to deposit the silver coin he still remembers the red telephone booth under yellow streetlights seemed like a shrine that had room for an outpoured prayer and grace

published in 1966
translated by Michelle Yeh and Frank Stewart

ANGELS

when the donkey brays, the roses bloom
you have come
from a gathering of angels
white like rain
wearing a blue dress

holding hands
I walk with the angels
their wings flap at me gently
making me look even more like a turtledove
the eucalyptus by the roadside
turns around in the drizzle
did it ever turn around?
the angels' hands are soft as if they are boneless
in my palms
they are only air, only smoke

published in 1972
translated by Michelle Yeh and Frank Stewart

Lin Ling (Helen Ong, 1938–2023)

Lin Ling, the pen name of Hu Yunshang, was born in Jiangjin, Sichuan, and spent her childhood in Xi'an, Nanjing, and Taipei. She graduated from the National Taiwan University with a major in chemistry and went on to receive her doctorate from the University of Virginia. For years she has worked as a scientist in the biochemical industry in the United States. Since her retirement, she has been living in New York. Lin started writing poetry in Taiwan in the 1950s and was closely associated with the Modernist movement.

In "Non-Modernist Lyric" Qilian is a rugged mountain range on the border of Qinghai and Gansu, and the Geng River is in Hebei. The background to "Notes on Spring Renovations" is the Rwandan civil war and the genocide against the Tutsi minority mounted by extremist Hutus in the early 1990s. According to the poet's note, "Major bloodshed took place in 1994, with a death toll that surpassed a million, yet developed countries in the West mostly turned a blind eye to the slaughter, like white termites hiding between cracks of wood."

UNTETHERED BOAT

Nothing can make me stay
—except destination
Despite the roses, green shade, and peaceful bay by the shore
I am an untethered boat

Perhaps someday
I will be tired of my travels through the galaxy
On an evening of blazing flame in May
I will wake
        and so will the sea
Then I will reconnect with the human world
And quietly return to the bounded from the boundless, before
I quietly leave again

Ah, perhaps someday—
I will be willpower itself, I will be an untethered boat
even if I am without wisdom
without ropes, a sail, or a mast

1955
translated by Michelle Yeh and Frank Stewart

NON-MODERNIST LYRIC

That landscape was no place to dwell
But I called it home.
It was the first latitude and longitude
To endow me with life, north of the Tropic of Cancer
It was the first soil
I set foot on
And set foot on again, and finally left

I remember, in that place
Animals weren't sacrificial, in the countryside
Silks weren't made into books, in the constellations
Blood
Wasn't drunk—
Promises had to be carved on bones
And the Modernist who drank from a bone
Did not want to, and could not
Be lyrical

I mean, such reckless lyrical expression
        (I mean, Oh, such reckless lyrical expression)
Like an infant taking steps, alone
In the spring wilderness at first light,
With an unbridled urge—
I mean, like the isolation of an infant
        By sleep
By time:
From all irreverent intellect,
Theory and classics
Inheriting—
Mountains and plains; let the winds of Qilian
Stop, and ferry across the Geng River
Let the winds of Qilian

Lead, everything fit for harmony
    Or unfit
Inhibit and indulge

(I mean . . . and what I mean is
A Modernist who has
Sworn an oath, does not want to
And cannot
Be lyrical)

Even silence would not do
Silence is the highest degree of intensity
Intensity is the highest form of stillness
Even a blank
Would not do. Blanks
Have over time clustered
Into shapes. (Easy to touch
               Tough to entomb)
They corrode
My slackened tension
Plasticity and tenacity
    In a small
Checkered cloth–covered
Twenty-four by twenty-five space
—In bygone days it was soil; I plowed
With age-old seeds
In the wrong sequence
While today it is a bed, is respite; the forbidden room
Of my nightmares.

In that place, every night, I interrogate
Some ancient passions
And contemplate
Their liberation—
Or execution; the final
And no longer pardoned
Execution. . . . If I can find
Gallows by the river
Then come spring, once the insects wake
The first sunny day shall bring

Death by a thousand cuts.

1981
translated by May Huang

NOTES ON SPRING RENOVATIONS

This ladder suddenly trembles: could it be
The flock of crows taking off outside   startling
An irrepressible spring day
Between branches; do the cherry pistils
Foreshadow somehow the fleeting lives
Of swiftly falling petals?
Or   is it a fretful fragrance
On the grassy slope; a fallen poetry collection
Spattering oil paint   Its mahogany
Dripping into the Hutu girl's open chest
Old news from 1994   New scars of '98
The yellowed newspaper quietly weathers away
On the grass   breathing life into aroused daisy and dogwood

(While my brown daughter softly sings
O Rwanda the beautiful   the beautiful Rwanda . . .)

Hiding   behind a tall ladder
I recklessly select
A partition perpendicular to the blue sky:
Garbage seen from an angle   A bird's-eye view
And history—
The cleanness of its filtered echo
Finally   like white termites, leaves me only sawdust

1998
translated by May Huang

Xi Xi (Cheung Yin, 1938–2022)

Xi Xi is the pen name of Zhang Yan (Cheung Yin in Cantonese), or Zhang Ailun, who was born in Shanghai and moved with her parents to Hong Kong in 1950. She graduated from Grantham College of Education and for years worked as an elementary school teacher. In 1970 she cofounded and edited the *Big Thumb* (first a weekly but later a biweekly) and *Su Yeh Literature* ten years later. Since 1978 she has been a full-time writer of not only poetry but also fiction, children's stories, prose, film scripts, film criticism, and translations. The recipient of numerous literary awards, she won the Newman Prize for Chinese Literature and the Cikada Prize in East Asian Poetry in 2019.

In "Memorials to the Throne," Jehol, or Rehe, is today's Chengde in Hebei. The construction of the vast mountain resort spanned the entire eighteenth century under three emperors of the Qing dynasty. Emperors spent much time here to meet with Manchu and Mongolian leaders, receive foreign envoys, and engage in such leisurely activities as deer hunting and archery.

MY FATHER'S BACKPACK

My father carries a backpack
As he treks along a rugged mountain

When he's hungry
My father pulls out
Paper-wrapped crackers
And a pinch of salt
For my little brother, who rides a wooden horse, to eat
On rainy days
My father pulls out
A rain hat and windbreaker
For my little brother, who spins a top, to wear

On the grassy slope of the mountain ridge
My father pulls out
A ladder
And four brick walls
Opens all the windows
So that my little brother, who flies a kite, can see the stars

Inside the backpack
My little brother, who rides a bicycle, says
Give me one hundred field mice
Give me twenty hedgehogs
Give me three rhinoceroses

My father says
That time he complained his backpack was too heavy
Was only because he was a bit tired
My father hangs the daytime on the ceiling
Beneath the sunlight
He pulls out my little brother, who wears a watch
Teaches him to draw a map

My father says
That time he complained the mountain road was too long and winding
Was only because he'd hurt his feet

While crossing the sea
Inside the backpack
My little brother with permed hair cries
Let me out
Let me out
My father opens his backpack
So that my little brother with bare feet can jump out
And run along the beach

My father slowly sits down on a rock
Pulls out
A group of white-haired friends
Listens as they finish telling a story about the spring tide
Then my father picks up the backpack and continues on his way
A smile spreads across his face
He waves to my little brother, who rows a canoe, saying his goodbyes

April 1976
translated by Jennifer Feeley

MEMORIALS TO THE THRONE

I respectfully wish
His Majesty everlasting years, everlasting blessings
Emperor writes in cinnabar ink:
WE ARE BLESSED

The Jiangnan region is warm this season
Crops are flourishing
The common people content with their lot   I'd sincerely like to brief
Your Royal Highness on   Suzhou and Yangzhou in the first and second
    months
May I respectfully present   a weather register
For Your Royal inspection
Emperor writes in cinnabar ink: YES

For the Dragon Boat Festival may I respectfully offer
A dragon robe   to specially wish
His Majesty great blessings
Additionally, please find several kinds of curios
Respectfully offered
For Your Royal viewing
Emperor writes in cinnabar ink: ALL OF THIS STUFF
IS FAR BETTER THAN GIFTS FROM YEARS PAST

In the city of Danyang in Zhenjiang under my jurisdiction
There has been a sudden plague of migratory locusts   the price of rice
Has soared   people worry about the scarcity of food
Sincerely submitted to His Royal Highness
Emperor writes in cinnabar ink: NOTED

I respectfully wish
His Majesty royal blessings
May I respectfully offer
Freshly picked loquat fruits   along with
The finest writing brush from Huzhou, a snuff bottle
And a porcelain bird feeder   May I humbly offer them
All together   bowing low on the ground
For your sage inspection
Emperor writes in cinnabar ink: OKAY
LEAVE THEM

Urgent news from Yanhai Pier in Taizhou
Pirates are firing cannonballs and rising in revolt
Looting from residents   resisting
Government troops   in seaside fields outside of Huai'an
Day after day of wind and rain
The tide surges and swells   the breakwater
Has burst   may I inform His Royal Highness
Of both matters
Emperor writes in cinnabar ink: NOTED

We have looked into roaming hoodlums in places such as Jinan in Shandong
The widespread bootlegging of salt   at Taicang's
North gate   there is a gang of thieves
Heads wrapped in cloth
Erecting flags
Assembling together
Additionally, hundreds of starving people have joined their ranks
With nothing to wear or eat
Encouraging each other to steal   by breaking into
The city's storehouse   may I inform His Royal Highness of these matters
All together
Emperor writes in cinnabar ink:
NOTED

I respectfully wish
His Majesty everlasting blessings
May I present twelve pots of golden Osmanthuses
Traveling north by waterway   per Imperial Decree
Sent under escort to your Jehol summer palace   bowing low I invite
Your Royal inspection
Emperor writes in cinnabar ink:
WE ARE GREATLY BLESSED
AT THE END OF THE SEVENTH MONTH
WE SHALL SET OUT ON A DEER HUNT

June 1979
translated by Jennifer Feeley

MY FRIEND'S CAT

the erudition of my friend's cat
is certainly unmatched
when it comes to books
my friend simply looks
while the cat is more than up to scratch

December 5, 2018
translated by Jennifer Feeley

Yang Mu (1940–2020)

Yang Mu, the pen name of Ching-hsien Wang, was born and raised in Hualian on the east coast of Taiwan. He received his BA degree in English from Tunghai University in Taizhong, his MFA degree in creative writing from the University of Iowa, and his doctorate in comparative literature from the University of California, Berkeley. For years he was a professor at the University of Washington but also taught at several universities in Taiwan and Hong Kong. He served as the dean of the School of Humanities and Social Sciences at the National Dong Hwa University in his hometown and as the founding director of the Institute of Chinese Literature and Philosophy at Academia Sinica, the premiere national research institute in Taiwan. The recipient of numerous awards, Yang Mu received the Newman Prize for Chinese Literature in 2013 and the Cikada Prize for East Asian poetry in 2016.

The eponymous poem "Jizi of Yanling Hangs Up His Sword" refers to Ji Zha (d. 485 BCE), a prince in the state of Wu during the Spring and Autumn Period (771–476 BCE). On a diplomatic mission, he passed through the state of Xu and befriended the king. Seeing how much the king admired his sword, Ji promised to give him the sword on his way back. However, by the time he returned, the king had passed away. Ji visited his grave and hung his sword on a nearby tree. Zilu and Zixia are among the closest disciples of Confucius.

In "Propositions of Temporality" Wu Gang, in line 12, is the Chinese equivalent of Sisyphus in Greek mythology. As a punishment, Wu had to cut down the cassia tree on the moon; however, each time the tree was cut, the wound healed immediately, hence condemning him to eternal futility. Line 22 alludes to "Sailing to Byzantium" by W. B. Yeats: "And therefore I have sailed the seas and come / To the holy city of Byzantium." The last line of the poem comes from Goethe's "Wanderer's Night Song II": "Über allen Gipfeln / Ist Ruh."

Philip Glass (b. 1937) is an American composer and pianist who is considered one of the most influential composers in the twentieth century and whose work is associated with minimalism. *Metamorphosis*, inspired by the story of Franz Kafka (1883–1924), is a series of five compositions for piano written in 1988.

WATER'S EDGE

I've been sitting here four afternoons
Not a single soul passes by—not to mention any sound of footsteps

(In loneliness—)

Spider Brake grows from the crotch of my pants up to my shoulder
    covering me for no reason
The cascade of flowing water is an indelible memory
All I can do is let it be scripted on a stilled cloud

Twenty meters to the south, a dandelion giggles
The pollen of the wind-pollinated flower lodges onto my bamboo hat
What can my hat offer you, come on
What can my shadow, lying down, offer you

Compare four afternoons of the water's sound to four afternoons of footsteps
Suppose they were some impatient teenage girls
Bickering endlessly among themselves—
Well then, let none of them come. All I want is an afternoon nap
Well, let none of them come

1958
translated by Michelle Yeh and Arthur Sze

JIZI OF YANLING HANGS UP HIS SWORD

I always hear the mountain's lament
At first I traveled on purpose. How can I explain
The lack of concern for so many reunions and partings?
Forget it. For you I dance
With eyes closed. Rustling
Reeds in water, chill
Of the crescent moon, and sound
Of beating clothes in a distant dusky land
Trails close behind my shadow and mock
My rusty swordsmanship. The forgotten scar
On this arm is still there
When I drink enough wine, it glows
As red as flower petals along the riverbank

You and I once sat withering
Under the scorching sun:
A pair of drooping lotus stalks
That was before my journey north, when
Summer's threat most grieved me. And
The delicate songs of southern women!
Like needle and thread, they stitched and joined
Making me draw sword from scabbard
And promise to give it to you on my return . . .
Who would guess that northern ladies, the glorious rituals of Qi and Lu
And endless chanting
Of the Songs would convert me
Into a dawdling Confucian . . .

Who would guess I'd put away my sword?
(People say you kept calling
Calling my name, and doing that
You died)
The bamboo flute's seven holes darkly retell
My disillusionment on reaching China's central plains
In early days, archery, horsemanship, saber and sword

Meant more than the art of rhetoric and debate
After the Master struggled in distant lands
Zilu's violent death and Zixia's appointment in the court of Wei
We all scrambled for places in great lords' houses
I set aside my sword
Tied up my hair, chanted the Songs
And acted like an eloquent scholar

The Confucian scholar!
He cut his wrist in the darkening
Woods by your grave—from now on
Neither swordsman nor scholar
Perhaps the blue glow of my precious sword will
Brighten you and me on this lonely autumn night
You died longing for a friend
I languish as a hermit
The tired boatman, once arrogant, once gentle
Is I

1969
translated by Michelle Yeh and Lawrence R. Smith

LET THE WIND RECITE

1.

If I could write you
A summer poem, when reeds
Spread vigorously, when sunshine
Swirls around your waist and
Surges toward your spread
Feet, when a new drum
Cracks in the heat; if I

Rocking gently in a skiff
Riding down to the twelfth notch
Could write you an autumn poem
When sorrow crouches on the riverbed
Like a golden dragon, letting torrents and rapids
Rush and splash and swirl upward
From wounded eyes; if I could write you

A winter poem
A final witness to ice and snow
The shrunken lake
The midnight caller
Who interrupts a hurried dream
Takes you to a distant province
Gives you a lantern, and tells you
To sit quietly and wait
No tears allowed . . .

2.

If they wouldn't allow you
To mourn for spring
Or to knit
If they said
Sit down quietly
And wait—
A thousand years later
After spring
Summer would still be
Your name—
They'd bring you back, take away
Your ring
And clothes
Cut your hair short
And abandon you
By the edge of the enduring lake—
Then at last you'd belong to me

At last you'd belong to me
I'd bathe you
And give you a little wine
A few mints
Some new clothes
Your hair would
Grow back the way it was
Before. Summer would still be
Your name

3.

Then I'd write you
A spring poem, when everything
Begins again
So young and shy
You'd see an image of maturity. I'd let you shed tears freely
I'd design new clothes and make a candle for your wedding night
Then you'd let me write
A spring poem on your breasts
In the rhythm of a beating heart, the melody of blood:
Breast images and the birthmark metaphor
I'd lay you on the warm surface of the lake
And let the wind recite

1973
translated by Michelle Yeh and Lawrence R. Smith

PROPOSITIONS OF TEMPORALITY

I inspect a gray hair under lamplight
was the snowstorm much more severe last winter?
At midnight I sat alone in the flickering world
hand on chest, repeating these words: I miss you

Perhaps I worry for the heavenly stars
some will be removed from Capricorn in early spring
I always recognize them in the mirror
for years they have returned home to my sideburns

You ask if the Osmanthus tree of my concern
may blossom in spite of its wounds
Before the autumn I never thought it would
when Wu Gang dies of exhaustion, I will replace him

See the morning dew rolling on the mallow leaves
and trying to keep balance among their venations
pearls like philosophy and poetry will beautify skulls
gracefully, more focused than the dew

In the northern hemisphere, scaly clouds reflect
the ocean surface where mackerel swim
soundlessly. I am exploring this waterway, seeking
to engrave the ages on my proud brow

Still in the days of my aging, I shall do so for you—
play the piano, see you to the ship bound for Byzantium
with music close to fading. Silence
here is beyond all summits

1993
translated by Wen-chi Li and Colin Bramwell

TALE (in the meter of *Metamorphosis II* by Philip Glass)

If the ceaseless tide at the speed of memory
If I, with the same heart, if the tide just once
In the days and nights of our parting
Tells the story just once to the end
The spiraling tune, the intertwined
Tale of life and death, rising and falling,
As though hurrying to a rendezvous

On the constantly cooling sea
Like a white bird gliding over the wake of a ship
Into the faltering breath of the season
If the tide just once
And I, with the same heart

1994
translated by Michelle Yeh and Frank Stewart

CLOUD SHIP

All the tangibles and the intangibles have been explored. Now we
With our bright hearts are determined to reach the other side of
The stars, on a ship with pure white sails or on the wings
Of the archangel, who has been waiting for us all along

Many years ago an ancient prophetic book
Foretold a time when all will be transported
In the melody of a song. In a steady twilight breeze
On a gently swaying ship of clouds, the joyful soul

2006
translated by Michelle Yeh and Frank Stewart

Underground Poetry, Nativism, and Women's Voices

_1970s–1980s_

After the initial period of pandemonium during the Cultural Revolution, Chairman Mao Zedong had no more use for the Red Guards and brought in the People's Liberation Army to suppress them. To diffuse discontent and revolt, he decided to send young men and women to remote rural areas to "learn from the peasants." Millions of them, referred to as "educated youth" or "sent-down youth," left home and lived and worked in harsh conditions. At a time when publications were strictly censored, writing in secret could have severe consequences. However, the youthful desire for self-expression could not be curbed, and poetry became a popular vehicle, and hand-copied poems were widely circulated across the country. Moreover, like-minded young people formed underground "salons" to read forbidden books, discuss literature and philosophy, and exchange their own poems.

The death of Chairman Mao on September 9, 1976, and the arrest of the Gang of Four (headed by Madame Mao) in less than a month marked the end of the Cultural Revolution. In 1977 the Higher Education Examination was reinstituted, after a decade of basing college entrance exclusively on class background. In December 1978 Deng Xiaoping took the reins of power and reversed the course of China from extreme leftism to "Reform and Opening Up" and the Four Modernizations (agriculture, industry, science and technology, and national defense). Under Deng the turn toward a market economy and "capitalism with socialist characteristics" could be summed up with the old proverb he loved to quote: "It doesn't matter whether a cat is black or white; if it catches mice, it's a good cat." The "thaw" that followed political reform led to a blossoming of literature and art—underground poetry, The Stars Art Group, "scar literature," realist drama, theater of the absurd, and film by "fifth-generation" directors—from the late 1970s through the 1980s.

As underground poetry found its way into official venues and attracted national attention, it also sparked controversy. Instead of politically correct content, the new poetry expressed personal thoughts and sentiments, directly or indirectly, in reaction against the Cultural Revolution. Instead of linguistic and formal features that had become familiar in the People's Republic, the new poetry employed a language that was individualized and filled with bold, refreshing images. For these reasons, it was critiqued by the establishment as "obscure" (*menglong*). However, the label only made it even more welcome across the nation, leading to a golden age of modern poetry in the 1980s.

On the other side of the Taiwan Strait, the social, political, and cultural transformations were no less dramatic. In 1970 the United States declared that the Senkaku Islands (Diaoyutai in Chinese) were part of the Ryukyu Islands and handed rule to Japan. This triggered a series of protests known as "Protect Diaoyutai" in Taiwan and Hong Kong, in which overseas students in the United States participated as well. In 1971 the Republic of China lost its seat on the Security Council and membership in the United Nations. In 1972 Japan ended diplomatic relations with the republic and recognized the People's Republic as the only legitimate representative of China. On January 1, 1979, the United States did the same; to show support for its longtime ally, the Congress ratified the Taiwan Relations Act.

The series of diplomatic setbacks led to shock and outrage among the people in Taiwan and spurred policymakers, intellectuals, and writers to engage in self-reflection. In reaction against what was perceived as overdependence on the United States, they advocated a return to the Chinese tradition, on the one hand, and an embrace of the Taiwanese society, on the other. In the cultural sphere, literature and art turned away from Modernism toward Nativism, which was to become the mainstream in the ensuing decades.

Finally, women poets gained increasing prominence, in both quantity and literary impact. While women were never absent among the pioneers in the pre-1949 period or the Modernists in the 1950s–60s, they were few and far in between. In the 1980s a new generation of female poets on both sides of the Taiwan Strait burst upon the scene to challenge literary conventions with innovative modes of writing.

Huang Xiang (b. 1941)

A native of Guidong County in Hunan, Huang was persecuted as a child and denied entry into the middle school because of his family background. His father was a Nationalist Party general who was executed in 1951. In 1956 Huang moved to Guiyang in Guizhou and made a living as a factory worker. In 1968, he and his friends formed an underground literary group called Wild Ducks. In 1978–79 he was a key player in the democracy movement known as the Beijing Spring. In October 1978 he traveled to Beijing and posted the poems he had written during the Cultural Revolution on the billboards along Wangfujing Boulevard in the heart of the capital. A month later, he founded the Enlightenment Society in Tiananmen Square; an eponymous journal was published in 1979. Between 1959 and 1988, Huang was imprisoned six times, for a total of twelve years, for his dissenting views and his poetry, which is banned in China to this day.

In 1997 Huang and his wife, Zhang Ling, left China and sought asylum in the United States. In 2004–6 he became the first writer hosted by the City of Asylum program in Pittsburgh. He stayed in the city as an honorary writer-in-residence and collaborated with the painter William Rock. Currently he lives in New York. In addition to poetry, Huang is well known for his calligraphy and philosophical writing. He was twice awarded the Hellman-Hammett grant, in 1994 and 2007.

BEAST

I am a beast being hunted
I am a beast captured
I am a beast trampled by other beasts
I am a beast trampling others

The era knocks me to the ground
With a sidelong glare
A boot on my face
It bites
And rips
And gnaws my body
Till only my bones remain

But even if only one bone of mine remains
I will stick it into the gut of this wretched era

1968
translated by Michelle Yeh and Frank Stewart

|

1.

I am a cry
Out of the raging years surrounding me

2.

I am a shattered diamond
In every facet a spark of sunlight

3.

I am I   I am my own obituary
I shall ransom myself from death

1978
translated by Michelle Yeh and Frank Stewart

THE DAY IS NEARLY OVER

There is a kind of space
That has its own vastness

There is a heavenly body
That has its own great orbit

Every cell in my body
Is impossibly distant

The unreachable constellations
Hide themselves in my flesh and blood

Death, which cannot be refused
Rises as it slowly sinks

Life, which cannot be refused
Waxes as it quickly wanes

In this world of dust under the luminous starry sky
I grow old one day at a time

In the space beyond space
I blossom alone like a child

June 29, 2002
translated by Michelle Yeh and Frank Stewart

Ying Peian (Yeng Pway Ngon, 1947–2021)

Born and raised in Singapore, Ying graduated from Ngee Ann Polytechnic, where he majored in Chinese. In the 1970s he founded the literary journal *Tea Booth* and ran a bookstore. In November 1977 he was arrested for his writings critical of the government and was released four months later. For years he worked as an editor and columnist for newspapers and journals in Singapore and Hong Kong. Ying started writing in middle school and published his first book of poetry in 1968, titled *On the Operating Table*. He acknowledged having been influenced by the Modernist style of Ya Xian in his early phase, before he turned to realism. In addition to poetry, Ying wrote fiction, plays, literary criticism, and social commentaries.

ON THE OPERATING TABLE

We can't find our face in the mirror
black sunshine bathes this impoverished land
toxic rain falls endlessly while riverbeds lie parched
heedless, we sow doomed seed
some fools trample the shoots coming up
while others hug the trunks of rotting trees
like cockroaches we gnaw at our culture's last crumbs

but we are televisions and bus stops and reinforced concrete
we hastily knot our ties and lace our shoes
hastily jot down phone numbers
drink Coca-Cola while debating a faraway war
our fingers count bills while our ears sift news of the market
an opera ticket can buy all manner of bombings

we ride up every elevator
we park in every lot
say hello, slap shoulders, give hands a firm shake, tug at smiling lips
lies fester between teeth, pride gets poked down noses
enthusiasm stamps every trademarked face
we stop at red lights, use calculators to count our money
words alone fail as symbols conveying feelings

years get hurled into a bottomless pit
one calendar poaches property from the next
lovers meet on the dance floor
rise from bed still botching each other's name
they flirt under overpasses, they kiss in movie theaters
but cross a street and one will turn a stranger's cold glance on the other
a week later, waiting for the bus, they study their separate newspapers
love is like a counterfeit coin that hits the cement with no sound
love is like a counterfeit coin
glittering eerily in the dark

life is a ledger, life is a slot machine eating every penny
life is the text of a prayer and a litany of wise words
life is a horse's cold muzzle and the features of a saint
life is a sleeping pill, life is a typewriter's chatter
life always tests us and always cheats us
life is a wrestling match with pillow and blanket, an illegal abortion and the pill
life is everybody sniping behind everybody's back

here's some fun
a flower blooms and before summer's arrival
each bright petal brews syphilis
green apples on the branch look innocent
even as worms swarm in their hearts
that first bit concerns the Bible and ethics, and the second bit
maybe biology
forests of scalpels surround you, your blood moans in your veins
yet you lie on the operating table and wait for a slow death
no sooner does your eye settle on an advertisement
than all your conscience, all your character, gets cut out and sold for pennies

in this market
corpses clad in sanctimony panic and take flight
in these trapped stagnant waters
every thirst awaits its moment to brew and decay
in this vast desert
all eyes lose track of the oasis
and when night falls
the tree trunk fills with serpent tongues and the branches bend with apples
before the cock crows
someone has betrayed Judas for a drop of water

all kinds of saviors get nailed into all kinds of mouths
various saviors drip blood onto various beds
but my sort of Jesus loiters under streetlights
smoking classy cigarettes and hitting bars before straggling home
to visit my fixed window, as miserable as a mangy cat
peering through to his portrait, he sees nothing but a handsome beard
within the portrait's whole frame, just a handsome beard

don't speak to Mary about her past
cross, nails, crown of thorns, and blood
pregnancy or no pregnancy, none of that matters
the dead are long dead
let him who was resurrected be resurrected again
how many veins could one drop of blood fill
how many mouths could a single loaf feed
even if someone were still foolish enough to kiss his ice-cold toes
his sleeve could never wipe clean our filthy bones

there is no Eden or Jerusalem
this is a wasteland, this is a shining city
this is Monte Carlo, this is your and my big fat casino
this is my hell and this is your heaven
they wager from the shoulder, use their own skulls for dice
they are monkeys in suits, animals wearing hats
trading a grain of wheat for a kilo of soul, buying with one coin every beast
    of the earth

at night under starlight the man holds his shadow and weeps
spends a sleepless ticking night lamenting the loss of his arm
the man lets diseased rats munch on his guts, vomits after a bender
floats his face into thorn-filled night
and next day his arms fill his sleeves again, although the shoulders are gone
and then the man spins his cocoon, weaves his web
and then he bequeaths sorrow to himself while spinning sorrow for others
there is no sadder tragedy than this

moss grows in the sunshine, and cacti, beyond the frontier
sunflowers grow in prison, and roses, down the alley
donors of blood get pushed to the bottom, bloodsuckers always rise to the top
there is no sadder tragedy than this

the cast of characters we will brew up tomorrow, the lecture we memorize today
the childhood names we dumped yesterday
we emerge from factories as identical loaves
and then one by one get swallowed up
we walk into hospitals and take up syringes
only to discover that we ourselves are leprosy's deadly bacterium

and so moss grows in the sunshine, and cacti, beyond the frontier
sunflowers grow in prison, and roses, down the alley
and so there is no sadder tragedy than this

beauty and his death
brilliance and his evil
the filth that glory brought him
who can let tongues of flame lick his blood dry
who can let the wind puncture his lungs
who can let the iceberg freeze his breath
who can shape his likeness in clay, and then use his own hands, resolutely
to smash the image to pieces

in a public restroom I hear silent weeping
over a blank gravestone hangs a nameless umbilical cord
he clenches his tiny fists, concealing his bewildered palm prints
and, with the white-furred reeds, issues a faint call to arms
on a bed lies a seventeen-year-old aspen, still dressed in her school uniform
she longs for someone to recite her flesh and read her blood
she longs for someone to interpret her

go march, go yell slogans, go attend birthday dances
go make out, go attend weddings or funerals, go participate
go off and do nothing
there is no path, no opposite shore, no temple
there is nothing called sweet
let alcoholics drink what they crave, let the profane curse at will
let the historians write their histories
let the politicians erect their monuments

we survive, we are a festival, we are a holiday
we survive, we are a wind out of season, a sightless cloud
we survive, we fake happiness and depression
and there is nothing called sweet

we sleep hearing the nails go into coffins, we use paper money to boil teeth
we make a living out of eating our words
we fill out forms for dying and pay taxes to lengthen our lives
we tear up years and call it a job
and then we pawn off our retinas to let other people see
use our throats to mimic other people coughing
and then, in murky sewage,
we kick bones that we have trodden into splinters

but we are televisions and bus stops and reinforced concrete
we hastily knot our ties and lace our shoes
hastily jot down phone numbers
drink Coca-Cola while debating a faraway war
our fingers count bills while our ears sift news of the market
an opera ticket can buy all manner of bombings

we ride up every elevator
we park in every lot
say hello, slap shoulders, give hands a firm shake, tug at smiling lips
lies fester between teeth, pride gets poked down noses
enthusiasm stamps every trademarked face
we stop at red lights, use calculators to count our money
words alone fail as symbols conveying feelings

May 5, 1968
translated by Randy Trumbull

Bei Dao (b. 1949)

Bei Dao, meaning "Northern Island," is the pen name of Zhao Zhenkai. Born and raised in Beijing, he started writing poetry in 1970. In December 1978 he and the poet Mang Ke (b. 1950) cofounded *Today*, the first underground journal devoted to literature in the People's Republic of China. Although it was banned after three issues, the journal had attracted national attention and helped usher in a renaissance in post-Mao China. Bei Dao has been the most famous representative of Obscure Poetry in post-Mao China. From 1989 to 2007, he lived in Sweden, Norway, and the United States as a writer-in-residence, lecturer, or visiting scholar. Since August 2007 he has been a professor of humanities at the Chinese University of Hong Kong.

Yu Luoke (1942–70), to whom "Declaration" is dedicated, was a native of Beijing. His father, an engineer at the Ministry of Water Resources, was persecuted during the Anti-Rightist Campaign in 1957. For this reason Yu was denied admission to college in 1960. On January 5, 1968, he was arrested for having published a series of essays that critiqued the fanaticism of the Cultural Revolution. On March 5, 1970, after a public trial, he was executed. In 1979 the authorities dropped all the charges.

DECLARATION

For Yu Luoke

Perhaps the final hour is come
I have left no testament
Only a pen, for my mother
I am no hero
In an age without heroes
I just want to be a man

The still horizon
Divides the ranks of the living and the dead
I can only choose the sky
I will not kneel on the ground
Allowing the executioners to look tall
The better to obstruct the wind of freedom

From starlike bullet holes shall flow
A blood-red dawn

ca. 1970; published 1980
translated by Bonnie S. McDougall

THE ANSWER

Debasement is the password of the base.
Nobility is the epitaph of the noble.
See how the gilded sky is covered
With the drifting twisted shadows of the dead.

The Ice Age is over now.
Why is there ice everywhere?
The Cape of Good Hope has been discovered,
Why do a thousand sails contest the Dead Sea?

I came into the world
Bringing only paper, rope, and a shadow.
To proclaim before the judgment
The voice that has been judged.

Let me tell you, world,
I—do—not—believe!
If a thousand challengers lie beneath your feet,
Count me as number one thousand and one.

I don't believe the sky is blue;
I don't believe in thunder's echoes;
I don't believe that dreams are false;
I don't believe that death has no revenge.

If the sea is destined to breach the dikes
Let all the brackish water pour into my heart;
If the land is destined to rise
Let humanity choose a peak for existence again.

A new conjunction and glimmering stars
Adorn the unobstructed sky now;
They are the pictographs from five thousand years;
They are the watchful eyes of future generations.

1976
translated by Bonnie S. McDougall

LOCAL ACCENT

I speak Chinese to the mirror
a park has its own winter
I put on music
winter is free of flies
I make coffee unhurriedly
flies don't understand what's meant by a native land
I add a little sugar
a native land is a kind of local accent
I hear my fright
on the other end of a phone line

1990
translated by Bonnie S. McDougall

THE LANDSCAPE ABOVE ZERO DEGREES

It is the sparrow hawk who teaches the song to swim
it is the song that retraces the earliest airs

we exchange fragments of delight
and enter the family from different routes

it is the father who has confirmed the dark
it is the dark that leads to the classics' lightning

the door of weeping shuts with a thud
leaving the echo to pursue its wail

it is the pen that flowers within despair
it is the flower that resists necessity's path

It is love's beam that awakes
to brighten the landscapes above zero degrees

published in 1996
translated by Clayton Eshleman and Lucas Klein

Liang Bingjun (Ping-kwan Leung, 1949–2013)

Liang Bingjun, also known by his pen name Yesi (Yasi in Cantonese), was born in Xinhui, Guangdong, and grew up in Hong Kong. He graduated from the English Department at Baptist University in 1970 and worked as a teacher and newspaper editor. In 1978 he went to the University of California, San Diego, where he earned his doctorate in comparative literature in 1984. After returning to Hong Kong, he taught at the University of Hong Kong and Lingnan University. Liang started writing poetry in the late 1960s and was involved in the founding and editing of several literary journals, such as the *Big Thumb*, *Chinese Student Weekly*, and *Four Seasons*. In 2011 he was diagnosed with lung cancer and passed away on January 5, 2013. Liang was arguably the most influential poet in Hong Kong in the twentieth century; he was also a renowned fiction writer, literary scholar, film critic, and cultural critic.

LOTUS LINK

I come to this lotus field by chance
Walking along old planks into foliage
The sound of silence rubbing against silence
How miraculous, green responding
To green, meeting in the morning of this world
Wind blows open that closed face
Swaying the furled leaves where I stand
Soon we'll make contact
And start to clumsily explain
The veins on a leaf that language can illuminate
Are the only world we know
Morning's gradually rounding dewdrops
Make me pause, and my silence
Prompts another leaf, who also bears
The weight of a perched insect
Meeting by chance in this world, side by side
But without taking pains to arrange a rhyme
We make the same sound then lose one another
Rather than searching the wind, why don't we
Look naturally, for meaning will slowly float up
The frost on leaves still weighs me down
Growing from the same shallow water
Exerting to stand straight with a hollow green stem
Extending toward a truer plane
I know we cannot leave this world's
Language, but we don't have to echo it
When we are silent, that place still brims with sound
Each of us shall tolerate the seasons' dust
While listening closely, and unfurling,
We feel the colors of distant waters

1983
translated by May Huang

THE OLD COLONIAL BUILDING

So much dust kicks up between sunlight and
Shadow in every corner scaffolding and wooden
Planks surround the old colonial building
As if to tear down every brick and board perhaps
In the end its basic shape will still remain
Perhaps to uncover the hardship buried in soil
Its lofty dome and spacious hallways still face
Clogged walls perhaps the cleaved and demolished
Staircase will lead to more ordinary houses

I pass the hallway's sometimes blooming and
Sometimes withdrawn flowers on my way to
Photocopy a paper and glance in the lotus pond's warped
Reflection where the spire's windows float like duckweed
Washed day and night until they are no longer pure or
Innocent but perhaps muddied while guileless goldfish
Collide everywhere searching for dying roots still
Entangled as orange scales flicker and fade
And half-open gills breathe by the windows

Can one reassemble images of ruins to
Construct a new architecture if portraits are absurd
And power always comical in the hallway we meet
Glancing by chance at the changing lotus pond
Thoughts don't avoid undulation or bend in wind
I know you don't believe in flags or fireworks
I give you fragmented words that don't represent reality
Or a center surrounded by skyscrapers but merely a pond
Of clear water rippling with swimming signs

1986
translated by May Huang

PAPAYA

You wrote down what you wanted to say and gave the paper to me
I had nothing to give you in return, so I wrote:

"Papaya!" When I sliced it open, there were so many
black, uncertain things inside

You once told me you liked eating papaya, but I don't know
if since then you've changed your mind

Every time I buy a papaya and put it in the fridge
it just so happens that you aren't here. Is it a language problem

or a papaya problem? I can only
pick a good one out by examining its greenish yellow skin

I can only answer at a greenish yellow
level; I have no idea what lies below the surface

What is inside? I'm positive it's sweet papaya flesh
Common sense tells me that. When I slice one open

there are a lot of seeds, which you don't
like. You say it would be best if there were nothing inside

nothing to cling to, nothing so sticky that you couldn't get rid of it
or so slippery you couldn't hold onto it if you wanted

Don't get hung up on so many commitments, don't
talk so much, let's just eat a wordless papaya

Fine, fine! But there is always something
to chew on before spitting out a word: Papaya

Now you are protesting. You say I talk too much
The mottled skin, the pulp filled with symbols

No, really, I just want to share a papaya
with you, but all the papayas that you and I

have shared are in this one papaya in front of us
When I slice it open, I see there are still many seeds

1990
translated by Michelle Yeh and Frank Stewart

TRAVELING WITH A BITTER MELON

I cooked it and ate it for lunch
I sliced it open and stir-fried it
It tasted good, slightly bitter, slightly sweet
With a trace of the kindness you brought from far away
It must have slowly picked up this kindness
By being next to you on the plane,
How did you carry it?
In your checked luggage or in a carry-on bag?
Did it peer around the airplane? Did it
Cry because it was hungry, did it get airsick?
I told you rain was falling hard where I was, you said
The sun was shining as you were getting ready to fly to my city
But you were sure the bitter melon would travel well
Across the different climate zones and customs
When I saw it, I realized you were right
You let me see that its unique color
Was because of where it was cultivated, the soil, and variety
This child of a poor family had grown up to have a body like jade
A good-natured personality, soft white
On the outside but not flashy, and glowing from within
It was only when I landed in a foreign country
Having brought the white bitter melon with me on the plane
That I thought to ask if you had been stopped at the Customs counter:
How come it isn't green like normal bitter melons?

They looked suspiciously at its strange passport, expecting trouble any moment
The innocent new arrival waited quietly, carrying the heavy baggage of his past
Good-natured and uncomplaining, with no sign of sourness or bitterness
It mildly indulged the immigration official, whose dull eyes and grim face
Were cheerless from the dismal work
I carry it with me as I travel farther and farther, like my words
The more they wander, the more they try to include
Because I don't want to leave out any details of how
A bitter melon tosses and turns at night, missing its own kind
Sighing heavily because it remembers
A familiar spot under a trellis loaded with other melons
A feeling that no one takes seriously
You always forgive my awkward habit of asking over and over:
When are you coming back? You reply simply:
And when are you leaving again? One leaving, the other
Returning. You put up with my verb tenses
Which are slippery and imprecise. I eat bitter melon all the time
I ate one before boarding the plane
Why has it traveled such a long way back to appear on my table again?
Does it want to tell me about the bitter feelings of separation and
    disappointment?
That it's developed a tumor? That the wrinkles on its face
Are from loneliness?
And that it has trouble sleeping, always waking up before dawn
And lying in bed, its eyes wide open, until the sun is up? In the silence
Like rippling water, does it say that illness has made it bitter?
Or a failure to fit together the pieces of a fragmented past?
Or is it bitter because it's consistently misunderstood by strangers,
Forever out of place in a hostile world?
But it still has the appearance of white jade
So translucent that one takes pleasure in chewing it
I am saying something confusing that I want to say clearly
The way everyone should speak. By myself
I set the plate and the cup on the table
I long to be sitting beside you, far across the ocean,
Eating a refreshingly bitter melon

There are always so many disappointments
There is always imperfection in the human world
Bitter melon understands

August 1998
translated by Michelle Yeh and Frank Stewart

He Furen (Ho Fuk Yan, b. 1950)

Born and raised in Hong Kong, He graduated from St. Paul's College and the University of Hong Kong, where he studied Chinese and comparative literature. He taught at St. Paul's College for years before retiring in 2010. In the 1970s He cofounded a number of literary journals, including *Big Thumb, Compass Poetry Journal*, and *Su Yeh Literature*. In addition to poetry, he has published prose, literary criticism, and historical studies.

THE BABY GIRL IN MY FAMILY

The baby girl in my family
asked for ice cream on her birthday
so I bought some and a candle to celebrate with her
I said she was the most beautiful, the most well behaved
She smiled a toothless grin
Then she began reciting "The Song of Everlasting Sorrow"; when she reached
    the line
"Raised in the inner chamber, she was unknown to the world," she hemmed
    and hawed
I pretended to be mad, that teaching her was like propping up a drunkard
when you steadied one side, the other side sagged. I impatiently finished the
    poem
for her, since I planned to slip out soon to get together with a friend
Then I tried to lull her to sleep. She touched her forehead, chest, and shoulders
    with her fingers

and prayed with her palms together: ". . . the Father, the Son, and the
    Holy Spirit"
Suddenly, as if recalling something, she burst out crying
saying how very much she missed her mother
"Where is she now?" she asked
"She has gone to a place where there are no more worries
So we shouldn't worry either," I said
I smoothed the comforter and closed the curtain
A dim light falling on her pale face
revealed her deep wrinkles. When I left her room
I called my friend: "I'm not coming tonight
My mother just had her seventy-seventh birthday
I'd like to spend more time with her"

1992

translated by Michelle Yeh and Frank Stewart

PANDEMIC PSYCHOLOGY

Pandemic is a psychological condition
says a psychologist:
It is an abandoned child
adopted by some kind of bat
Raised in seclusion
in extensive inhibition
No lights at all
Autistic, and unavoidably narcissistic
it is really more feminine in this regard
He concludes, with evidence most scientific
that all female writers are claustrophobic
Male, on the other hand, will become
masters in their field
It is no surprise that when it meets its kind
(or it deems to be its kind
based on similar inclination
or sexual orientation)

they become intimate
But love of this nature
invariably ends in hate
In teary eyes, the psychologist says:
Separate they must
at sunrise
one dies
the other survives

2020
translated by Teresa Shen

SICK SHIP

A ship is sick
It may infect other ships, it seems
No island allows it to berth
Island after island disappears
from the map
No lighthouse either
It keeps wandering
drifting, wearily, till kelps grow hither
Webs develop too
Extended use of mask
makes gills the only way to breathe
But no fish consider it their kind
not even the humble plankton

Poor thing, a fisherman observes from the shore
Please, don't pollute the ocean

2020
translated by Teresa Shen

Mang Ke (b. 1950)

Mang Ke is the pen name of Jiang Shiwei, who was born in Shenyang and moved to Beijing in 1956. In 1969, in the midst of the Cultural Revolution, he was relocated to Baiyangdian, a fishing village about a hundred miles from Beijing. There he became friends with Duo Duo and Genzi (b. 1951), and the three young men started writing poetry in friendly competition. In 1976 he returned to Beijing and two years later cofounded the underground journal *Today* with Bei Dao. Since 2004 Mang Ke has been a professional painter.

NIGHT ABOVE SNOWY GROUND

The night above the snowy ground
is a dog with a black-and-white coat
the moon its tongue flicking out
the stars its teeth flashing

It's this dog
this dog unchained in winter
this threatening dog circling our house
with its barking
and the howling of the north wind
that startles us out of our sleep

causing me to thrust open the door
and rush angrily outside
causing me to shout into the darkness:
Get away from here now!

But the night does not leave
and this dog in the snowy darkness
circles continuously, never resting.
I hear its persistent barking
until, exhausted, I drift off to sleep
and dream of flowers blossoming in the warm spring

1973
translated by Michelle Yeh and Frank Stewart

SUNFLOWER IN THE SUN

Do you see it?
that sunflower in the sun?
Notice how it refuses to bow its head
but instead twists away
as if trying to bite through
the rope around its neck
held by the sun

Do you see it?
See that sunflower
with its head held high, glaring back at the sun?
Its head almost eclipses it
Even when there is no sun
the sunflower still blazes forth

Do you see that sunflower?
You should go up to it
When you do, you will notice
the soil it grows from
Squeeze a handful in your fist
and blood will ooze from it

1983
translated by Michelle Yeh and Frank Stewart

A MAN CONTINUES TO AGE AFTER DEATH

the white hair of the dead sprouts from the earth
convincing me that a man continues to age after death

and that after he dies, nightmares continue to pounce on his chest
even now, he wakes with a start, eyes wide, trying to see

another day hatches from its egg
and begin pecking hungrily at the ground

even now, he still remembers the sound his steps made
the joys and sorrows of when he had legs

even now, though his skull is empty he remembers
the people he loved, who have all decayed under the earth

even now, he sings eulogies to them and to his beloved
whose face he gently holds in his hands

as he lays her back softly in the grass
and watches her clumsily, erotically undress

even now, he anticipates the sunrise
that the wind will blow away like a shabby straw mat

even now, he waits for the sunset that will flee from him
as though being pursued by a wild beast

the night, though, tamely lets you take it in your arms
lets you dandle it playfully without making a sound

even now, overcome with weariness, he closes his eyes
and listens to the howling beasts at war in the sky

even now, he worries that in a single night
all the blood of the heavens might pour over the earth

even now, he will rise to mourn the absent face
of one whose eyes are still fixed on you

even now, he hopes and wishes he could live forever
wishes he were not merely a predator's quarry

nor merely a carcass roasted over a fire and eaten
in unbearable pain even now

the white hair of the dead sprouts from the earth
convincing me that a man continues to age after death

1985
translated by Michelle Yeh and Frank Stewart

Duo Duo (b. 1951)

Duo Duo, the pen name of Li Shizheng, is a native of Beijing. In 1969–75, during the Cultural Revolution, he was relocated to the fishing village Lake Baiyangdian, a hundred miles from Beijing. After returning to the city, he worked as a librarian and a reporter for the *Peasant Daily*. On June 4, 1989, he flew to London after witnessing the government's crackdown on the student movement in Tiananmen Square, thus beginning an exile of fifteen years in Europe, mostly in The Netherlands. In 2004 he was appointed as professor at Hainan University, a position he held until 2017. Currently, he lives in Beijing and, while continuing to write poetry, has established himself as a painter. Duo Duo won the Neustadt Prize in 2010.

Marina Tsvetaeva, to whom "Craft" is dedicated, was one of the greatest Russian poets of the twentieth century. She experienced the 1917 Revolution, exile in Paris, and persecution in the Soviet Union. Jobless and getting no help from her friends, she hanged herself on August 31, 1941.

CRAFT—*AFTER MARINA TSVETAEVA*

I write poems of degenerate youth
(poems of infidelity)
written in narrow, long rooms
raped by poets
poems discharged to the street by coffee shops
that indifferent poem of mine
with no resentment left
(itself just a story)

that poem of mine no one reads
like the history of a story
the one that lost pride
and lost love
(my aristocratic poem)
she will be married off to a peasant
she is my discarded moment

1973
translated by Lucas Klein

NORTHERN NIGHT

bats' soundless screams shake the dusk's drumming
the setting sun, dignified as a tiger pushing a millstone
air, air returned to us through a horse's nostrils
light, bright light that has passed through the eye of a keyhole
        hiding like an arrow
every dusk has hidden this way
what night has stored is too much, what's flowed away with water too little
the always unsettled is battering. In its battering
there are nights that have begun but not yet ended
rivers that shimmer but their colors can't be seen clearly
there are times in strong opposition to night
there are times that only arrive at night
        the night a woman meets a docile little pet
        language begins but life goes away

snow holds the whole afternoon looking out from the window
an afternoon that will not end
a group of fat women taking a rest in the sky
everything they remember is resting
the scenery is covered by a great leaf
morning exhibits all the idiocy it wants
        circumstances like a ship sinking in a fish's stomach
        the heart has the silence of ice flying into a beehive

where the pasture ends and the city begins
crops hate to grow, and grapes are exhausted
the stars extinguished, like bags of rocks
the moon seeps inside, the walls are full of holes
we know, but we should know
time is on its way home, but life is a child let out from school
       the world is a window, outside which are horses
       who neigh after they've eaten ten thousand lamps:

a large foot passes over the field, crosses the mountain ridge
prehistoric humans hold up fossils and smash in our heads
in our brains as bright as lamps
even now all is a wild forest
deer are bleeding, still skiing on snow trails
tones are trembling, trees keep on giving life
       the beginning is a beginning before it's begun
       farewell a farewell in the time of farewell

1985
translated by Lucas Klein

RESIDENTS

only when they drink beer in the depths of the sky do we kiss
when they sing, we turn out the lights
when we sleep, they use their silver-plated toenails
to walk into our dreams, when we're waiting to wake
they've already formed a river

in timeless sleep
they shave, and we hear a violin
they row a boat, and the earth stops spinning
they stop rowing, they stop rowing

it's impossible that we'll ever wake

in sleepless time
they wave to us, we wave to children
when children are waving to children
stars wake from their distant hotel

all that know pain have woken

the beer that they've drunk has flown back to the sea
the children who walk on the sea
all earn their blessing: flow
flow, it's only the yielding of the river

with tears that flow in secret, we have formed a river

1989
translated by Lucas Klein

OFTEN

often the women occupy the metal chair in the park
just as they often own many clothes
in the homes they own there have been lives
often this city is dreamed by them
this world, too

just as they have spent long years
often they still feel hungry when reading the paper
a hunger from a far-off place
which makes them feel like they could get fat, it's only a pain
though their lives won't change because of it
when they read the paper, the map does get larger

they have been lovers, wives, mothers, and still are today
but no one is willing to remember them
even the pillows they slept on with others
no longer remember them. so
the time they spend talking to themselves gets longer and longer
as if they were talking to god. so
they are nice now, if they weren't before

they are willing to listen, whether to people
or animals, or to rivers, and often
they feel that they are a port
waiting for boats to depart from or arrive at
they may not want to go to Africa
but want just to sit on that fixed metal chair
the exile across from them might be covered in apple leaves
and sleep, sleep and dream
of their wombs as the churches of tomorrow

1992
translated by Lucas Klein

EVENSONG

as is the sower to the reaper
a pair of parents, apart from each other
hang their heads, to see a boy
looking at them from below the ground
the light granted to the living
is pushed now a little farther away

a field of crops cut and dropped
turns a bent waist landscape
into evensong—night's grain made
sunset on the spade, against
the setting sun in the boy's eyes, go
concentrate this bitterness—that entire ray of light

made a funeral, spade-shaped waves
sunset's serene fruit, demanding
we accept anew the binding of wheat

2004
translated by Lucas Klein

Chen Yuhong (b. 1952)

Born in Gaoxiong into a family that hailed from Nanhai, Guangdong, Chen grad-
uated from the Wenzao Ursuline University of Languages in Gaoxiong in southern
Taiwan. She lived in Vancouver, Canada, for more than a decade, then moved back
to Taiwan in the early 2000s and started publishing poetry. In addition to poetry,
she has translated into Chinese such poets as Margaret Atwood, Anne Carson,
and Louise Glück. She won the Cikada Prize for East Asian poetry in 2022.

   In "Tales no. 14: Reset to Zero," *wabi-sabi* is a Japanese term describing the
aesthetics of finding beauty in the imperfect, the impermanent, and the incom-
plete in nature.

PARENTHESIS

   —*Parenthesis: insertion; digression; interval, interruption*

days empty out
hands empty out
no one in sight
house empty (skylighted
) heart empty too
at night in the mountain in dream frogs croak come co(mecomecomecome
i say if between if oh between if
merely a blue piece of silk our) rolling sea
at night in the mountain in dream
fog in the air whom to tell to tell the thunder sounding heavy
weightless tintless lead-gray thud

where could it reach at last such an (emp-
          ty whirring thud) indication
where are you the midnight dark gloomy thunder
sounding unspeakable unspeakably
)   where are you
('cause of the heat the humidity of the indocile
movement up and down and rubbing the perception of black
energy the solar star burns and blasts (off) collapsing
memory splashes all over the bed comecomecome oh empty calls
          overlapped) such stretching holding releasing connecting overlapping
you say all the same (the same
drawing up the hasty paints of night not yet dry
tomorrow will not come frogs croak gonegonegonegone
non-volatile the sound last night rain (slim
                    winds gusty at night in the mountain in dream
dream has 1,000 hands rousing 1,000 nights and mountains is you)r hands
                                        where) are you

2008
translated by Chen-chen Tseng

AT THE BEGINNING

Willing to return to the beginning
of an extinct fern, or a raindrop

long before volcanoes and glaciers were formed
winged dragons flew in flocks across the dateline
and musk whales and Qilins frolicked on grasslands

Return to a pair of eyes without a grit of sand
a pair of hands without calluses

Look, touch, and smell
the hybrid night like a solitary cat
tasting the forest-green wind of chewed mint

Willing to once again
return to the very beginning, a pair of ears

like river clamshells
so thin and translucent
they filter your algae breath

2011

translated by Michelle Yeh and Frank Stewart

TALES NO. 14: RESET TO ZERO

I have asked again and again
Am I free? Can I, unhindered,
Define my own role?
Created, molded, regulated,
Can I still have a true self?
I refuse to repeatedly misread the coding.
I must reset to zero
Partition off the black hole of memory
Reset the password, restart,
And rebuild the self unimpeded

This is my epiphany: creation
Is no more than order amid chaos
A temporary balance
By necessity everything will return to wabi-sabi
The undifferentiated, one
This is my universe:
Neither good
Nor evil
Forces for and against life
Antithetical and parallel

Untamed by the ribcage
Dust or mire
Amid imagined imperfection
I create temporary perfection
I, we, destined to be in the minority
Destined to rewrite over and over again
The self, rewrite the future history
Without end . . . the future
How it
Stares at me

2021

Michelle Yeh and Frank Stewart

Ling Yu (b. 1952)

Ling Yu, the pen name of Wang Meiqin, is a native of Taipei. She received her BA degree in Chinese from the National Taiwan University and her MA degree in East Asian literatures from the University of Wisconsin–Madison. In 1991 she was invited by Helen Vendler to Harvard University as a visiting scholar. She was a lecturer at the National Yilan University in 1992-2015. Ling Yu started out writing fiction but began writing poetry in 1982 when she became a copyeditor for the revived *Modern Poetry Quarterly*, for which she served as the chief editor from 1986 to 1992.

"Rivers and Mountains" depicts Li Yu (937–78), the last emperor of the Southern Tang dynasty, which lasted from 937 to 976, a small kingdom with its capital in Nanjing. Li was a brilliant poet and artist but an inept ruler. After his kingdom fell to the newly founded Song dynasty in 975, he was taken captive in the capital, Bianliang, today's Kaifeng, in the north. During the few years he lived there, Li wrote his best poems and died from poison at the order of the Song emperor.

A POTTED PLANT

Those things that have nothing to do with the heart—
are no better than a potted plant

Those that have something to do with the heart—
are no better than a tree

Tree is God
mother
hometown
an abbreviation of these words

I pass by a tree in a village
I ask it—"Do you have God?"

It says: "What is God?"
"A widower who loses things endlessly"
"Like me"
"Like me, howling in a low, dry voice"

It smiles, a bitter smile
then we turn silent

2010
translated by Michelle Yeh

THE PACIFIC OCEAN

we are in the process of losing. in the ocean carrying all the things
we have lost. flowing to the east. to the other shore
of glamour

feelings. beliefs. memories. drifting farther and farther away—

that's when our tears will pour like rain. insignificant
they will flow into the mighty ocean. then we'll turn around. someday
we will turn around. to welcome what flows from another place—

feelings. beliefs. memories. and we will feel an
excitement. our blood will surge anew. and we'll be astonished by
the secretly replaced moment. how. that moment.
is forgotten by time

by then
I will have a son
you will be on my breast
sucking

2010
translated by Michelle Yeh

MONTH OF MAY

Green lions are climbing mountains
numerous green lions are climbing mountains
newly born
with bushy manes

They are determined to sit quietly in the mountains
practice meditation and maybe become vegetarians too

Wildness untamed
they want to race with springtime
to see who can run faster from one peak to another

"Wait for me! I am wearing pink
and it's slowing me down"

2010
translated by Michelle Yeh

AUTUMN IN SEPTEMBER

Above the green a touch of yellow
Gray birds bringing back grayness

Scallion green pale green celery green
But the green of banana is a bit old

Some strands of white hair
Appear
In the paddies the country roads the furrows
Announcing a harmony of colors

They move—
Through the fuzzy spring day

Now the orchard dims a little, because
The fruits are getting larger, leaves plumper
A deep green
Is spreading

White—
The secret visitor—

Since he came from the wild that day
He has never left

Here—
I like that he has no design—

Walking up to me quietly
Some people hear it some
Don't

2010
translated by Michelle Yeh

RIVERS AND MOUNTAINS

In the small courtyard in twilight—
I issue a self-reproach edict—I find shelter
Under the most intimate tree, rereading it in the shade

Leisurely reading it, all things
Are no longer my concern. Inside and outside the palace
Those who walk by, those specks of dust
Make me wonder
About those about to arrive

Sometimes I go upstairs to the window
To gaze afar at those gray clouds
That are about to betray me and escape

Then I will be imprisoned
In darkness. But my heart will not be troubled

—Darkness is also my
Rivers and mountains

2013
translated by Michelle Yeh and Frank Stewart

Shu Ting (b. 1952)

Born in Longhai, Fujian, Shu Ting, the pen name of Gong Peiyu, spent her child-hood in Xiamen and has lived on the Gulang Island (or Kulangsu) off the coast of Xiamen most of her life. In 1969, while a sophomore in junior high, she was sent to the countryside and started writing poetry. In 1972 she returned to the city to work on a construction site, then at a textile mill and a light bulb factory. She published her poetry in the underground journal *Today* in 1979 and soon won national fame for writing about love from a woman's point of view. A leading Obscure poet in the early 1980s, she has been a prolific prose writer in recent years.

Goddess Peak, in Shu's poem, derives from an old Chinese legend about the Goddess of the Witch Mountain, who faithfully waited for her lover, the King of Chu. As time passed and he failed to return, she turned into a stone.

GODDESS PEAK

Among the colorful handkerchiefs waving at you
whose hand is it that suddenly withdraws
to cover her eyes
When the crowd moves on, who
remains standing at the stern of the ship
her skirt fluttering like a cloud
the river's waves roaring
as they leap high
and murmuring as they recede

A beautiful dream preserved the story
of a beautiful sorrow on earth and in heaven,
and passed it down for generations
But can the heart
really turn into a stone
forever gazing at the cranes that vanish into the distant sky
instead of at the river's returning spring tides and the bright moon

Along the riverbank
a torrent of golden coneflowers and privets grow
I'd rather have my love's shoulder to weep on
than be memorialized on this cliff for a thousand years

June 1981
translated by Michelle Yeh and Frank Stewart

SELF-PORTRAIT

She is his little schemer.
When he begs for an answer, she doesn't say a word;
When he needs silence, she laughs and clowns around
Making him dizzy.
She destroys balance,
She despises concepts,
She is a headstrong fairy in the woods
Circling him with quirky dance steps.

She is his little schemer.
What he craves in his dreams, she won't give him;
What he never imagines, she wants him to have.
She is drawn to tender love but evades expressing it,
She is afraid of losing what she has not yet received.
She herself is a whirlpool
Creating many whirlpools;
No one understands her magic power.

She is his little schemer.
She won't come when he calls, won't leave when he asks her to;
She is close but seems far, she is hard to quit.
Sometimes she is like an iceberg,
Sometimes a sea of fire,
Sometimes a wordless song
He listens to it but has no idea if it's real or unreal;
He recalls it but can't tell if it's sweet or spicy.
She is his, his,
She is his little schemer.

1981
translated by Michelle Yeh and Frank Stewart

Zhong Ming (b. 1953)

Born in Chengdu, in Sichuan, Zhong served in the military in Manchuria in the 1970s before entering the Chinese Department at Southwest Normal University in 1977. He has worked as a college teacher and editor. Zhong started writing in college and founded the underground poetry journal *Second-Growth Forest* in 1982 and another journal *Persona Invisible* in 1990. He has been recognized not only for his poetry and prose but also for his antique collection, photography, and archaeological research on Three Star Mound, a Bronze Age cultural site in Sichuan.

Ruan Ji, in the second of Zhong's poems here, was a poet and musician who lived in the Three Kingdoms Period, which lasted from 220 to 280. One of the eccentric, Daoist-leaning literati known as the Seven Sages of the Bamboo Grove, Ruan was known for showing the whites of his eyes to people he despised and the black irises to the few he approved of. Infantry lieutenant was the highest official rank he held.

CHINESE ACROBATICS: A HARD CHAIR (1 of 4)

2.

[What does the emperor fear most—the chair.]

The chair's tight Chinese silk makes him slide as though over slippery snow
toward winter, his own hard winter. Recondite vision will
handle him, turn him like a broom, lean him against the chair and he
speaks the wrong words in precise tones, the authority of illness.

But who can say what people ought to do?
These good-hearted people avoiding freedom after the overthrow,
rigidly, intensely staring at his dirtiness,

and so we have a duty to make sure our mouths and chairs are aboveboard.
In the white but snowless chill and void,
atop a thousand people stretched tight like clay
he sits out green, yellow, purple, the system, hard living and the soft life,

employing both violence and benevolence. He makes a face with hard *qigong* practice,
he can produce heat, placing his imperial lectern like a huge jar on our spinning
heads, and then we have a reading month, we have heavy snow portending a
   good year,

our work and the sovereign's metaphorical tilling of the land will both be
   recognized,
military and literary mouths stand up straight and haggle over gains and losses,
while the sovereign, on an ancient chair of trivial matters, takes note of the
   seating arrangements.

1987
translated by Eleanor Goodman

DUELING WITH RUAN JI

Your Excellency, come, set your sword shining, make your move,
there are terrible customs that can only be guarded at sword point!
The generous light is like an ear of corn,
and with a little shake, I step into the mystical kingdom of Jiuye.

You have merely to shout, a bloodied throat,
and I perceive the infinite, spread my hair on the vast ocean.
Secretly cut the birds some slack, let them flap forward a few feet,
what's the difference if you break a few more twigs?

The quivering and cruelty that don't really resist me
return to the pine forest, ascend and think of someone.
Two sleeves flap in boredom,
the spirits sit alone in the hall amid the scenery,

and that's yet another song of your regal bearing!
Whereupon I know the betrayal, know
that you aren't moved by a woman's beauty, an old oxcart,
bringing the well-studied swordplay to the end of the road.

Your Excellency, your bow made of wooden omens,
can it dispel the boredom of courtly successes,
it envelopes your beautiful beard, your deep grief,
one white eye like a burning sun, one black eye like a tiny flame.

I want to follow you as you pick up that ivory-handled knife,
learn from the singing phoenix. Daoist priest, infantry lieutenant, Excellency,
sadly the song and dance are gone, burning desire suddenly fades,
in the duel everyone turns to dust,

as though just absentmindedly groomed. Your Excellency, Sir,
we dress up again as the dead in a stone mirror,
surmounting the boring diseases of the saints,
come, come, let us slice open each other's palms!

1993
translated by Eleanor Goodman

Chen Li (b. 1954)

Chen Li, the pen name of Chen Yingwen, is a native of Hualian on the east coast
of Taiwan. After graduating from the English Department of the National Taiwan
Normal University, he taught at Hua Gang Junior High for decades, retiring in
2005. In 1999 he was invited to the Poetry International Festival in Rotterdam. He
was the organizer of the annual International Pacific Poetry Festival in Hualian
from 2006 to 2018. Chen published his first book of poetry in 1975. In addition
to poetry, he is a prolific prose writer and literary, art, and music critic as well as
translator of world poetry into Chinese, working alongside his wife, Fen-ling
Chang (Zhang Fenling).

   "War Symphony" is a concrete poem composed of four Chinese characters.
Bing 兵 in the first stanza is a pictograph of "soldier." *Ping* 乒 and *pang* 乓 in the
second stanza are onomatopoeic words; together *ping-pang* means "ping-pong."
The two characters also resemble one-legged soldiers. *Qiu* 丘 in the third stanza
is a pictograph of "mound," or "grave." In "Little Deaths" Jiří Kylián is a Czech
former dancer and dance choreographer.

THE EDGE OF THE ISLAND

On the world map with a scale of one to forty million
our island is an imperfect yellow button
dangling on a blue uniform
My existence is a transparent thread
thinner than spider's silk, going out my window facing
the sea to bind the island and ocean together

At the edge of lonely days, in the crevice
between the new year and the old
thought is like a book of mirrors, freezing
the ripples of time
Thumbing through it, you'll see pages of an obscure
past, flashing upon each mirror

another secret button—
like an invisible tape recorder, pressed against
your breast, repeatedly recording and playing
your and all of mankind's memories—
a mixed tape of love and hate
dream and reality, sorrow and joy

What you hear now is
the sound of the world
the heartbeats of all the dead and living
plus your own. If you call with all your heart
the dead and the living will speak to you
in clear voices

At the edge of the island, on the boundary
of sleep and awake
my hand is holding my needlelike existence
threading through the yellow button polished and rounded
by the island people, piercing hard into
the heart of the earth beneath the blue uniform

January 1993
translated by Fen-ling Chang

WAR SYMPHONY

兵兵兵兵兵兵兵兵兵兵兵兵兵兵兵兵兵兵兵兵兵兵兵
兵兵兵兵兵兵兵兵兵兵兵兵兵兵兵兵兵兵兵兵兵兵兵
兵兵兵兵兵兵兵兵兵兵兵兵兵兵兵兵兵兵兵兵兵兵兵
兵兵兵兵兵兵兵兵兵兵兵兵兵兵兵兵兵兵兵兵兵兵兵
兵兵兵兵兵兵兵兵兵兵兵兵兵兵兵兵兵兵兵兵兵兵兵
兵兵兵兵兵兵兵兵兵兵兵兵兵兵兵兵兵兵兵兵兵兵兵
兵兵兵兵兵兵兵兵兵兵兵兵兵兵兵兵兵兵兵兵兵兵兵
兵兵兵兵兵兵兵兵兵兵兵兵兵兵兵兵兵兵兵兵兵兵兵
兵兵兵兵兵兵兵兵兵兵兵兵兵兵兵兵兵兵兵兵兵兵兵
兵兵兵兵兵兵兵兵兵兵兵兵兵兵兵兵兵兵兵兵兵兵兵
兵兵兵兵兵兵兵兵兵兵兵兵兵兵兵兵兵兵兵兵兵兵兵
兵兵兵兵兵兵兵兵兵兵兵兵兵兵兵兵兵兵兵兵兵兵兵
兵兵兵兵兵兵兵兵兵兵兵兵兵兵兵兵兵兵兵兵兵兵兵
兵兵兵兵兵兵兵兵兵兵兵兵兵兵兵兵兵兵兵兵兵兵兵
兵兵兵兵兵兵兵兵兵兵兵兵兵兵兵兵兵兵兵兵兵兵兵
兵兵兵兵兵兵兵兵兵兵兵兵兵兵兵兵兵兵兵兵兵兵兵

兵兵兵兵兵兵兵兵兵兵兵兵兵兵兵兵兵兵兵兵兵兵兵
兵兵兵乒乒兵兵兵兵兵兵乒兵兵兵兵乒兵兵兵兵乒乒
乒乒兵兵乒乒兵乒乒乒乒乒乒乒乒乒乒乒乒乒乒乒乒
乒乒乒乒乒乒乒兵乒乒乒乒乒乒乒乒乒乒乒乒乒乒乒
乒乒乒乒乒乒乒乒乒乒乒乒乒乒乒乒乒乒乒乒乒乒乒
乒乒乒乒乒乒乒乒乒乒乒乒乒乒乒乒乒乒乒乒乒乒乒
乒乒乒乒乒乒乒乒乒乒乒乒乒乒乒乒乒乒乒乒乒乒乒
乒乒乒乒乒乒乒乒乒乒乒乒乒乒乒乒乒乒乒乒乒乒乒
乒乒乒乒乒乒乒乒乒乒乒乒乒乒乒乒乒乒乒乒乒乒乒
乒乒乒乒乒乒乒乒乒乒乒乒乒乒乒乒   乒乒乒   乒
乒乒乒   乒乒乒乒乒   乒乒   乒乒乒   乒乒   乒乒乒
乒乒乒   乒乒乒   乒乒   乒乒   乒   乒乒乒乒   乒乒   乒乒
乒乒乒   乒乒   乒乒乒   乒乒   乒乒   乒乒   乒乒
乒乒   乒乒乒乒   乒乒   乒乒   乒乒
乒乒   乒乒   乒乒   乒乒   乒乒
乒乒乒   乒乒

乓乓乓乓乓乓乓乓乓乓乓乓乓乓乓乓乓乓乓乓乓乓乓
乓乓乓乓乓乓乓乓乓乓乓乓乓乓乓乓乓乓乓乓乓乓乓
乓乓乓乓乓乓乓乓乓乓乓乓乓乓乓乓乓乓乓乓乓乓乓
乓乓乓乓乓乓乓乓乓乓乓乓乓乓乓乓乓乓乓乓乓乓乓
乓乓乓乓乓乓乓乓乓乓乓乓乓乓乓乓乓乓乓乓乓乓乓
乓乓乓乓乓乓乓乓乓乓乓乓乓乓乓乓乓乓乓乓乓乓乓
乓乓乓乓乓乓乓乓乓乓乓乓乓乓乓乓乓乓乓乓乓乓乓
乓乓乓乓乓乓乓乓乓乓乓乓乓乓乓乓乓乓乓乓乓乓乓
乓乓乓乓乓乓乓乓乓乓乓乓乓乓乓乓乓乓乓乓乓乓乓
乓乓乓乓乓乓乓乓乓乓乓乓乓乓乓乓乓乓乓乓乓乓乓
乓乓乓乓乓乓乓乓乓乓乓乓乓乓乓乓乓乓乓乓乓乓乓
乓乓乓乓乓乓乓乓乓乓乓乓乓乓乓乓乓乓乓乓乓乓乓
乓乓乓乓乓乓乓乓乓乓乓乓乓乓乓乓乓乓乓乓乓乓乓
乓乓乓乓乓乓乓乓乓乓乓乓乓乓乓乓乓乓乓乓乓乓乓
乓乓乓乓乓乓乓乓乓乓乓乓乓乓乓乓乓乓乓乓乓乓乓
乓乓乓乓乓乓乓乓乓乓乓乓乓乓乓乓乓乓乓乓乓乓乓

July 1995

TANGO FOR THE JEALOUS

If you embrace love as if it were a dishwasher,
ignore the greasy scars left on the dishes
licked by others' tongues or slashed by
the lengths of their knives and forks. Start the cycle
and flush them: forgetting is the best detergent.
Remember only the glorious, beautiful, shining parts,
because platters, especially china, are delicate.
Wash them, dry them, and, like a brand-new man,
greet tomorrow's breakfast as if nothing had happened.

Especially when your life is approaching or has passed
noon, youthful anxiety comes back to you again.
You pick up the phone and dial her in vain.
Suspicious and fretful, you make even more mute
and aimless phone calls to your invisible rivals in love.
You call that one again and again (oh, how convenient
modern communication), only to be answered
by an afternoon empty as a big bowl. Now, please
unplug the dishwasher for the moment, and swallow
the tangled phone wires like a mass of noodles,
splashed with a little of enmity's soy sauce.
The dishwasher will quickly rinse off your disgrace.

However, the dark night is an even bigger dishwasher,
when you're aggrieved and all the past dishes are flung at you—
unwashable bits of starlight stuck to the dish bottoms.
Ah, ignore the noise of the machine in operation,
the hum of the dark universe that won't go away.
Ignore the shadows which encircle you like leftover
fish bones, if the one you love is not by your side.
If you still feel like spitting out those irritating fish spines,
rearrange them, stroke after stroke, into new lines of poetry.

May 1998
translated by Arthur Sze

LITTLE DEATHS

Based on Jiří Kylián's dance title

Under the wind's quilt, each day
little deaths

Under the quilt's waves, you and I
brandish a sword of nothingness

A sword stabs into the body
to kill you, kill me

A sword stabs into the heart
to kill time, to utterly kill time

Where the tip of the sword points, little
orgasms belong to the quilt

Where the flashing sword passes, little
triumphant shouts and sobs

Little deaths make us
gradually accustomed to the humble triviality of living

Little conquests and surrenders
where neither enemy nor allied troops are on time's plain

Killers and instigators to the other
Assassins and pilgrims to the other

In the lifelong, indolent process of living,
process of dying, indolently

Inverting the sword handle into a pendulum, each day
little vibrations, little deaths

January 2002
translated by Arthur Sze

ADAGIO

Grandma sitting by the window
(she was seventeen
then, she says)
waiting for the distant clouds
to move slowly to the mountaintop
and become her hair in the mirror
A cat walks across the lawn
(so can a pig
but not now)
knocks over the rattan chair
she often sits on
in the middle of the lawn
She turns on the radio
to listen to reports of snowfall
but the grass is so green
Suddenly she craves
vanilla ice cream
The bread tree stands at the end
of the lawn the whole afternoon
not moving one bit
The Oriental sesame flower stands
at the other end of the lawn
chitchatting with her sisters
Grandma thinks to herself
the silent tree is poetry
so is the talking flower
She raises her head and sees me
with a backpack of books cross
the lawn, set the rattan chair on its feet
open the door, enter the house, and see

Grandma sitting by the window
(she was seventeen
then, she says)
waiting for the distant clouds
to move slowly to the mountaintop
and become her hair in the mirror
A cat walks across the lawn
(so can a pig
but not now)
knocks over the rattan chair
she often sits on
in the middle of the lawn
She turns on the radio
to listen to reports of snowfall
but the grass is so green
Suddenly she craves
vanilla ice cream
The bread tree stands at the end
of the lawn, the whole afternoon
not moving one bit
The Oriental sesame flower stands
at the other end of the lawn
chitchatting with her sisters
Grandma thinks to herself
the silent tree is poetry
so is the talking flower
She raises her head and sees me
with a backpack of books cross
the lawn, set the rattan chair on its feet
open the door, enter the house, and see

March 2006
translated by Michelle Yeh and Frank Stewart

Luo Dayou (Ta-yu Lo, b. 1954)

Born into a family of doctors in Taipei, Luo graduated from China Medical University in Central Taiwan and practiced medicine while pursuing his interest in music. He started composing and performing professionally in 1976 and went on to become one of the most influential songwriters in the Chinese-speaking world. Equally adept in rock and roll and folk, love lyrics and social critiques, Luo has set to music several modern poems, including "Four Rhymes of Homesickness" by Yu Guangzhong and "Mistake" by Zheng Chouyu.

"The Orphan of Asia" was taken from the title of the novel written by Wu Zhuoliu (1900–1976) in 1943–45 and first published in Japan in 1946. The story depicts the plight of the Taiwanese people under Japanese occupation, from 1895 to 1945.

CHILDHOOD

On the banyan tree by the pond, cicadas' humming calls for summertime
On the swing in the playground just a single butterfly perches
On the blackboard the teacher's chalk is busily screeching
A childhood of waiting—for class to end, for school to end, for fun to begin

The school store has everything, but I haven't a penny
The hero Zhuge fights the Demon Squad—who will capture the precious
	sword?
Why hasn't the girl in the classroom next door passed by my window yet?
Snack in my mouth, manga in my hand, my first childhood sweetheart

Always just before bedtime I remember my homework isn't done
Always after an exam I remember I should have read the books
Inch of time, inch of gold, the teacher says time's worth more than gold
Day after day, year after year, my muddle-headed childhood

No one could explain to me why the sun always sets beyond the same hill
No one knew if immortals live deep in the mountains
So many days I would sit alone staring at the sky just dreaming
So many questions and fantasies in such a lonely childhood

Dragonflies in the sunlight, the rice paddies shining green
Crayons and kaleidoscopes could never match the rainbow
When will I ever have a big person's face like the senior-class boys
Longing for vacation, for tomorrow, and for growing up
Day after day, year after year, longing for the end of childhood

originally released in 1982
translated by Michelle Yeh and Frank Stewart

THE ORPHAN OF ASIA

The orphan of Asia is crying in the wind
His yellow face streaked with crimson mud
In his black eyes the fear of Whites
The west wind sings a sad song in the east

The orphan of Asia is crying into the wind
In games, no one plays fair with you
They all want to steal your favorite toy
Tell me why you are crying, my sweet boy

How many weep over questions with no answers
How many sigh in helpless loneliness each night
How many wordlessly wipe away their own tears
Dear Mother, can you tell me the meaning of this

The orphan of Asia is crying in the wind
His yellow face stained with crimson mud
In his black eyes the fear of Whites
The west wind sings a sad song in the east

1983
translated by Michelle Yeh and Frank Stewart

ROILING RED DUST

At first, you were indifferent and I was young and naive
In the roiling Red Dust our young love came to a silent dead end

It must be a flaw in human nature or karma from a past life
But I'd die for Yin and Yang to be in harmony for one moment

Coming together is easy, parting is hard—drifting in the dusty world
Parting is easy, reunion is hard—forever hurt by love and grieving

This heart that should be yours is still locked tight in my chest
All because of a faithless mind behind an untrue face

So you who were reluctant to part said goodbye to me forever
A humming in the world still whispers the legend of us together

originally released in 1990
translated by Michelle Yeh and Frank Stewart

Yang Ze (Hsien-ching Yang, b. 1954)

A native of Jiayi in southern Taiwan, Yang Ze, the pen name of Yang Xianqing (Hsien-ch'ing Yang), received his BA and MA degrees from the Department of Foreign Languages and Literature at the National Taiwan University and his doctorate in East Asian studies from Princeton University. After teaching at Brown University and working for the *China Times* in New York for several years, he returned to Taiwan in 1990 and became an editor at the *China Times*. For years he was the chief editor of the literary supplement of the newspaper. Yang started writing poetry while in college under the mentorship of Yang Mu and published his first book of poems in 1977. In addition to poetry, he has written literary essays and cultural critiques and has edited books of critical essays and poems.

OH, MY HOMELAND IS A MYSTICAL RADIO STATION

I stood on an avenue in the center of the lowland, when
darkness descended again. This dead end street
suddenly lost its direction
Beyond the confused frequencies of the city—
oh, my homeland is a mystical radio station
always beckoning me from across the dark expanse
with its timbre of malevolent night
its mournful rivers and mountains

Just arrived from Tel Aviv, it seemed,
a Jewish prophet, his heart full of the glories of his ancient country,
appeared at a New York airport, crying:
"Hear,
O people of Israel!"
I stood on a street corner with peculiar shadows in the lamplight, when
night came, I thought I heard it—
my homeland in the distance
calling the names of its sons and daughters

Across the dark expanse, across
this superficially novel but messy age
My homeland is a radio station that once broadcast joy
crossing the straits, bringing final victory
and the return of an island to the continent's embrace.
I stood on an avenue in the center of the lowland—
Oh, my mother and father also heard that mystical dialect
identical to the one I was hearing now

Across the distant expanse, across
the atmosphere blockaded above the straits
Now it was a sound wave's journey
full of hardship and grief: blood and tears
sprayed into the wind, amid the malevolent night's sonic boom
(The mournful rivers and mountains are the only testament, only echo)
Before it had traveled halfway,
ah, it was already freezing cold . . .

I stood in vain on the avenue, when
night came deeply. The straits surged and crashed
The city moaned its own name in masturbatory ecstasy, amid its disordered
    frequencies—
oh, my homeland is a radio station occupied by rioters
its staff slaughtered, its human voices replaced
by the squawking of bloodthirsty parrots
I stood in vain on the avenue,
"Hear,
O China!"
I thought I heard the broadcaster's urgent dying gasp
from the pools of blood
But the street teemed with noises, it was only—
mountains and rivers full of resentment
abandoned to the dust of the city . . .

1977
translated by Brian Skerratt

LIFE ISN'T WORTH LIVING

Life isn't worth living.
A little earlier, I may have
had a foreboding premonition.
A little earlier, before your lovely
Body patterning, like a young animal's, against
the papaya tree in the dark,
the highly perfected balcony and stars,
before the night—the night of the magic flute
and unicorn that belong to all lovers;
when the magic flute has sounded through
the magic flute has sounded through the house and things turned chilly
The trumpet returns to that last
and first grassland dawn . . .

Life isn't worth living,
A little earlier, I had this premonition.
A little earlier, before my relativity
your absoluteness—like a wild hare,
that honest, brave instinct for love
and that multifarious, impure bearing
(which makes it so hard to let go)
tending toward sentimentality, tending toward speed,
and tending toward the slight overindulgence and madness
that fantasy brings.

No, life is not worth living.
A little earlier, before books,
music, and painting—from the beginning,
I had a dark premonition.
Green glow and blue rose
Rings of pot smoke and Zen
I dreamed of you: the girl on the electric bicycle,
imitating the headless horseman in the painting
holding in her hand a severed head with long, black hair, racing toward
the grassland dawn . . .
When the magic flute sounded through again
the magic flute sounded through again and things turned cold
The knockout drugs of love and death are
Like the setting sun over the sea—
a kind of eternal violence
and madness . . .

Life isn't worth living.
The elephant herd stampeding on the shore
Before the sea and the sky grow old together:
Young animal, secretly licking your wounds,
to protect your first and last sentimentalism
I'd ride into battle with nothing but an axe handle,
your untiring,
unvictorious hero

I will
go on living, marmot-like
Even though, before your dreams,
my nihilism; before
your cave, my light—
even though life is not worth living.

1993
translated by Brian Skerratt

HAVE NO DOUBT

The hour grows late
No time for regrets
A cold wind rises
When you wake up one morning,
push open the window and look out
to discover the autumn sidewalk
impressively splattered with sunlight and shadow
and rustling leaves
The better part of your life
up and left you long ago

Please have no doubt
A cold wind stirs
Sunlight and shadow on the grass
Each day shorter than the one before
When the old apartment building hides itself on the front lines of midnight
dripping and
trembling in the rain
The one on the bed tosses and turns, remembering
things that happened he was powerless to resist
It rises and falls like the tides

The hour grows late
You rush back
onto time's track
to roam the interstices between so many gears
to rediscover
all the illusory truths
that belong to you, and the entire century
until, like a message from the gods,
the intermittent sound of a weeping piano
flows emptily from above the apartment

The one on the bed cries out, sitting upright:
like a secret ritual for the end of night,
the cold, clear music
carries you
barefoot across the flame
and in an instant, rescues you!

2013
translated by Brian Skerratt

The Anti-Sublime
and Multiculturalism

———————

1980s–1990s

The 1980s in mainland China are rightly regarded as the new Age of Enlighten-
ment and the era of High Culture Fever. After decades of power struggles and
draconian policies during the Mao era, a hunger for new knowledge, a zest for
intellectual debates, and an eagerness to experiment in literature and art exploded
in the New Era under Deng Xiaoping. In the liberalizing atmosphere, translations
of Western literature and philosophy were extremely popular, on the one hand,
and, on the other hand, various efforts to reexamine and redefine Chinese identity
were manifested in the Roots-Seeking movement in literature, painting, and film.

However, the opening of China amounted to a balancing act. As new knowl-
edge and values poured in from abroad, the Communist Party found it necessary
to reign in certain domestic tendencies. The Anti–Spiritual Pollution campaign
in 1983 and the Anti–Bourgeois Liberalization campaign in 1987 represented the
tension between reformism and conservatism. In 1986–87 college student protests
erupted in various cities. In April 1989 college students in Beijing gathered in
Tiananmen Square, ostensibly to mourn the passing of Hu Yaobang (1915–89),
the reform-minded general secretary of the Communist Party who had resigned
under pressure. The student-led movement for more freedom and democracy
gained support from other sectors of society and spread all over China. On the late
night of June 3, shots were fired into the crowd in Tiananmen Square. By the early
morning, the square was "cleared." Reporters and Western diplomats estimated
that hundreds to thousands of protesters were killed, and many more were injured.
The crackdown on the student-led pro-democracy movement—known as the
Tiananmen Massacre, or Tiananmen Incident—brought to an end the New Era
characterized by openness and optimism. As China adopted a market economy
and promoted private entrepreneurship in the 1990s, prospects of political reform
were dim. To this day the term *June Fourth* remains a political taboo in China,
strictly enforced by censorship in print media and the internet.

The underground poetry that had emerged during the Cultural Revolution became a national sensation in the early 1980s, aided by the fact that it was critiqued by the establishment for its alleged obscurity. Veering away from the politically correct model, "Obscure Poetry" addressed personal feelings that had been repressed in the past, such as romantic love and existential angst. It also paid tribute to the young men and women who had been persecuted during the Cultural Revolution for speaking up against leftist extremism. Obscure Poetry inspired a new generation of poets, who, like their predecessors, published underground poetry journals, which were circulated in minuscule numbers of mimeograph copies. Numerous groups thrived in the mid- and late 1980s and were collectively known as post-Obscure, the Third Generation, or the Newborn Generation. In contrast to its predecessor, post–Obscure Poetry shifted from affirmations of personal dignity and idealism to depictions of mundane details of everyday life and the powerlessness of Everyman, often in an irreverent or self-mocking tone.

In Taiwan political reform made great strides in the 1980s. On September 28, 1986, the first opposition party in Taiwan, the Democratic Progressive Party, was founded. On July 15, 1987, President Chiang Ching-kuo (1910–88) lifted martial law, which had been in place since May 20, 1949. The act put an end to the era of White Terror, ending censorship of mass media and allowing civilians to travel to Mainland China. In 1988 Lee Teng-hui (1923–2020) became the first native Taiwanese to be president, and in 1996 he went on to be the first president elected directly by the people. Four years later Democratic Progressive Party candidate Chen Shui-bian (b. 1950) won the presidency, which represented the first transfer of power from the Nationalists since 1945.

The nativist turn was also reflected in literature and art. For example, poetry reexamined the repressed history of Taiwan and exposed social and political injustices. It also gave voices to various marginalized groups, including women, homosexuals, indigenous peoples, and Nationalist veterans. Finally, ecological consciousness arose and found expressions in nature writing in multiple genres.

Yu Jian (b. 1954)

Born in Kunming, Yunnan, Yu held a number of manual labor jobs from age sixteen to twenty-six. In 1980 he entered the Chinese Department at the University of Yunnan, where he founded the literary journal *Ginkgo* in 1983. After graduating in 1984, he was assigned to the journal *Yunnan Literary Criticism* as an editor. In 1985 Yu founded the underground journal *They* with Han Dong and others and began publishing his own poetry. In the late 1990s he advocated a "populist poetry" that avoided dense, metaphoric language and drew on everyday life for its subject matter. In addition to poetry, he has published prose. Currently, Yu is a professor at Yunnan Normal University.

WORK NO. 16

the snow came   higher than the door
everything is warm inside
some things need to be thought about in silence
some things in the past and some in the future
so far no letter in reply
the postman is green
he delivers newspapers and colorful magazines
i've given him a lot of stamps on a lot of envelopes
so far no letter in reply
it's a good year for getting married
lots of people have gotten wedding invitations on red paper
maybe i should get married too
like my friends
go traveling   across the north in springtime
i have sung of the poplars there
in a fifty-line poem
a bit sweet   a bit bitter   a bit lost
coming home from work in the factory
i liked to watch movies with little lei
i forget the scene we were watching   he started crying softly
the woman next door came home
she slipped under her covers quietly
like a gentle cat (i'm guessing here)
her sighing is light as snow
the walls are thick as snow
her husband is a gunner

this summer on the second floor   i saw them
the snow is sleeping the night has a white pillow
the cold wind blowing makes the moon brighter
december stands silently on the street
a bit sweet   a bit bitter   a bit lost

1983
translated by Josh Stenberg

THANK YOU FATHER

twelve months of the year
out of your pipe poppies bloom
family warm like spring   no talk of divorce
no meddling   no lending money   no loud laughter
quiet as mice   cleaner than a hospital ward
ancestral virtues   smooth as stone
never to bleed   in the flood of centuries
patterns simpler by the day
as father   you brought home bread and salt
at the long black table   you sit in the center
the place of emperors professors and editorials
sons tied to either side   not negotiators
but golden buttons   making you glitter brightly
from there you caress us   your eyes full of fatherly love
like a stomach   tender and lasting
making us understand how to behave
when you were young you often had a stomachache
when it acted up   your sons turned into beetles
together morning and night   I've never seen you from the back
only when I grew up did I see your work file
proactive and willing to work   enthusiastic and sincere   affable and easy to
    approach
respectful of leaders   never complaining   never leaving early
once you told me   as a kid you liked soccer

especially dancing   the two-step kind
that really surprised me   I thought you were talking about a sea lion
ever since I was little I knew you were a good man   in an uncommon era
there were more jerks than good guys on the streets
when these infidels were arrested, exiled, never to return
you came out of the park   to be a bridegroom
in 1957 you became a father
as a good man   dad   you had a really hard life
confession   exposé   reporting   informing
when you finished all that   you left work with a briefcase under your arm
at night you couldn't sleep   always strained your ears and listened
quietly you got up   checked your sons' diaries and what they said in their sleep
as assiduously as the gestapo
the tiger cubs you sired   made you worry sick
if the young ones were careless   the whole family would be implicated
late at night you stood in line to buy coal   exchanged rationed oil for milk
    powder
you went all the way to Shanghai   an exhausting journey   to procure
    clothes and shoes
you knew doctors principals drivers and the guards at the gate
cunning and astute   knowing when to bend   smooth as stone
that's how   through the dark era   in the turmoil
you raised me   got me an ID card
I grew up   far from easy   dad
I am an adult now   just like you
industrious and assiduous   simple and unassuming   spotless in character
when he was born this kid looked suspicious   had an inauspicious horoscope
might have a nervous disorder or die of a brain infection
might run a red light   break his leg and become a cripple
might be seduced by a bad egg   and get sentenced to hard labor in the end
might be a drunk brawler a gambler an addict an AIDS patient
dad   I never did any of these things   I did not kill myself
as long as my parents are alive   I won't go far   I study hard   to get better
    and better
I go to bed at nine-thirty   wash my clothes on Sundays
a virgin   I passed the prenuptial physical exam at twenty-eight

a three-bedroom apartment   both my parents alive   surrounded by
    children
the whole family at the round table   warm as spring
it hasn't been easy   my father with a head of white hair

December 21, 1987
translated by Josh Stenberg

THE SOUND OF FALLING

i heard the sound of falling   that sound
of falling from a certain height   straight down   i heard its beginning
and its ending below   the echo in my room   i turned around
i could tell the sound was behind me   i thought it was on the floor
or between the floor and the ceiling   but nothing's loose there
nothing is out of place   that's what i expected   everything is fixed
with cement   nails   ropes   screws or glue
and the inexorable descent of objects   descent   to get caught on the table
    on the floor
descent   to get caught in the book on the table   descent   to get caught
    in the words on the pages in the book
but at that point in time   at eleven twenty what was falling
through the wall clock and the rattan chair what was falling
surely it passed through the bookshelf and the porcelain horse on top of the
    bookshelf
i'm sure it fell from a room on another floor   i heard it go through all kinds
    of things
rays of light   carpets   cement boards   plaster   sand and
    nailheads   going through wooden boards and cloth
like in the revolutionary era   secrets passing from one jail cell to another
it's far from the orchard here   far from stone or anything spherical
this isn't the rainy season   nor gusty spring
so what was falling   in the time between eleven twenty and eleven twenty-one
i clearly heard its fall which might so easily be ignored
because nothing was damaged   nothing was connected to it
its falling was not like a large pane of glass shattering all over the place

or like a meteorite that makes everything around it quake
the sound   was quite crisp   enough to be audible
but not clear enough to be described   sketched or acted out   not enough
    to be corroborated by another pair of ears
what was falling   this falling connected only to me
it halted there   behind me   at some point in space and time

August 1991
translated by Josh Stenberg

ELEPHANTS OF 1966

red elephants in droves strutted across the square
their long, shrieking trunks swaying
the speed at which the sun turned was like the immense void
for their captives   who at last found a superficial contentment
so united   so pleased with themselves   so brilliant
crazy school kids revised the slogans on the tips of their tusks
I sharpened the last pencil of my adolescence while I
waited for the rain to fall   words on the blackboard gone
a white high-heeled shoe belonging to teacher Fan Yuying had been dropped
    in the hallway
It was the first time I had seen a flattened shoe

2016
translated by Michelle Yeh and Frank Stewart

Luo Zhicheng (b. 1955)

Luo was born in Taipei into a family that had come from Hunan. He graduated
from the National Taiwan University, where he majored in philosophy and went
on to earn an MA degree in East Asian languages and cultures from the University
of Wisconsin–Madison in 1983. He has worked as a newspaper editor, publisher,
television producer, radio host, director of Kwang Hwa Information and Culture

Center in Hong Kong, and director of the Central News Agency in Taiwan. Luo started writing poetry and founded a poetry club in high school. In college he was involved in the founding of NTU Modern Poetry Club, along with Yang Ze (b. 1954), Liao Xianhao (b. 1954), and other schoolmates. In addition to being a poet, he is an illustrator and designer of books.

The bodhisattva referred to here is Guanyin, Goddess of Mercy in Chinese Buddhism. In the poem it may also refer to the mountain in the western part of Greater Taipei. Yelü Abaoji (872–926), in the eponymous poem, unified the Khitan tribes and founded the Liao dynasty, which ruled northern China, Manchuria, Mongolia, and parts of present-day Russia and North Korea from 916 to 1125. Han Yanhui (882–959) was a minister of Han descent who served the Liao court.

BODHISATTVA

Graceful Bodhisattva is sleeping soundly in a circle of candles.
Her supine pose is a dark, folding screen of dreams:
Hiding under her hair, I cast my fishing line—
Heavy snow is falling on every distant star

August 1975
translated by Michelle Yeh and Frank Stewart

A CANDLE FELL ASLEEP IN ITS FLAME

A candle fell asleep in its flame
My child, let's tiptoe quietly down the stairs,
Straighten up the world you toppled before you fell asleep
Put away the little tantrums you left behind on the rug
And let them fade away beneath the blankets
A candle fell asleep in its flame
Time's cradle gently rocks you
While death softly slumbers
It doesn't notice us tiptoeing by
My child, clutching our secret SOS to eternity

Let's go fly a kite beside the ocean!
Peek through a hole that a meteor has poked in night's curtain
And marvel at the constellations making their rounds
Let's ski down the slope of your hair—
Careful we don't wake a living soul.

A candle fell asleep,
like a magic brush painting a dream-sky
Let us go to the bakery before it closes
To buy breakfast for tomorrow
Afterward, if you are willing
We'll steal the Earth's celestial blueprints

A candle fell sound asleep in its flame
Sweet child, blow it out with your perfect, O-shaped mouth
Our deaths we've tended day by day inside us like a garden
Kept apart in our love
What do they say to each other?
Beautiful, sleepy child, when you wake, all your feelings
Will still be waiting for you here on your bedside table

December 1977
translated by Michelle Yeh and Frank Stewart

YELÜ ABAOJI

But Yelü Abaoji is more ferocious than his half-brothers
When he yanks his horse's mane and overtakes
A shooting star
So swift there's no time to make a wish
With his bare hands he defeats the ten best wrestlers
As easily as dandling his favorite concubines
And when he runs
He punches a hole in the wind

He loves to overeat, overdrink, and compete in everything
Loves to slap people hard on the shoulder
Loves to sleep and snore
When in high spirits he sings loudly, off-key
Because he is great, he tolerates the flaws in others
No one can alter his kindness, calculation, and
confidence

He orders Han Yanhui to spread Sinicization throughout
While he also promotes the new Khitan writing system
And writes love letters and war declarations in its script:
"Greetings from the Supreme Celestial Emperor"—
Is how he begins all his letters.

He puts his grandsons and their playmates on his shoulders
And allows their muddy hands to soil his court robe
Of gold-threaded brocade.
He tickles them and laughs
And so he trains his stout wolf cubs
He rerolls all maps with care
And looks past borderlines and others' opinions
He uses the latest ideas to refute the old ones
In his military tent, when he sits musing
As upright as a border stake driven three feet deep in earth
Even time hesitates to disturb him
For the look in his eyes is sharper than an arrow
And whomever it strikes will shudder
and surrender

But Yelü Abaoji is forgiving—
A virtue only the strong
can afford to display—
Which is why he never puts aside his leather whip

Every day, the brutal sandstorm from the northland
Trims the golden nails of the setting sun
Undaunted by a solitude as ancient as the dawn of civilization
Yelü Abaoji leads his horse-loving tribesmen

Leaving deep hoofprints in the rapidly passing
Saga of Chinese history
Long familiar with looting and battles

"Greatness contains conflicts and failings
Which lesser minds cannot bear."
At the head of his marching troops
He exhorts his followers
Their colorful standards flutter, as he
Strides powerfully through their veins

1984
translated by Michelle Yeh and Frank Stewart

DESOLATE CANDY STORE (opening section)

Yes, no matter how old we are,
We are like children when it comes
To solving the mysteries of time.

Such as traveling back a hundred years
To the old, idealized part of the quiet city
Where as in a fairy tale a candy store stands
At the corner of a deserted, cobblestone lane
Which it makes glimmer with beauty
Looking like a small train station that has lost its way
And is waiting for a train that never arrives
Like an exquisite, mysterious music box
Forgotten in the back of an old closet
In which feelings no one has ever understood are locked
And sealed alongside melodies that were never written down

The little store has gilded, pastel-colored windowsills
Above them an awning of royal blue
Every window facing the street
Overflows with welcoming happiness
And a delicacy that insists on its gracefulness
If you peer in the window from the shadowy lane

You'll see an enchanting carnival is rehearsing:
Toffee, lollipops, fruit-flavored candies
Nougats, mints, chocolates, and a medley of gummies
Are neatly displayed, waiting to be sold
Oh, even many years afterward when the carnival is no more
We require such small splendors
Life, uneventful and fleeting as it is,
Still longs for joy's momentary cure

A weary traveler, I have come a long way
As if from the border of memory
To the home of my banished soul—
The familiar yet so strange scene
And the lonely fantasy of my childhood
Gaze at each other across the vast span of time
At this moment they gently take me into their arms
With a solitude and melancholy I cannot escape
But I quickly turn against to the candy store
A part of my unrealized dream
Transforming nectar into honey in a secluded beehive

Under the cover of the children's excitement
I start visiting this little store
I linger unseen in a corner
And browse the shelves
Of bottles and jars of every shape. I gaze into glass cabinets
At the sparkling sugar fairies that seem to be
Slumbering together as at a pajama party—
Put one after another of these gems in your mouth
And fireworks burst on your taste buds
Like the frozen Northern Lights
Wrapped in sheer, radiant gowns,
Dancing silhouettes in the gilded, dressed-up windows—
No one would ever want to leave

published in 2020
translated by Michelle Yeh and Frank Stewart

Wang Xiaoni (b. 1955)

Of Manchu descent, Wang was born and raised in Changchun, Jilin. She was relocated to the countryside during the Cultural Revolution. In 1978–82 she studied in the Chinese Department at Jilin University. After graduation, she edited film scripts at Changchun Film Studio, before moving to Shenzhen in 1985. From 2005 to 2012, she taught at Hainan University. While in college, Wang and six friends—including her future husband, the poet and literary critic Xu Jingya (b. 1949)—founded a poetry club called Child's Heart, and in 1980 she started publishing poetry. In addition to writing poetry, she is a prolific writer of fiction and nonfiction.

HALF OF ME HURTS

A pretty little insect
wants to eat through my teeth

The world's
right side is suddenly poignant.
The body was once
just a ramshackle house.

Half of me leaps with black fire.
Half of me is filled with the sound of medicine.

You put out your hands
one grabs me
the other grabs the opaque air.
Pain is also life.
We can never control it.

Sitting then standing
letting the breeze blow here and there.
Only when pain flickers up
do we realize the world is far from ordinary.
We aren't well
but
we still want to walk around.

I use the half that doesn't hurt
to love you.
My left hand pushes the door for you.
The world's right side
is bright and magnificent.
The long hair of pain
disperses into a forest.
That's also me,
that's another good woman.

1988
translated by Eleanor Goodman

PEOPLE WAITING FOR THE BUS

The early morning sun
illuminates the bus stop.
Some of the people are painted with its luster.

They're suddenly pleasant.
What a wonderful group of people.

Light
falls on
the people waiting for the bus.
Unmercifully
dividing them in two.
I assume

those in the back being outshone by the good must be bad.
The bus doesn't come for a very long time.
The radiant sun can't wait forever.
Good people and bad people revolve inch by inch.
The brightly lit bodies overheat and deteriorate.
The spot that was wretched and unlit
gleams and turns beautiful.

God
your light keeps moving
you poor old
blind man standing in the firmament.
The goodness that you see is also evil
and the evil is also goodness.

1993
translated by Eleanor Goodman

INSIDE WHITE PAPER

Inside white paper
the sunshine moves outside the house
inside the house is merely me
a tranquil idler.

Three meals a day
rule over the docile cabbage hearts
my hands
float in a semitranslucent porcelain basin.
When my breath reaches somewhere far away
the white-colored rice grains
will be cooked into white-colored rice.

The screen door is like an attendant standing tall in the wind
gazing at the flickering afternoon I've napped through.
My mailbox

holds only the fine down of bats.
The people in their homes
aren't waiting for anything.

Throughout the house
are dangerous winding conduits.
Bringing either water or electricity
they revolve around me intimately.
Casually flip a switch
and all around me
just the right amount
of water or fire flares up.

The sun and moon are both in the sky
these are days that leave no mark.
Behind the backs of the brown farmers
I bend low to thump an oval watermelon
whose back is slightly yellow
from the setting sun curving beyond me.

Meaningless,
just living.
Just casually turning on a dribble of water.
The fragrance of rice floats through the house
and only I try tasting
the precariousness in its scent.
Some knife
is cutting open the outer layer of the world.

Living breath by breath
my paper
forever holds my fire.

1995
translated by Eleanor Goodman

VERY WHITE MOONLIGHT

The moon in the deep night lights every sliver of bone.

I inhale blue-white air.
The world's trifles and smatterings
turn into sinking fireflies.
The city's a carcass.

No living thing
matches this pure nighttime color.
I open curtains at the window:
before my eyes, heaven and earth join in argentine white.
In moonlight, I forget I'm a human being.

The last scene of life
is quietly rehearsed in a shadow of plain color.
Moonlight reaches the floorboards:
my two feet have already whitened beforehand.

2016
translated by Arthur Sze

Yang Lian (b. 1955)

Born in Bern, Switzerland, Yang returned to Beijing with his family at the age
of six. In 1974 he was relocated to Changping, near Beijing. In 1979 he started
publishing poetry in *Today* and became a leading Obscure poet. During the Anti–
Spiritual Pollution campaign launched by the government, his poem sequence
"Norilang" was criticized for its sexual images. In 1988 he, along with Mang Ke,
Duo Duo, and Tang Xiaodu, founded the underground poetry journal *Survivors*
in Beijing. After the Tiananmen Massacre on June 4, 1989, he left China and since
then has lived in Australia, New Zealand, the United Kingdom, and Germany.
Currently, he divides his time between London and Berlin. He has won numerous

international awards, including the inaugural Sarah Maguire Prize for Poetry in Translation in 2020 for *Anniversary Snow*, with his translator, Brian Holton.

"The Cry of Cranes in Bassdorf" was inspired by the poet's stay in the summer retreat of his friend Cornelie von Bismarck, who is a direct descendant of the early-nineteenth-century composer Felix Mendelssohn. According to Yang, "The Mendelssohn family were Jewish and were ennobled following the success of the Mendelssohn Bank: the bank's badge is a crane, and Bassdorf is on the cranes' migration route. As guests there one summer, we were regularly woken in the early morning by the crying of the cranes, and we seemed, in the darkness, to have been set inside a painting of a flock of cranes by Song Dynasty Emperor Huizong (1082–1135). Cranes migrate endlessly, always coming home by the same route. Yet, for us, with painful memories of German Jewry, and with our own wandering from place to place, the meaning of 'home' is so complicated, and so serious."

MEMORIAL TO A TREE AT THE STREET CORNER

last night   my poem moved to the street corner
enacted a tree   waved
small white flowers that suddenly turned their faces like ghosts

screaming on tiptoe   permeated the air
ankle bones sparkled like crystals
the Tang dynasty like a lantern suddenly switched on

already it's been so many years   along a redbrick wall
I turned a corner it was the old country   at branch tip
familiar bloodshed finds again its stand-in

throws out tons of quicksilver colors
but I am no longer scared of shriveling   since a spring night
washed away   at the tree stump the lingering sound of an electric saw

2001

translated by Arthur Sze

ISLAND

2.

You're right   in life's chamber music
either listen with total attention   or else switch off
Water   one drop can perfectly lock up these shores

The crash of waves has no gap   is like a tailored body
still sitting on the rock   the lilac-scented surrounding ocean
still striking at a little girl's unceasing gaze into distance

Purple or white   petals are stored in the eyes
all through the springtime night, dark rings around the eyes
keep opening   torn by where she looks far away

Suffering is that waiting, underwater pearl
what turns old is salt   low sobbing in every wave
The fierce wind is a jade bracelet on the wrist

Island   like a boat sailing since the day you were born
never slowing down its disconsolate speed
always arriving yet, underfoot, drawn away by the ebbing tide

Purple   wounds the turbulent, close-up scene
sets off white   the horizon like land cutting, above snow line, into fate
exposing the snow flower you've caught for life

Still wet   tears run halfway down the girl's cheeks
After so many years   play the cold rain you've brought back
A seagull plunges   then flies back up   You hear clearly this kiss

2003
translated by Arthur Sze

BABY GIRL

—to a deliberately drowned baby girl

you're so small you're not worth the chill   water choking
pocket-sized lungs   pocket-sized explosions fresh and tender
you're so small you're not worth breaking   in an eyeblink
bloody streaks diffuse into red flowers   each one welcoming mother

splashed hands   still the loveliest
hands in the world   each droplet a toothmark
when you're half-sunk   your snowdrift collapses
pressed under water   a sea so small it doesn't shudder

tied to the womb   your eyes
closed to witness your final moment   your fate
is a chain of bubbles of denial   the wailing bulge of your sex
all of your organs stamped prohibited

you have to die   for the possibility of a younger brother
die right away   water quicker than love   nip off this cycle
small eddy stirred by smaller limbs
and silenced   mother dissolves into a toxic epithet

2008
translated by Brian Holton

THE CRY OF CRANES IN BASSDORF

For Cornelie von Bismarck

life has one string
darkness has one string
twisting a tiny throat   go back home

lake water is vacant land
put into hearing so early   a tongue tip
opens the red pine woods   a Song Dynasty fan

cranes waking   notes bivouacked in the score waken
light-years carve with care a
sopping wet dredged-up feather

there are wingtips   the journey begins dangling in the air again
there are eye pupils   the skyline is still a wound
inviting you to fall endlessly into the impulse

cries toward home in voice after voice
home   records the waiting immensity
how often quieted   to be shattered so often

crane necks curve down   dive into   the dull pain of waterweed
upstairs bedroom window covered by dense foliage
ears expect bass green   fate green

elegy is coming back   elegy never goes away
until the shyest bodies
move into and fill our growth rings

2015
translated by Brian Holton

Zhai Yongming (b. 1955)

Born in Chengdu, Sichuan, Zhai volunteered to be sent down to the countryside
in 1970 during the Cultural Revolution. After returning to her hometown, she
entered the University of Electronic Engineering and Technology of China in
1976 and graduated four years later. She started publishing poetry in 1981, and her
sequence titled "Woman" appeared in 1984, sparking a widespread discussion of
female consciousness and women's poetry in China. Zhai lived in the United States

in 1990–91 and, since 1998, has run a saloon, called White Night, in Chengdu, where writers and artists gather.

THE SUBMARINE'S LAMENT

starting work at 9:00 a.m.
I ready my coffee my pen
poking my head outside to check on the latest
typhoon warning
whether I need it or not
my submarine is always ready its lead gray body
hiding beneath the windless surface of a shallow pool

at first I wanted to write this:
currently the war hasn't touched us
currently curses   are taking a different tack
rom my listening post   I hear
the gentle rush of silvery fragments

crimson shellfish   still catch my fancy
in the tumult of world   events it flushes a deeper red
and we eat it   the hand grasping the data shuttles back and forth
when I start writing   I see
cute little fish   encircling the shipyard

state enterprises are going under   what's more
here's economic panic next door   and those girls with stylish painted faces
these volatile receipts   encircle
our shallow pool

so this is what I write:
let me see
where should I launch   my submarine this time
in whose veins will it weigh anchor
the starstruck, the hipsters, metalheads in discos
analyzing the periscope of writing

alcohol, nourishment, high in calories
as if prepositions, pronouns, exclamations
were sealing up portions of my skin
submarine   it will plunge to the bottom of the sea
urgently   but it's diving for nothing
no longer subject to orders

I've written this before, and I'll write it again:
it doesn't add up
you're still building your submarine
that memorial to war
that tomb of the war dead   lying dormant at the bottom of the sea
 but it grows ever more distant over time
in its self-imposed isolation

you can see for yourself:
that now   I've built my submarine
and yet   where is the water
it's lapping over the world
and now   I must create water and fashion an elusive wholeness
for the lament that lies in everything

2000
translated by Andrea Lingenfelter

NEW SWAN LAKE

Onstage, another ladder is erected
men bearing milk pails advance in a line
This is a battle scene they know

On the other side, the swans have built their nests
their limbs hang limply
This is a tender scene they love

Men like to conceal guns everywhere
from under their arms to farther down   they loiter all over the world
Men also like to wear all sorts of bulletproof vests
from their pecs to their groins
crushing their dreams flat

The young men are about to take flight
their eight-pack abs   are highly suggestive
of eight lips
Their black scalps and
pima cotton shorts are stunning

The young men wear only feathers
only ride on the back of the moon
only give their bodies to
another dude with wings

Those men with their eight-pack abs
skin smelling of sweat   cigarettes and funk
Heaven knows   why they
were made ready but not for us

May 19, 2001
translated by Andrea Lingenfelter

REPORT ON A CHILD PROSTITUTE

Some people call a child prostitute pretty baby
She wears lacy embroidered lingerie
Her thighs already inviting
Her mother is even prettier
They look like sisters   "But she is the gazelle . . ."
Men love a pretty baby
And she loves gazing at herself in the mirror

But the child I saw wasn't like that
She's twelve years old   thin and dressed in rags
Her eyes take in the entire world
And perhaps   there's no room for even a single tear

Her father is a peasant   he's young
But his hair is already gray
He's spent three months already
Searching everywhere for his
Lost baby

Three months for a child prostitute
That's nearly one hundred days
Over three hundred men
Not an easy number for a child
She's never understood why
So many old, ugly, filthy men
Want to press themselves to her belly
She doesn't understand what it's all about
She only knows her body
Is becoming light and empty   that something's been taken from it

Some people think child prostitutes are pretty but dumb
But she wouldn't know about that
She spends her nights counting
She counts over three hundred
Nameless figures   residence unknown
Collectively they're consumers
Their numbers like ancient symbols in a graveyard
Vanishing   before dawn

Reading the paper I keep thinking:
You can't write a poem about this
You can't turn poetry into something like this
You can't chew up a poem
Or hammer words into teeth   to eat away
These diseases   these incisions
These large sums added to her twelve years

Poem, bandage, photo, memory
They scratch at my eyes
(Here in the retinal zone where dark and light meet)
Everything becomes clear: it's useless
No one cares about this damage
It's just a daily quotient   of data
Creating a life of misery for someone else

In part she's just a picture in the paper
Twelve years old   standing in a group of girls
You can't see   she's missing an ovary
You could say   it's just a story in the news
Every day   our eyes take in thousands of pieces of information
That control our pleasure as consumers
That stream past us   just like this item
Masses of information   hotlines   global perspectives
Like a huge rough rag   wiping away one person's feeble suffering

People like us   take a glance and that's all
Crumple up the paper   stuff it in a metal bin

April 21, 2002
translated by Andrea Lingenfelter

Bai Hua (b. 1956)

Born and raised in Chongqing, Sichuan, Bai Hua graduated from the English Department of Guangdong University of Foreign Studies in 1982 and attended graduate school in the Chinese Department at Sichuan University in 1986–87. After teaching English in Chongqing and Nanjing, he relocated to Chengdu in 1992. Since 2004 he has been teaching at Southwest Jiaotong University. Bai started writing poetry in 1979 and cofounded the underground journal *Make It New*. In addition to poetry, he has published prose, literary criticism, and translations.

"Last Emperor Li" refers to Li Yu (937–78) of the Southern Tang dynasty. In the same poem, cutting wine refers to a Daoist from the third century named Zuo Ci, who parted wine in the cup to share with the hegemon Cao Cao and then threw the cup up to the rafter, where it floated like a bird. The poem "Reality" refers to Lin Yutang, a twentieth-century writer and translator who introduced Chinese literature and philosophy to the West. He published dozens of works in English, including such bestsellers as *My Country and My People* (1935) and *The Importance of Living* (1937). From 1935 to the end of his life, he lived mostly in the United States. Lu Xun was friends with Lin but criticized his writing as bourgeois and ineffectual. For the poet to call them identical is to question Lu's socialist mission.

EXPRESSION

I want to express a kind of mood
a kind of white mood
this mood can't speak
and you can't sense its existence
but it exists
it came from another star
specifically for this night
it has come to this strange world

It is mournfully, beautifully
dragging a long long shadow
but can't find any other shadow to talk to

If you say it is like a stone
icy and silent
I'll tell you it is a flower
its fragrance slinks through the night sky
not until the moment of your death
does it enter the field of your awareness

Music can't bring out this mood
dance cannot reveal its forms
you can't know the length of its hair
or why it must be combed into this style
You love her, she doesn't love you
your love started at nightfall last spring
why wasn't it this year's winter dawn?

I want to express a mood of cellular locomotion
I want to consider why they revolt against themselves
produce in themselves ineffable passion and rage

I know this mood is quite difficult to express
for example the night, why has it come at this hour?
She and I, why do we love each other at this hour?
Why are you dying at this hour?

I know the spilling of blood is silent
although tragic
it can't dissolve this iron-wrapped land

Flowing waters send out a sound
splintering trees send out a sound
snakes throttling toads send out a sound
what do these sounds portend?
Do they prepare the transmission of a mood?
Or do they express a self-contained philosophy?

Or those sobs
those sobs you can't describe
the ones Chinese children cried under the walls of the old city
the tears Christ's faithful children cried in Jerusalem
thousands upon thousands died in Hiroshima
and the Japanese once cried
the victims, the weaklings, they cried too
but all of this is so hard to understand

A kind of white mood
a kind of inexpressible mood
on this night
has come into this world
outside our vision
inside our spinal nerve
quietly shrouding the whole cosmos
it can't die, it also can't leave us
in our hearts it is persisting, persisting . . .
can't settle down, can't perceive
because we don't want to die

October 1981
translated by Nick Admussen

SUMMER IS STILL FAR AWAY

—to Father

A day passes, another
Something sneaks up to you in the dark
Sit a while, walk a little
See the leaves fall
the rain drizzle
See that man walking past, in the street
Summer is still far away

So swiftly, vanished as soon as born
all the kindness an October evening can hold
Beyond beautiful, imperceptible
A vast calmness like your clean cotton shoes
Beside your bed, the past lingers, tenderly
like an old wooden box
a faded bookmark
Summer is still far away

Chance encounter, vague reminiscence
A hint of chill outside
The tired left hand reaches
in secret, farther left
to somewhere deep and far off
to a single-minded longing
Summer is still far away

No more—the quick temper, and quicker passion
Gather up these bad habits of old
Feel disappointment year after year
The bamboo hut, the white shirt—
were you not at the prime of your life?
Time to finally make up your mind
Summer is still far away

winter 1984
translated by Luo Hui

LAST EMPEROR LI

The distant man, so fair, so bright
in the slender autumn of the year 997
full of voice and wine
sleepless all night, guilty
loyal tears drifting across the lake's surface

The small boat in his dreams like an old tune
longed for his profligate years
the smoke of debt
the wounds of lost love
the fall of an empire

Oh, last emperor
arbor's shade and rain's mist, sunset on the palace roof
the banisters you stroked
now a detail in a poem or a pearl
you cut wine with a knife, cut your sleeve
with the lamp you lit in your little window
you breathed aflame the wind in the bamboo forest,
the scholar's ambition, and your breath ignited
a free-spirited, dissolute witch

1986
translated by Nick Admussen

IN THE QING DYNASTY

In the Qing dynasty
carefreeness and idealism became more and more profound
cows and sheep had nothing to do, people played chess
the imperial examination was impartial
every place had its own currency
grain could be used to barter
for tea leaves, silk, porcelain

In the Qing dynasty
landscape painting had attained near perfection
paper was abundant, kites flew everywhere
lanterns grasped the essentials
temple after temple faced south
the wealth was seemingly excessive

In the Qing dynasty
poets didn't work for a living, concerned with reputation
drinking under falling petals, in warm sunny weather
the lakes brimmed with water
two ducks swam against the wind
everything was at odds

In the Qing dynasty
one person dreamed of another
read the Grand Historian at night, swept at dawn
the court created a Military Office
each year selecting officials with long fingernails

In the Qing dynasty
men with beards and men without beards
taught by example instead of with words
farmers didn't want to learn to read
the young respected the old
mothers submitted to their sons

In the Qing dynasty
taxes inspired the people
and built irrigation works, schools, temples
books were printed, gazetteers collected
architecture designed with an antique flavor

In the Qing dynasty
philosophy fell like rain, science couldn't adapt
one man changed his mind night and day
always unreasonably anxious
resentment became his lifelong vocation
until his death in 1842.

1986
translated by Eleanor Goodman and Wang Ao

REALITY

This is mildness, not the mildness of rhetoric
this is boredom, boredom itself

ah, the future, reading, turning around
it is all slow

in the long night, we do not reap out of necessity
in the long night, speed should be discarded

and winter perhaps is just like spring
and Lu Xun perhaps is just like Lin Yutang

December 11, 1990
translated by Nick Admussen

Gu Cheng (1956–1993)

Gu was born in Beijing, though his father, Gu Gong, a writer serving in the military, hailed from Shanghai. In 1969 his family relocated to the countryside in Shandong during the Cultural Revolution. Gu started writing poetry at the age of eight, and his earliest extant poems are dated 1968. In 1974 he returned to Beijing and worked as a carpenter and painter. He contributed poems to the underground journal *Today* and became famous as a leading Obscure poet in the early 1980s. In 1983 he married Xie Ye (1958–93) and had a son five years later. The family moved to Waiheke Island in Auckland, New Zealand, while Gu continued to give readings around the world. Brewing marital crisis led to tragedy on the night of October 8, 1993, when Gu killed his wife and then himself.

ONE GENERATION

Even with these dark eyes, a gift of the dark night,
I go seeking that shining light.

April 1979
translated by Joseph R. Allen

ACCESSORY TO THE CRIME

You are forever looking at the world outside
Your feet are seeking slippers
You are married
There is a small patch of wheat
And in your dreams you are a thief

You are once again looking at the steps outside

July 1984
translated by Joseph R. Allen

FICTION

X
The earth is a drop of blue water
Within it breathes a faint flame

XX
All you can do is to urge
The fish to sun itself on the beach
And birds to sleep in the air

XL
We were the ones to raise high the stars
And decide to gaze at them from below
Though we wanted to live high above them

L
How could you have thought I was human?

.

LXX
My dear
The earth has fallen again
At the time when life comes
You will keep her safe

October 1990
translated by Joseph R. Allen

GHOSTS ENTER THE CITY (2 of 8)

The ghosts
Of midnight
Walk carefully along
Afraid to fall on their heads
And change
Into men

Monday

Ghosts are fine folk
They sleep   then awake
They scan bulletin   go for a swim
Standing tall beside the river
Swimming out a stream of gold from the earth
Flip fish   flip head over heels   blow on weeping bottles of wine
They like to watch things up above
And to catch, all at once, the golden
            Leaves

Ghosts too can sometimes read:
"Indeed, they're well acquainted"
Then place their hands underneath the document
"This old rose beside the river"
They say in unison exhaling a cloud of smoky mist
At dusk people say
"It's time to go home"

Along the road the streetlights cast their shadows
The ghosts don't speak   the wind blows through the streets
Writing at the station   grazing   faces turning gray
A gust of wind turns over the mist

Sunday

"The dead are the beautiful people"   after saying so, the ghost
Looked into the mirror   and he was actually only seven inches tall
He was pressed down by a pile of glass   the glass

Brushed clean

"The dead are all pretty"   like
    Glass without shadows
           White projection screen   lit by lights
           Passing through the slides   layer upon layer
The dead are at the emergency door
A huge pile of glass cards

He stuck his finger in one nostril
The light shone   he stuck it in the other
Shadows cast by the light, the city disappears from sight
• She still cannot see •
You can hear the sound of bricks falling to the ground
The ghost is very clear
The dead make the air tremble

There are stars far away   and farther still
There are stars still   only after a long time
Did he know there was a transparent poplar tree above the chimney?

October 1992
translated by Joseph R. Allen

Ouyang Jianghe (b. 1956)

Born in Luzhou, Sichuan, Ouyang Jianghe is the pen name of Jiang He. Upon graduating from high school, in 1975, Ouyang relocated to a rural village and then served in the military. He started publishing poetry in 1979; in 1983–14 he became well known for the long poem *Hanging Coffin*, which started a trend of writing "contemporary epics." In 1986 he worked at the provincial Chinese Academy of Social Sciences, and in 1993–97 he lived in the United States. After spending six months in Stuttgart, Germany, in March–September 1997, he returned to Beijing. Since 2015 he has taught at Beijing Normal University. In addition to poetry, Ouyang writes widely on literature, music, film, theater, and art.

GLASS FACTORY (1 of 5)

5.

In one factory I see three kinds of glass.
Substance, ornament, symbol.
They tell me glass is the child of muddled stone.
In the void that is stone, death is not ending
but original, mutable fact.
Stone crumbles, glass is born.
This is real.
But there is another reality that lifts me from this height
to another height, where glass is nothing
but water, a fluid made boned and unflowable,
where flame is a bone-chilling cold,
where for a thing to be beautiful it must also be fragile.
All lofty things of this earth
and their tears.

September 6, 1987
translated by Austin Woerner

STRAWBERRY

If a strawberry is ablaze, she will be the white snow's little sister.
She touches your lips, but she loves someone else.
No one can tell me if anything ever existed before a strawberry was given.
In this long life, my every step begins with a strawberry.
A group of children gallop in bright-red thoughts against the wind.
When they are tired, they glance back without thinking
—it is such a beautiful yet bewildering moment!

I was young then, stuffing my mouth with strawberries.
The green field I have long forgotten,
Teardrops about to fall yet never quite falling,
Once, a little boy clinging to his parents cried bitterly under the sky.
I turn and walk into the dark clouds so he can't see me.
The loneliness of two is only half of loneliness.
Can first love be communicated by a strawberry?

Childhood's dizziness has lingered to this day.
Lovers glow violet as moonlight fills their bosoms.
This is not an age of lyricism,
A strawberry is merely the speed from the bite to the body.
Nothing is closer to dying than tasting a strawberry.
Oh, this generation of premature aging, old dreams that never return,
Who will hear my elegy of endless self-pity?

November 6, 1988
translated by Michelle Yeh and Frank Stewart

CROSSING THE SQUARE AT DUSK

Where does the square of a bygone era
begin? Where does it end?
Some cross in an hour, others spend
a life in the crossing:
children in the morning, at evening old men.
How long must they walk on into the sunset
before they can rest?

And how long must they gaze on into the sunset
before they can close their eyes?
When speeding cars turn on their blinding lights.
I see faces: those who once,
on a bright and beautiful morning, crossed the square—
in rearview mirrors, they flash
and disappear.
At dusk, they get in their cars and leave.

A place no one leaves is not a square.
A place where no one falls is not one either.
Those who have left will come again,
those who have fallen will stay forever.
There is a thing called stone: it piles swiftly, stands—
it is nothing like bone, does not take a century to grow
and is not so weak.

Every square has a mind of piled stone,
making the empty-handed people above
feel the weight of survival.
No lighthearted thing, to gaze up and hope with a giant's mind of stone.
The weight of stone
lightens our burden of sacrifice, duty, love.

Cold and darkness rise.
Office buildings loom on all sides, dressed in the latest styles of tile and glass.
All is made miniature. The world of stone
floats lightly, reflected in the world of glass,
like a scribble in a child's assignment book,
a small dark thought
to be crumpled and thrown away.

Cars hurtle past, fluid speed
pouring through a vast system of steel-tendoned concrete,
silence assuming the shape of a horn.
In rearview mirrors, a square of a bygone era
flashes and is gone.

Gone, forever—
an acne-covered, adolescent square, square of first loves,
a square never figured into ledgers and death counts,
a square of squared shoulders, tightened belts, rolled-up sleeves,
of washboards and hand-me-downs, stitches and patches—

a square that saw youthful blood flow outside of its veins—
a square licked and pounded, knocked by knees and foreheads, covered
    in flags—

an imagined square, a square that ceased to exist
as a night's snowfall ceases at morning.
A pure and mysterious melting
glistening by turns in consciences and eyes:
one part becoming a thing called tears,
the other hardening into a thing called stone.

The world of stone has crumbled.
Now a cellophane world is rising
like water leaving mineral, creeping up the tube
into a distilled, sealed, charmingly packaged space.
I am riding a high-speed elevator up the handle of an umbrella.

Back on earth, I gaze up at the rooftop restaurant
like an umbrella turning in the sky above the city.
A sorcerer's hat, its dimensions unfit
for a giant's head of piled stone.

The arms that held up the square have let it down.
A giant props himself up with a little sword.
What will he stab? A frail revolution
once incited on paper, plastered on walls?

There is no power
that can keep two worlds pasted together for long.
A paper mind will soon be ripped down.
The gargantuan thigh of a mixed-blood model
bestrides a whitewashed wall
alongside ads for hair restoration, ads for artificial limbs.

A baby carriage stands in the twilit square,
nothing to do with a world nearing madness.
I imagine a distance of about a century
separates this child from the sunset.
A century: ruler of almost infinite length, long enough to measure
the span of solitude, the length of a shuttered era.

Fear of solitude
brings the people out of their homes, brings them pouring into the square,
turns life's loneliest hour into a raucous holiday—
but in their darkened homes, where the gazes of love and death meet,
lies a vast empty square, heart's hoard, shadow square
like a shuttered confessional, thing of secrets within.

Before we cross the square, must we first cross the darkness within?
The two halves of darkness have come together.
A mind of hard stone has been cleft in two.
The blade of a sword glitters in the night.

If a strange cleft night can account
for two feet on the ground, for one bright and beautiful morning—
if I am allowed to mount sun-strewn steps
and survey the giddy void from a giant's shoulder
not that I may rise but that I may fall—
if words engraved on gold plaques are not meant to be sung
but to be rubbed out, to be forgotten, to be trampled—

as a trampled square must one day fall upon the heads of the tramplers,
the footsteps of those who once, on a bright and beautiful morning,
crossed the square
will fall upon the blade of a sword,
fall heavy, fall as a coffin's lid must fall.
Who lies within? Not me, and not
those who walk on the blade's edge.

I had not thought that on bright and beautiful mornings, so many
had crossed the square, sundering solitude
and eternity. I had not thought
that at dusk they would leave
or fall.

September 18, 1990
translated by Austin Woerner

Zhang Shuguang (b. 1956)

Born in Wangkui County, Heilongjiang, Zhang graduated from the University
of Heilongjiang in 1982 and has worked as an editor for journals and publishing
houses. Since 2004 he has been teaching in the Chinese Department at his alma
mater. Zhang started publishing poetry in 1980. In addition to poetry, prose, and
literary criticism, he has published Chinese translations of Dante's *Divine Comedy*
and the poetry of Czesław Miłosz, among others.

HUMAN WORK

Taking a whole morning to split wood.
Stockpiling vegetables for winter.
Sealing the windows well
so not a breath of storm comes in.
The trees by the window have shed all their pretty leaves
I don't know if that grieves it.
Humans must do the work of marmots
and learn how to wait a long time.

1985
translated by Eleanor Goodman

ULYSSES

It's a question of metaphor. When an old wooden boat
pieces together the scenery and all its meaning, waves of starlings
sweep over the cold mast, and the sound of the breakers
gurgles like a flushing toilet, and it shrinks a whole morning

down to a piece of paper. Sometimes, it seems like a word
appears from a far distant shoreline, gradually approaching us
and turning dusk's face unfamiliar and indistinct,
you cannot estimate them, sometimes they are wrung dry by time

or merged into history as a whole. But all of our questions rest in
whether or not we can turn that page again
or from a withered rose petal
gather a sweet fragrance anew and bring back happy times

I imagine Homer in his old age or James Joyce
searching for a giant's castle between islands of words and torrents,
do they hear the sirens' song? At midnight we walked
the dark dirty streets, from the gaps in leaves

and mollusks, a pop song, lighting up
our dim lives, like candles on a birthday cake
our fear comes from within ourselves, and in the end we go from a lover to a
    wife's
coldness and chasteness, carrying a history smelling of virtue

1990
translated by Eleanor Goodman

PHOTOGRAPHS OF DYING TIME

One by one I see you, friends from my youth
still lively, optimistic, cracking tasteless jokes
it's as though time hasn't cast its spells upon your bodies
or perhaps you've somehow found a prescription for eternal youth
but the forest and sky behind you maintain the same
shapes, without a single alteration, as though bravely holding out against time
and all that time brings. Oh, young knights, we
had our brilliant age, drinking, chasing women, staying up all night
discussing a poem or novel. We acted out *Hamlet*
now imagining crossing the wasteland, seeking out the long lost Holy Grail
looking for Eliot's lonely shadow by the campus flowerbeds at dusk
back then I didn't like Yeats and didn't understand Lowell or Ashbery
of course I didn't know you then, but each day on the way to class or the
    cafeteria
I'd catch sight of you hurrying by, your expression solemn or dejected
I once went mad because of an unreal portrait, acclaimed
the spring, but was thrown into a deeper snowdrift, until my heart was
    exhausted
some of those old squirrels are dead, others have lost their teeth
and occasionally let out a furious cry, to prove they still exist
we've reconciled with our fathers or become fathers ourselves
or sunken into one of life's deeper traps. And all that beautiful time
we yearn for, which once existed but now has passed? Or
was it only a mirage or something we imagined in the midst of our pain?

Perhaps we are only witnesses to time, like these old photographs
yellowing, becoming brittle, but still holding certain things that
people once called history but were not real

1993
translated by Eleanor Goodman

Liu Kexiang (Ka-hsiang Liu, b. 1957)

Born in Taizhong County in Central Taiwan, Liu Kexiang, the pen name of Liu
Zikui, received his BA degree in journalism from the Chinese Culture University
and for many years worked as an editor for the *China Times*. Since July 2017 he
has served as the director of the Central News Agency in Taiwan. Liu started
writing poetry in the 1970s. In the early 1980s, he became widely recognized for
his "political poetry"—poetry that critiqued the ruling Nationalists and dealt
with political taboos, such as the February 28 Incident and the White Terror. At
the same time, Liu also wrote about native birds and won himself the nickname
"Bird Man." He went on to become a prolific and important nature writer who
has published poetry, nonfiction, fiction, picture books, and photography.

   In "Young Revolutionary" the background is the April 6 Incident of 1949, in
which some students at the Taiwan Provincial Normal College (today's National
Taiwan Normal University) were arrested following a protest against police brutal-
ity in a minor traffic accident. *Marcuse* refers to Herbert Marcuse, the twentieth-
century German American philosopher of the Frankfurt School of critical theory,
who critiqued capitalism, communism, and mass culture in the modern industrial
world. Xing Tianzheng, in "What Is Indescribable about Mount Indescribable" was
a native of Hebei who moved to Taiwan in 1949. He started mountain climbing
when he was forty-seven years old and became a pioneering mountaineer. Atayal
is an indigenous tribe.

YOUNG REVOLUTIONARY

That day, none of the students from our village
who attended the city's Teacher's College returned
except for my panic-stricken father
If what people say is true, he was the only survivor
For years afterward, he was depressed and joyless
Later, he married my mother, and I—his naive son—was born
When I got older, Grandma said I looked just like him

At the end of the 1970s, I attended the university
Perhaps because it was destined by historical determinism
By then, I might have been reading Marcuse, and I probably knew
something about socialist theory. It was a period of political upheaval
and with my fellow students, I circulated underground journals
and dissident flyers. The authorities gave me many warnings
I gave up the dream of studying abroad. Seeing what's going on
around me, I felt I had no right to leave. Father found it hard to understand
and we got into heated arguments

At the end of the 1980s, everything changed—or ended
I got married. She . . . I can't describe her
As for me, I got a job at a transnational corporation,
bought my own apartment, and now we have a son
I've already saved tens of thousands dollars
so someday I can send my son to study abroad

1983
translated by Michelle Yeh and Frank Stewart

HOPE

Someday there will be a spring
When our children and grandchildren may read
A front-page story like this:

The small water ducks are returning north from their winter migration
Cars passing by the Tamsui River
Are forbidden to honk their horns

1984
translated by Andrea Lingenfelter

TROPICAL RAINFOREST

Took a tour to a small island between the equator and the Tropic of Cancer. Wet, humid green, ceaselessly fattening in the air. For five days running, we pass through the rainforest. There is no snow or prairie nor hibernation, even in dreams. An ornithologist in our group is here to look for a horned osprey particular to this place, a species on the brink of extinction. Every evening as dusk descends, we call out in imitation of this bird, but all we hear is our own weak voices, sent out unanswered. The aboriginal guide says: without sound, the forest will disappear. And I am once again too upset to sleep; awake for the entire night, I press my cheek to the Earth, spreading out my arms into a curve and holding it tight.

1986
translated by Andrea Lingenfelter

WHAT IS INDESCRIBABLE ABOUT MOUNT INDESCRIBABLE

Perhaps it would be more precise to start with the leaf tip of a cold Japanese
    cedar
That's the moment of contact with the dry edge of a long-maned mountain
    goat's nose
That's an azalea's petals finally dropping
That's an almost intolerably quiet winter dawn
That's a Mikado pheasant cock stretching its neck to feel the warmth of
    sunbeams
That's the day when the louse reunion again fills the lean-to

I stand on a mountain that maps don't name
Shoulder to shoulder with the gaunt clouds, with the Han Chinese Xing
    Tianzheng
Looking upon winter's most remote likeness
The vast world of a single Japanese cedar on the horizon
An old Atayal man blows on a mouth harp

My pocket journal has again grown light
The pent-up feelings in my left ventricle have once more grown heavy like
    stones
All my desires turn into ice

1992
translated by Nick Kaldis

Wang Jiaxin (b. 1957)

Born in Danjiangkou, Hubei, Wang entered the Chinese Department of Wuhan
University in 1978, where he began writing poetry. After two years in the United
Kingdom as a visiting scholar 1992–94, he became an associate professor at the
Beijing Institute of Education. From 2006 to 2020 he served as professor of
creative writing and literature at Renmin University. In addition to his many
volumes of poetry and literary criticism, Wang is a prolific translator, rendering
collections of the work of Paul Celan, Osip Mandelstam, and Marina Tsvetaeva.

Wang's poetry has appeared in multiple languages, such as German, Dutch,
Croatian, and English. *Darkening Mirror: New and Selected Poems*, edited and
translated by George O'Connell and Diana Shi, with a foreword by Robert Hass,
was a finalist for the American Literary Translation Association's Lucien Stryk
Prize.

The subject of the first poem, Boris Pasternak, was a Russian poet, novelist, and
literary translator. Best known for the novel *Doctor Zhivago* (1957), he received the
Nobel Prize in Literature in 1958. The second poem depicts the Mexican poet and
diplomat Octavio Paz late in his life. Paz won the Nobel Prize in Literature in 1990.

PASTERNAK

I can't leave a bouquet of flowers at your grave
But I am destined to pour my life into reading your poetry
With the passage through thousands of miles of driven snow
A shattered holiday, and the trembling of my soul

I'm finally able to write as I want
But I'm unable to live my own life as I would
This is our common tragedy
Your lips grow more reticent, that's

The secret of fate, you cannot tell of it
You can only bear it, the scars deepening under your pen
For the sake of obtaining, you give up
For life, you demand your own death, to die completely

That is you, from one catastrophe to the next, you find me
You test me, making pain shoot abruptly through my life
From snow to snow, on a bus in Beijing rumbling through the mud
I read your poems, silently in my mind

I shout the lofty names of those who were
Banished, sacrificed, and who bore witness, those
Souls who join together in a trembling mass
Those shining in death, and my own

My own land! The shining tears in the northern livestock
The maple leaves burning in the wind
The darkness and hunger in the people's bellies, how
Can I ignore this just to talk about myself

Like you, I must bear fiercer blizzards
Before I can defend your Russia, your
Larissa, that beautiful, unbelievable miracle
That can no longer harm you

Cover yourself with snowy coldness, there before our eyes!
And Levitan's candlelit autumn
The death, praise, and sin in Pushkin's rhymes
Spring arrives, the vast land's blackness exposed

Open the soul toward all of this, poet
This is happiness, the highest law rising from the heart
Not suffering, it is ultimately what you bear
Ever unstoppable, coming in search of us

Seeking us, it demands symmetry
Or a requiem more vibrant than an echo
And us, how do we deserve to walk to your grave?
This is shame, this is December, winter in Beijing

This is the sadness in your eyes, seeking and questioning
Like a bell tolling, oppressing my soul
This is pain, this is happiness, to speak out about it
I need ice and snow to fill my life.

December 1990
translated by John Balcom

PAZ IN OLD AGE

Last year, stunned, he watched
As a fire at dusk
Burned down his home in Mexico City
Consuming all his treasures collected over a lifetime
Years of manuscripts and unfinished poems
That ancient Mexican mask
And a painting by Picasso
The family furniture handed down over generations and
All the photos and letters from childhood onward
That pleasure dome, the rafters like

A ribcage, every last thing
Reduced to ashes
In a towering inferno

That fire still burns
Burns in the dark
Scorching the wings of the birds rising from his poems
Consuming a man's previous existence
Consuming the burdens of the years
And also consuming the emptiness and the ashes themselves
The vanities and desires of life
And the unfulfilled ambitions
Crackled in the fire of old age
The firemen
Shouted in the choking darkness
Like shadows running here and there

Now he is free
As if freed from long torture
Once again he sits on a Paris street
Fallen leaves silently curled at his feet
His forehead illumined by a more distant shaft of light

2004
translated by John Balcom

ORANGES

That whole winter, he ate oranges,
Sometimes at the dinner table, sometimes on the bus,
Sometimes while he ate
Snow fell from inside, inside the bookcase;
Sometimes he didn't eat, just slowly peeled them,
As if something lived inside.

That's the way he ate oranges all winter,
While eating, he thought of the heroine in some
Novel, who carried a plate of oranges,
One of which kept rolling to the end of the story . . .
But he couldn't remember who wrote it.
He just ate oranges in silence.
The orange peels on his windowsill piled up.

He finally remembered the oranges
Placed by his hospital bed when he was a little boy,
He had no idea where his mom got them:
His little brother wanted to eat one, but his mom said no,
It was he who shared them with his brother;
But neither one of them could bear to eat the last one,
So there it remained on the nightstand.

(But what finally happened to that last orange?)

He ate oranges that way all winter long,
Especially on snowy days, or in gray weather:
He ate very slowly, as if
All he had was time,
As if he were swallowing darkness;
And so he peeled and ate oranges, looking up
The snowy radiance shined though his window.

February 2006
translated by John Balcom

Sun Weimin (b. 1959)

Born in Jiayi, in southern Taiwan, Sun received his BA degree in Western languages from the National Chengchi University, MA degree in English from Fu Jen Catholic University, and doctorate in English literature from the National Cheng Kung University. He taught for years before retiring from Far East University of Science and Technology in Tainan. Sun started writing poetry at the age of fifteen and is also a prose writer and literary critic who has published a book-length study of T. S. Eliot's *Four Quartets.*

In "Peacetime" the street in Taipei is named after Dr. Sun Yat-sen, who led the revolution that overthrew the Qing dynasty and founded the Republic of China in 1912.

THREE POTTED PLANTS AND THEIR MASTER

I.

A creature on the lower rung of the hierarchy:
He's rootless. He shits. He consumes lots of air and food.
Good at faking. Dioecious.
His mind is inclined to darkness and solitude.

Each night, I perch on the windowsill
and hear his snores and somniloquies.
I watch the broadcast of his rainbow-colored dreams
repeatedly—I also see Death

passing by the window several times,
prying.

II.

I am aging quickly.

Unable to resist the hypnotizing gravity,
the flower petals on branch tips finally sink
into a deep slumber.
The fogged world rotates at high speed,
silently decoupling from the colorful dreams . . .

He is aging quickly.

Drizzle gently decorates the deciduous tree
he often gazes at from the window.
Farther away, a flock of wild geese
fly according to some secret plan.
He stubs out a cigarette, paces back and forth in the room,
coughs.

Then he makes two phone calls: a literary supplement and his publisher—
"Recently I've not been writing much," he says, "but
I have sensed the urgency of writing."
His glasses reflect the simple interior of the house.
His eyes show fatigue:
"I must write something truly good, and fast . . ."

He hangs up the phone. One hour later
he leaves his study, still pondering over the syntax of a sentence.
He brings me outside to have some raindrops,
and with a silence that afflicts him,
he picks up a fallen flower from the living room floor.

III.

I listen. Sometimes I open my eyes.

The man who waters me daily has changed the pace
of his breath and footsteps, apparently.
Today he is sluggish, turbid, heavier than yesterday.
His lineaments are more obscure.
Today he is further removed from his species.

I am naked. Sometimes I breathe deep.

The man who deworms me daily has a body temperature
apparently different. The skin too.
Today he is colder and coarser than yesterday.
The smell of his decay gets stronger.
Today he's becoming more like me.

published October 28, 1992

translated by Wen-chi Li, Colin Bramwell, and Sun Weimin

SPRING 1985

That year in the spring, I suddenly took sick,
an illness not particularly grave. Willow catkins
rose and fell in the wine of the air;
sparrows brushed lightly past damp, gleaming roof tiles.
I was still confined to the sick ward; every day
injections, drip IVs, and doctors
who discussed past and future bacteria.
In the end, I came to know my roommate well,
the history of his illness, and his family.
Blue-uniformed staff punctually brought the meals
and cursed, cleaning up the day's garbage—
every day, until I left the hospital.

Every day, before I left the hospital,
I passed through the evening corridors,
arriving at fir trees and the little rose garden,
where other patients and their relatives and friends
together sat on wrought-iron chairs. Sparrows
flew in the small rain of the setting sun and perched
in their own shadows. In the end,
I became familiar with even more bacteria,
past and future, as well as
present strains, realizing
that I myself, perhaps, was really not so sorrowful—
I suddenly took sick in the spring of that year.

published September 1993
translated by Mike O'Connor

MISSING SOMEONE

I miss you, but this doesn't mean I need to talk
on the phone to you, or meet up with you somewhere—
In this world soaked in twilight colors, I just want to thank you
for always giving my thoughts a branch to perch on.

July 1999
translated by Michelle Yeh and Frank Stewart

PEACETIME

When Dawn is rising, her rosy fingertips
Touching the hills and valleys in northern Afghanistan,
A juvenile, just leaving the internet café, starts
His motorcycle before a convenience store on Yat-sen Road.

March 2002
translated by Weimin Sun

Lü Dean (b. 1960)

Born in Mawei, Fujian, Lü graduated from the Fujian School of Art and Craft in
1981. He was a cofounder of the Friday Poetry Society in Fuzhou and a member
of the They Poetry Society in Nanjing in the 1980s. In 1991 he lived in the United
States, where he made a living by selling his paintings. Since then he has divided
his time between New York City and Fuzhou in China. In 2011 he cofounded
the Friday School of Painting.

WHALE

On a winter night, a pod of whales breaks into the village
quietly occupying half of the land
it's like the nearby mountain, which cannot be convinced to move
what can we do, they don't want to leave
dark, persistent, refusing to answer. Might as well go
and howl right into the dark holes of their mouths
but mostly it's just our own voices we hear
shine our lamps into their eyes: an imprisoned sea
probe their mysterious weight with our hands
losing strength, becoming nothing, borderless and vast
what can we do, they don't want to move at all
they want to come live with us
so much so that they won't let us
call the tide for them before breakfast, that's how it is
These enormous godlike bodies
immobilized there in front of us, delaying time
open the windows, the sea is a few meters away,
but in their eyes, they're not welcome,
they've manufactured a historical suicide
and died. Death added to their weight
will constrict the earth's heart for a very long time
like on the nearby mountain, people bring tools
and set up ladders, vowing to turn their fat
into lamp oil, and give it to the church
and give the rest to their families, the people seem to dig holes
dig one hole into another, all facing the direction of the sea
it's like digging dirt, but the more they dig the more dirt there is
if they hit rock (those contentious
bones) they'll pull them out, and build them into a wall, turning
inconspicuous, turning historical, turning into an archaeological site—oh,
a fishy stink permeates the air everywhere
along with the peppermint taste of truth, no matter how

convincing these actions still are today
at the very least they don't seem like whales, they come suddenly at night
suspicious, and depressing

1992
translated by Eleanor Goodman

THAW

The stone is believed to stay on the mountain
never rolling down, but that's a lie
in spring, it really starts to move
the summer before it was on a higher mountain peak
and I was on guard against its tiniest movement
the shadows on the ground, its suspicious support
weren't like in my dreams, in my dreams it held me down
or toppled me into a world devoid of people
but now there are little clusters of lizards everywhere
fleeing, as though each movement of the stone
held a silent curse
ordering you to disappear from the world, carrying
dappled light and a few clumps of old snow on your body
and as soon as the stone starts to yell, the plants tremble
its long-prophesized innate craziness
and its stony hoariness and stubbornness
will immediately be revealed, and it will begin to jump again
when that happens, you'll no longer be able to say: just
stay right there. You need to escape
you'll see a weird stone popping up
here and there, breaking in half along the way
in the end it's like a hungry family
bumping and thumping down the mountainside
to reunite in a stream. That's a stone's life
as they roll down the mountain
one drops straight into a terraced field
one gets bruised on the steps of the mountain path

and from a dark thicket of grass takes off again
one is round and smooth and its lithe blue shadow
moistens the grass tips like drops of fresh blood
I think it's these stones—unlike in the sky
or in a church—that can become our idols
they're just rolling, here for a while
then there, then in our dreams,
then up on our roofs, where our eyes are drawn,
and only after all of that do we realize the mountainside
is thawing, and prevent a disaster

1993

translated by Eleanor Goodman

Walis Nokan (b. 1961)

Walis Nokan was born and raised in Mihu Tribe, a northern branch of Atayal Tribe, in Heping District, Taizhong County. In 1980 he graduated from the Taizhong Normal College and taught at several elementary schools. In 1989 he cofounded the *Indigenous Post* in Pingdong in South Taiwan, which was the first newspaper devoted to the news, literature, and oral history of indigenous peoples in Taiwan. In 1990 he and his wife founded the journal *Hunter Culture*, which evolved into a research center. In 1994 he moved back to his hometown and changed his Chinese name, Wu Junjie, to Walis Nokan. He published his first work of prose in 1979 and has since published a wide range of poetry, fiction, reportage, history, and biography. In 2019 he was invited to the International Writers Workshop at the University of Iowa.

Baya Saddle, which appears in "Family Genealogy VI: Three Generations," is situated between the Central Range and the Jade Mountain in Taiwan.

RED FLOWER

In foggy G Port, I run into Red Flower, the one who left the tribe. She came to this strange city many years ago. She took to wearing cheap perfume, having various men take turns sleeping on her pillow, changed her name to—Maria. She goes in and out of fancy hotels; naturally someone is watching from behind a column.

Last year, with her health broken, she came back. Her father, who led a degenerate life (oh yes, his contract with his pimp was for five years), shut the door of his new mansion in her face, as if he were afraid of catching a disease. Has he forgotten that Red Flower is his daughter?

Today I run into Red Flower once again in foggy G Port. Her hands on the silent windowsill, with their garish nails, look like the spreading wings of a bat as she solicits the passersby. Five years from now, maybe we will all have forgotten Red Flower.

1986
translated by Michelle Yeh and Frank Stewart

FAMILY GENEALOGY VI: THREE GENERATIONS

1900, we assembled in the forest to brew up fresh fairytales, we chased fowl and beasts in the Baya Saddle, gathered around the enchanted campfire and drank the rice wine of last year's vintage; in the winter after logging we waited for the beginning of the coming spring.

1945, we came to an island with a name unknown to us; amid lofty but empty slogans we slowly approached the center of suspicion; in the black forest, bullets chased our defenseless bodies. Ah, how I missed another island where the beautiful wife and maybe the hunter's newborn child lived!

1980, on an island without bullets or fear my tribesmen live, attesting in a karaoke bar to their song-loving nature; some barter newly cultivated mountain land for a day of pleasure, eager for the next game of chance, in which money plays the role of the skilled hunter and we play the role of the fleeing prey.

published in 1994
translated by Michelle Yeh and Frank Stewart

HUSBAND-GAZING ROCK

In our tribe there are many old women
Who refuse to live in the twentieth century
Other than chitchatting and combing hair, they rarely stir
Each has a husband who does not come home
So each has an extraordinarily bad temper
One day when we tried to climb over the bamboo fence
They flew at us like a swarm of bats

Smoking tobacco, they sit in the yard
Always with a letter or photograph in their hand
Or nothing at all
Snarled in their hair like a ribbon of smoke
They are not the sort of women who sacrifice for love
And they never remarry
In the end, they either die or live
As hard as stone

published in 1994
translated by Michelle Yeh and Frank Stewart

Chen Dongdong (b. 1961)

Born in Shanghai into a family that hailed from Wujiang, Jiangsu, Chen graduated from the Chinese Department of Shanghai Normal University in 1984 and has worked as a teacher and editor in Shanghai. In the 1980s and 1990s he took part in the founding of several unofficial poetry journals. Since 1998 he has been a full-time writer.

HORSE IN THE RAIN

In the dark, pick up an instrument. Sit steadily in the dark
the sound of a horse drifts over from the far end
a horse in the rain
this obsolete instrument, glittering
like the red freckles on a horse's nose, glittering
like the far end of a tree
the cotton roses begin to bloom, startling a few gray robins
the horse in the rain is doomed to gallop through my memory
like an instrument in the hand
like cotton roses blooming on a warm fragrant evening
at the far end of the passageway
I sit steadily like rain falling all day
I sit steadily like a flower blooming all night
a horse in the rain. The horse in the rain is doomed to gallop through my
    memory
I picked up the instrument
and strummed the song I wanted to sing

1985
translated by Eleanor Goodman

LIGHT THE LAMP

Light the lamp inside the stones, let them see
the expressions of the sea, let them see
the ancient fish
and let them see the light
a lamp raised aloft on the mountainside

The lamp should be lit in the river too, let them see
the living fish, let them see
the silent sea
and let them see the setting sun
a firebird rising from the forest

Light the lamp. When I block the north wind with my hands
when I stand between the valleys
I think that they'll crowd around me
that they'll come to see my lamp-like
language

1985
translated by Eleanor Goodman and Wang Ao

LOW BANK

Dark Heihe is dark to its zenith. The compass rose haltingly
the conical evening star inherited by the night is like
a navigator, correcting the neon lean of the needle—
its sharp radiant language relies on the wind
stabbing into the pupil that reads on the dam

the pages turn the gradual dusk, now displaying
the chapter of excessive street scenes along the river
from above sea level and below the embankments is the rising tide of streets
from even higher: the dizzying arched lamplight of the Sichuan Road Bridge—
the city's diction and architecture are slipping, piling up

on the two banks—with the eyes' puzzlement, profusion and nerves
like being tangled up in European syntax, the complex grammar
drowns out expression. In the confusion, a boat carrying manure
speeds toward the bridge, forcing aside the tranquil and reflective water
sweeping the hubbub and purgatory back to the heart of the river

watching comes from weariness, and more weariness; watching means drowning
the visual field inclines up the asphalt ramp, or jumps
the cooling railing. And at the far end of the railing and the asphalt ramp
under the warehouse's church portico, people stand around, light cigarettes
and inhale deeply, their bronchi choking down Heihe's melancholy matter

1998
translated by Eleanor Goodman

Chen Kehua (Ko-hua Chen, b. 1961)

Born and raised in Hualian, Chen graduated from Taipei Medical School in
1986. He was a visiting researcher at the Schepens Eye Research Institute at Har-
vard Medical School in 1997–2000. Since 2018 he has been director of General
Ophthalmology at Taipei Veterans General Hospital. Chen writes poetry, prose,
fiction, plays, and song lyrics; he is also a photographer and painter. He published
his first book of poems when he was twenty years old and has won numerous
awards for his poetry and song lyrics. A leading LGBTQ+ poet in Taiwan, Chen
has written a large number of poems about homosexuality and has been an activist
for the cause of gay rights.

A STRANGE TALE OF NANJING STREET

I witness my birth into such a street:
The Vietnam War three thousand miles away
Spurred the prosperity of the bar alley—
Young girls of Hualian, with their cheongsam slit up to their waist
Became one after another Suzie Wong who glowed from falling out of love

I witness my birth into a thin-walled womb
A fallow placenta, contracted eyeballs
An overly loose vagina
A mother with pigeon toes

Once she was a popular young widow—a white-skinned
Blonde-haired sperm with his youthful ignorance
Broke through layers of the gold chastity belt and
Settled in her lower abdomen which fell in love for the first time

This is how I see two clashing blood types mixed in me
When Nanjing Street unnoticeably got out of prostitution
I became a witness to the straying sperm
Those kids from good and pure families accost me:
Hello OK blah blah blah.
I always gently answer:
Fuck your mother fuck your mother's old cunt.

1985
translated by Michelle Yeh and Frank Stewart

WEDDING VOW

My dearest love:
after putting on your expensive ring
I will authorize you to use my cunt.

You will feed me with
food from China, the West, Japan,
Korean kimchi, Cantonese dim sum, French dinner
and, of course, with your cock, your spunk,
your toes and body hair
your STD and genital warts. My love . . .

I am a graduate: I am mature and financially independent.
From today I will be your one and only wife—
I will deny that my fingers ever touched
other similarly swollen veiny cocks,
I will forget the joy of being raped by my father
and only ever admire your throat, your body odor.

I will persist with my diet and regular exercise,
but I will not give up watching soap operas and playing with myself:
I have cherished my hymen
and diligently trained my vaginal sphincter
though both of us have failed to understand the concept of virginity . . .

My dearest love,
please accept my leather whip, branding iron
handcuff, torture equipment, and lube in return

(Why weren't you a Nazi officer in black?)

After our pure white wedding
I shall long for a hairy little baby who looks like you
who will grab my nipples and squeeze the milk from them
who will endow my boring and sad life with some heavenly bliss

1986
translated by Wen-chi Li and Colin Bramwell

RAIN IN KYOTO

All the ghosts, strolling through the city in April,
bleak, despondent, and jittery,
tears like drizzle—finally, by turning to deluge,
rain awakens the dreamer to morning's blear—
sprinkles over a serpentine path to the blanketed temple gate,
dampens a nap that slips from the arm.

In this rain, the monks are poor, and so are the aristocrats.
Flowers flourish in extremities,
blooming into umbrellas—now comes the moment
where the bell sound crashes into the heads of the pilgrims
who cover their heads with their hands and flee into the shower.

Bells flee too, to wherever they stop chiming.
The fresh wet ghosts rush by the temple
like tombstones standing, small
and engraved with death-haiku:
He who is rinsed with
tears, knives, nails, and kerosene
must grow into fear.

Come. Come with me.
Come, follow the rain back to the sea,
the ocean of infinite ignorance, come—
imagine raindrops silently falling on dark water
peacefully and quietly,
like a ghost that weeps at night
and cannot wake the dreamer come morning . . .

2001

translated by Wen-chi Li and Colin Bramwell

Cui Jian (b. 1961)

Ethnically Korean, Cui was born and raised in Beijing. At the age of fourteen, he learned to play trumpet from his father, and at twenty-one he was invited to join the Beijing Orchestra. In the late 1970s and early 1980s, he was exposed to rock and roll and jazz; Bob Dylan, Simon and Garfunkel, the Beatles, the Rolling Stones, and the Talking Heads inspired him the most. On May 9, 1986, Cui performed "Nothing to My Name" at the first World Peace Concert in Beijing and became an overnight sensation. Dubbed the "Godfather of Rock" in mainland China, Cui combines traditional Chinese instruments with rock and roll. His lyrics are bold and sardonic responses to the social and political environment, and they have continued to speak powerfully to the disenchanted youth. In 1991 he won MTV's first International Viewers' Choice Music Video Award for "Wild in the Snow."

FAKE MONK

I wanna walk south to north, I wanna walk from day into night
I want everyone to notice me, and no one to know the real me
If you see I'm weary, please pour me a bowl of water
If you have fallen in love with me, please kiss me on the mouth

With my feet and legs, I've ten thousand mountains and rivers to cross
I want to have everything and to regret nothing
If you love me, don't resent me the day I leave and keep walkin'
I won't stay anyplace too long and want no one tagging after me

I wanna walk south to north, I wanna walk from day into night
I want everyone to notice me, and no one to know the real me
I wanna look at your face when it's pretty, and never when it shows pain
I want heavenly rain to fall on me, but never your tears
I don't believe in evil and don't want anyone to hate me
You'll never see who I really am, nor how deceitful

1989
translated by Michelle Yeh and Frank Stewart

A PIECE OF RED CLOTH

With a piece of red cloth, on that day
you blindfolded me and the sky
You asked me what I could see
I said I was seeing happiness

It felt so good
that I forgot I had no home
You asked me where I was goin'
I said wherever you wanted

I can't see you, or the path we're on
You grasp my hands in yours
You ask what I am thinkin'
I say only about obeying you

I know you are not made of steel
but you're tough and fierce as metal
I feel the blood pulsing in your
Strong hands warming mine

I think this isn't a wilderness
though the earth is cracked an' dry
I am parched and thirsty
but you cover my mouth with a kiss

I can't go back and I can't cry
for my body has dried up
I will stay with you forever
for I know your pain more than anyone

Doo ... doo ... doo ...

1991
translated by Michelle Yeh and Frank Stewart

EGGS UNDER THE RED FLAG

Suddenly an opening
Actually, it's not so sudden
and the chance is here
but no one knows what to do
The red flag still waves
billowing in uncertain directions
The revolution goes on
the old man is stronger than ever

Money is fluttering in the wind
but we've lost our idealism
Though the air is new and fresh
we can't see the distant future
Though now is the right time
we are so timid
We are round and smooth
like eggs under the red flag

A head suddenly pokes out
for a long time we've been hoping for this
Puff out your chest, raise your head an' shout
we've inherited this in our genes
Of course we know in our blood
who our forefathers were
So whether our actions are honorable or not
inside our hearts we are pure

A power is hovering around us
sometimes it taps us on the shoulder
All at once a thought arises
don't be just followers anymore
though our bodies are soft as babies
and the only thing we know how to do is yell
Look up at the morning sun
like an egg hatching under the red flag

1994
translated by Michelle Yeh and Frank Stewart

Han Dong (b. 1961)

Born in Nanjing, Han was relocated to the countryside of northern Jiangsu with
his parents during the Cultural Revolution. In 1978 he was admitted to the Phi-
losophy Department at Shandong University and, after graduating, taught in
Xi'an and Nanjing. In 1985 he cofounded the underground poetry journal *They*
with Yu Jian and Ding Dang. Since 1992 he has been a full-time writer of fiction
and film scripts in addition to poetry.

Great Wild Goose Pagoda is located in the Temple of Great Compassion in
the city of Xi'an, Shaanxi. Built in 652, the five-story pagoda was the site where
Buddhist sutras were translated and stored in the Tang dynasty. Simone Weil was
a French philosopher, mystic, and political activist.

AS FOR GREAT WILD GOOSE PAGODA

as for great wild goose pagoda
what can we know about it
lots of people travel great distances
just to climb up it
to be a hero for just once in their life
some even come a second time
or more

those discontented people
those well-fed people
every one of them climbing the pagoda
to be a hero this one time
then they come down
into the street below
and are gone in the blink of an eye
then there are some who have the guts to jump
to become red blossoms on the stone steps below
those really did become heroes—
heroes of our times

as for great wild goose pagoda
what can we know about it
we climb up
glance round at the scenery
then we come down again

1983
translated by Josh Stenberg

THE SIDE OF ME THAT IS TENDER

I once lived a lonely life in the country
which shaped the tender side of my character
every time I get world-weary
a fresh breeze revives me
at least I'm not so naive
that I don't know where my next meal is coming from
and you'll see that I'll live this wretched life all the way to the end
experiencing every bit of the joy in it
and my habit of getting up early and home late
I do that as easily as picking up a hoe
except I can't harvest anything anymore

can't relive every precious detail
life will forever carry some real sorrow
like a farmer crying bitterly over his crops

March 1985
translated by Josh Stenberg

THESE LAST YEARS

these last years, I've been doing fine
I love, but don't fall in love anymore
I sleep, but don't sleep with women anymore
I write, but don't write poetry anymore
I often have harsh words with people, but don't fall out with them
I'm usually in Nanjing, though sometimes I
leave town and wander around
I'm still alive, but not keen on living a long life

these last years, I've been short on money, but don't feel like earning any
don't get enough sleep, but won't take sleeping pills
don't eat enough meat, but won't eat chicken drumsticks
if I'm going bald, then I'll be okay with being bald
if my teeth are rotting, then let there be holes
there'll be enough left
my beard's going gray, and so is the nether beard
my eyebrows are getting long, so are my nose hairs

these last years, I've been to Shanghai once
don't think Shanghai has changed much
went to some grassland once, but didn't feel
at one with heaven
I read, just the one book, but I've read it seven times
listen to music, just the one CD, I listen to it every day
words no longer torture me
and I no longer torture language either

these last years, one friend died
but I feel like he's still alive
another friend has achieved immortality
well, bye then, I'll take my leave
I'm still Han Dong, but people call me Old Han
Old Han's hale and hearty, goes hiking every week
no gazing into the distance, no fucking in the wild either
just halfway up the mountain and sauntering down

August 11, 2008
translated by Josh Stenberg

READING SIMONE WEIL

she tells me: desire absence
she tells me: fall in love with love itself
they're not just words, her heart beat fiercely
then she grew calm, also more radical
her intensity was pure, her certainty
bore the scars of her struggle
she died of hunger, leaving behind a white sheet on her deathbed
her purity and agony—just like the sheet
white, chilly, who could lie upon it without shivering all over?

"Whatever else may happen, we know that the universe is full."

May 6, 2003
translated by Josh Stenberg

Jiaya (Boon-Swee Tan, b. 1962)

Jiaya, literally "False Teeth," is one of the pen names of Chen Wenrui, or Boon-Swee Tan, who was born in Malacca in southwestern Malaysia. He graduated from the Malaysian Institute of Art and has worked in advertising and journalism. Since the early 1990s, he has been living in London. In addition to poetry, he writes fiction, film scripts, and film criticism under the pen name "Sent from London." His first book of poetry, *The Little Bird of My Youth*, which contains a hundred and four poems, was published in Malaysia in 2005 and broke sales records. The phenomenon was repeated in 2018 in Taiwan, where the book went through eight printings in six months. The book gives the dates of his life and death as "1962–2063"! In 2019 Jiaya's poems were adapted to the stage by Razor Experimental Theater.

HOMESICKNESS

That year they traveled to Africa
His dad was eaten by a lion
His mom was eaten by a crocodile
His kid brother was eaten by a black panther
His kid sister was eaten by a python
Now whenever he gets homesick
He pays a visit to the zoo

published in 2005
translated by Michelle Yeh

UNTITLED

He is a kindhearted man
he has a kindhearted wife
a kindhearted son
a kindhearted daughter
a kindhearted dog
a kindhearted cat
a bowl of kindhearted fish
and a row of kindhearted potted plants

They are all starving

published in 2005
translated by Michelle Yeh

ONE-ACT PLAY ON THE SUBWAY

The woman, from the moment she plants her butt on the seat across from him, starts putting on her makeup. He watches her skillfully apply the foundation, eyeliner, and lipstick. By the time the train reaches the terminal, she has transformed herself into a goddess.

Perhaps because of her shameless candor, perhaps because he just witnessed a process of artistic creation, he has fallen in love with her.

published in 2005
translated by Michelle Yeh

Lu Yimin (b. 1962)

Born in Shanghai, Lu graduated from the Chinese Department at Shanghai Normal University. She became one of the representative poets of the Newborn Generation in the second half of the 1980s and 1990s.

In "*Sylvia Plath*" Lu writes that the American poet was thirty-one when she died, though she was actually thirty. (Plath was born in October 1932 and died in February 1963, four months after her thirtieth birthday.) This is perhaps because of the way Chinese count age: one is a year old at birth.

AMERICAN WOMEN'S MAGAZINES

Peering out this window
You know, there's everything under the sun
Beneath the flowerless tree, you see
That crowd of lively people

Ladies who coil braids around their right temple
Who wear their hair down covering both cheeks
Who gaze straight ahead, or who deride and sneer
You recognize that crowd of people, one by one

Who used to be me
Who was one day of mine, an autumn day
Who was my spring, many springs
Who? Who used to be me

Now and then we fall in the dust, or rush here and there
Armed with a dictionary, flipping to the page of death
We cut and paste this word, embroider it
Rip apart its nine brushstrokes and reassemble it

People notice this commotion
They've noticed it for centuries
They commend us on our good job, our bravery, our composure
That's how they describe us

You recognize that crowd of people
Who used to be me
I stand in front of you
My hands washed of it all

1984
translated by Jennifer Feeley

SYLVIA PLATH

At this moment, I only feel a twinge of sadness
At once, it surges in my heart, then flows across my lips
At this moment, it's merely someone gathering a wisp of wind
(Her virtue was greater than mine)
Dense clouds thirst to drip   to drop
Onto the white stones of the twilight street
I mourn for an entire forest
In my softest voice
(A voice soaked with tears)
I sing of her constant smile
I sing of her unaffected smile

Thirty-one when she died   heart content
Her corpse and soul
The purple berries sold by the side of the road
Her breath congeals in her poems
Becoming dark red
Fine rain and burning lamplight
Melt into a nighttime forest
People turn back to admire its glistening beauty

She spoke loudly about death, and pondered it silently
I see purple sunset clouds
And think of their accidental deaths
Her shadow so distinct
Slowly approaching my body

1993
translated by Jennifer Feeley

Wang Yin (b. 1962)

Born in Shanghai, Wang graduated from the Chinese Department of Shanghai
Normal University in 1984 and has been a teacher, reporter, and editor. He started
publishing poetry in 1983 and was active in the unofficial poetry scene in the 1980s
and 1990s. He published his first book of collected poems in 2005. Today he is a
full-time writer and currently resides in New York.

THINKING ABOUT A CZECH FILM,
BUT I CAN'T REMEMBER THE TITLE

Cobblestone streets, soaking wet
Prague, soaking wet
On a corner by the park a girl kisses you
You do not blink

Later as you face the guns you still don't blink
Waffen-ss rain slickers inside out
like shiny leather overcoats
A three-wheeled motorbike speeds by
When you and your friends fall to the ground
rain is still falling
I see one raindrop and another raindrop
chasing along a power line
and finally tumbling to the cobblestone road
I think of you
lips moving
No one sees

1983
translated by Andrea Lingenfelter

GIFTS FROM ON HIGH

How will you thank the setting sun, god-given talents
How will you come to see these roses of politics
these springtimes bereft of independent thought

How will you listen for the hour hand's insurrection
What will you do about the flames burning through paper
or the raging river that surges beneath the city

The illusions hidden up your sleeves
exceed the limits of reason
The sick man's gaze and the cackling of banners
are so very alike
Promises are so hollow
and secrets so nimble

Grieving skulls, the heart of a summer day
sorrowful fragrances, along with
the cries of children in the Milky Way

How can you ever answer

February 1992
translated by Andrea Lingenfelter

THE EVENING OF MY LIFE HAS COME TOO LATE

The evening of my life has come too late
There's wine in abundance
but no cups to be found, and nightfall
has drained the grapes of their color

October sunflowers are dazed raindrops
smoldering silks and satins
Magnified grains of time
fill the photo album of night

Bobbing straw hats screen off
a landscape gone incognito
the fear that haunts life, the pain beneath a sweater
The storm gathers to it every scattered soul

The evening of my life has come too late
I still abide by prophecies of love and death
just as my heart long ago
became inured to grief and its shame

June 6, 2011
translated by Andrea Lingenfelter

New Lyricism
and Postmodernist
Experiments

_____

The New Millennium

The twenty-first century has witnessed the dramatic rise of China as a world power. If China went through a metamorphosis from a closed, backward society to a reform-bent, outward-looking country under Deng Xiaoping in the 1980s and 1990s, the new millennium has witnessed its transformation from the "factory of the world" to a global leader in advanced technologies, such as artificial intelligence, quantum computing, semiconductors, and aerospace. Today China is the second-largest economy in the world, next only to the United States, and, with its economic muscle, it has become a major player in global politics. Some Western media outlets have dubbed the twenty-first century as the "Chinese Century."

Understandably, the Chinese people take great pride in the prosperity and prestige that China has achieved. The return to Chinese rule of Hong Kong (a British colony since 1841) in 1997 and Macau (a Portuguese colony since 1887) in 1999 mark the end of a century and a half of defeat and humiliation by Western imperial powers.

On the other hand, the nationalist sentiment the Communist Party fosters through the educational system and the media underlines tensions between China and democratic countries in the world. China's human rights abuses in Tibet and Xinjiang, crackdowns on massive protests in Hong Kong, sweeping claims of sovereignty in the South China Sea, and repeated threats to Taiwan through the use of fighter jets have raised concerns and have been widely criticized by the United States and its allies.

The cultural scene in China has also evolved in new directions. Popular culture, from film and television to computer games and anime, has expanded by leaps and bounds. The film industry has become so lucrative that it is overtaking Hollywood in box office. The internet is ubiquitous and has significantly impacted not only the economy and consumerism but also sociocultural practices and the vernacular language. Paradoxically, although literature has lost its halo and has been marginalized in the public view, it continues to thrive on the internet. An example is poetry by migrant workers, which would not have caught on but for its enthusiastic online reception. Poetry has also been the subject of controversy in the mass media from time to time.

In Taiwan the past two decades have seen the presidency held alternately by the Democratic Progressive Party and the Nationalist Party. Regardless of which party rules, nativist discourses have become the mainstream through de-Sinicizing policies and educational reform since the presidency of Lee Teng-hui. Compared with the turn of the twenty-first century, more people in the 2020s identify themselves as Taiwanese than as Chinese or both Chinese and Taiwanese. However, economically, Taiwan is closely tied to—and dependent on—China. It is estimated that Taiwan's trade surplus with China in 2020 totaled 86.7 billion US dollars.

Culturally, the marginalization of highbrow literature has also taken place in Taiwan as in Mainland China, although, compared with the West, the numbers of literature readers in Asia are still much larger. In the same vein, conventional publishing has shrunk due to competition from the internet. Since the 1990s, the site of digital literature has evolved from the Bulletin Board System (BBS) and blog to Facebook, Instagram, Line, and other services. More importantly, these new platforms have made possible new modes of creation, such as hypertexts and video poems. While poetry is the dominant genre in digital literature, the platforms have also proven productive for fiction and nonfiction prose.

Zhang Zao (1962–2010)

Born in Changsha, in Hunan, Zhang received his BA degree in English from Hunan Normal University and his MA degree from the Sichuan University of Foreign Languages. In 1986 he went to study in Germany and received a doctorate from Trier University, then taught at Tübingen University. He moved back to China in 2005 and taught at Henan University and the Minzu University of China. Zhang started writing poetry in college and was active in the underground poetry scene in the 1980s. On March 9, 2010, he passed away from lung cancer.

Liang Shanbo and Zhu Yingtai, known as "the butterfly lovers," are the protagonists of an old folktale. Zhu disguised herself as a man in order to attend school away from home; there she met the poor scholar Liang, and they became close like brothers. After discovering Zhu's true identity, Liang expressed his love for her. However, Zhu's father had arranged her marriage to a rich man. Taken sick and brokenhearted, Liang passed away. Zhu cried so hard that his grave opened up, and she threw herself into it before it closed again. The lovers turned into butterflies and flew away together. The opening line comes from *The Book of Songs*, the first poetry collection in China, compiled in the sixth century BCE. *Blue collar* refers to the garment worn by students in the Zhou dynasty (1045–221 BCE).

IN THE MIRROR

When a lifetime of regrets comes to mind
plum blossoms begin to fall
Just like seeing her swim across the river to the other shore
Just like going up a pinewood ladder
What's dangerous is admittedly beautiful
Better to see her return, riding on a horse
her cheeks warm
abashed. With downcast eyes, she answers the Emperor
A mirror waits for her always
Let her sit inside the mirror in her usual seat
gazing out the window. When a lifetime of regrets comes to mind
the falling plum blossoms blanket the Southern Hill

1984
translated by Yanting-Leah Li and Nick Admussen

LIANG SHANBO AND ZHU YINGTAI

"O you, with the blue collar, lasting is the sorrow of my heart!" Each day they read and riddled, inseparable like body and its shadow, like brothers.
He didn't expect the beauty of lit candles inside her,
never considered stroking that exquisite face.

The pair of butterflies had long existed, watching them
in their fresh robes, crossing a little bridge for an outing.
She hooted from behind to tease him, waving her long sleeves.
She sensed that he was like a picture, inlaid in the afterlife.

She wanted to tell him a lonesome metaphor,
but felt herself replaced by some sort of litheness.
Foreign whispers echoed a thousand strands of thoughts.

That was the butterflies emptying out their existence,
so as to accommodate their most fragrant evening:
they entered each other deeply, shuddering the flower veins.

translated by Yanting-Leah Li and Nick Admussen

CONVERSATION WITH TSVETAEVA (1 of 12)

C'est un chinois, ce sera long.
—*Tsvetaeva*

2.

I dream every day of eternal sorrow. White clouds are drifting.
Marina, you bring a private pot of coffee to a boil,
the sugar cubes are distant, beyond the blue myopia,
guilty like a houseboy. He longs for cardinal right and wrong.
Poetry is laboring, like workmanship, its outcomes
are silent objects, symmetrical to the human lot.
Perhaps functional? But its measures won't exceed
the parentheses whose two shadowy ends are in love. A round hand mirror
can make poetry too, if someone is willing, but he has to
guard against its habit of mixing up the left and right wing.
Face to face, two fronts turn against each other, and yet
the Reds and the Whites duel over the word *No*. One is at a loss,

looks into the mirror, the houseboy of the revolution takes the same road back;
Smashing it, one feels a sudden emptiness, the coffee startles, falls . . .

1994
translated by Yanting-Leah Li and Nick Admussen

DRIFTING

Top floor, language lab.
          Autumn arrives with a boom,
a cool sheen covers the walls with a cosmic sheet of new glass.
The gang put on their headsets in unison, their faces as gentle as jade.
The pregnant teacher is also listening. Glittering fragments of
          misty sounds:
"Evening news, evening news," whistling cassettes fast forward around the globe.
Tense words refuse to fade away, like street scenes and
fountains, like a few aliens standing firm at some margins
fiddling with the twilight, suddenly releasing a cascade of brocade
Emptiness is less than a flower!

She looks around at the
new configuration, everyone has in their mouths a loom
murmuring as they tell the same
good story.
Everyone is immersed in listening,
everyone baring their organs, working,

utterly unaware.

1997
translated by Yanting-Leah Li and Nick Admussen

Xi Chuan (b. 1963)

Xi Chuan, the pen name of Liu Jun, was born in Xuzhou, Jiangsu, into a family that hailed from Shandong. In 1985 he graduated from the English Department at Peking University and for years has taught at the Central Academy of Fine Arts in Beijing. He was involved in the founding and editing of the poetry journal *Tendency* in 1989–91. In 2000 he played the role of a "sent-down youth" from Beijing during the Cultural Revolution in *Platform*, directed by Jia Zhangke (b. 1970). He was a visiting professor at the University of Iowa in 2002 and at the University of Victoria, Canada, in 2009. He has given readings in many countries around the world. Some of his poems have been adapted to music and theater.

Ha'ergai is a small town in Qinghai on the Tibetan Plateau near the western border of China. Jorge Luis Borges was a twentieth-century Argentine poet, short story writer, essayist, and translator. He worked as a librarian in his early career; by the age of fifty-five he went completely blind. In Chinese mythology, Nüwa created humankind and repaired the Pillar of Heaven.

STARGAZING ON HAERGAI

There is a mystery you cannot master
and for which you can only fulfill the role of observer
allowing that mysterious force
to emit its signals from afar
to send out light, piercing your heart
like tonight, on Haergai
in this desolate spot so far from any
city, beside a train station the size of a fava bean
on the Qinghai-Tibet plateau
and as I gaze up at the stars
the cosmos is so silent, even wings are rare
grass grows wildly toward the constellations
the horses have forgotten how to fly
the wind blows through an empty night and blows through me
the wind blows through the future and it blows through the past
and I become somebody, lighting a lamp
in some hovel of a room as its

icy roof is trampled into an altar by the billion feet of the constellations
and like a child taking communion
I am holding my breath, trying to be brave

1985
translated by Lucas Klein

REREADING BORGES'S POETRY

—for Anne

The precision of this statement emerges from the chaos of the past
this pure force, like the rhythm of a dripping faucet
annotates the aporia of history
touching starlight I leave night to the earth
night that licks the earth's crevices: that forked memory
No Man is a man, No Where is a place
a No Man in No Where has written these
lines I must decipher in the shadows
I give up scouring the world of dust for the author, and lift my head to see
a librarian, lethargically, and only for his livelihood
preserving the order of the universe and books

1997
translated by Lucas Klein

NOTES ON THE MOSQUITO

Ten thousand mosquitoes unite into a tiger, reduced to nine thousand they
unite into a leopard, reduced to eight thousand they unite into an immobile
chimpanzee. But one mosquito is just one mosquito.

The hematophagous mosquito, the female of the species, is in the same category as the leech and the vampire, to which could be added the bloodsucking bureaucrat, the landlord, the capitalist. Were all creatures under heaven arranged according to diet, they would be arranged as carnivorous, herbivorous, and hematophagous.

In the crevices of history, mosquitoes are everywhere. They have witnessed and even participated in beheadings, human quarterings by horse cart, busted embankments on the Yellow River, and the peddling of sons and daughters, yet not once do the twenty-five books of the dynastic histories mention the mosquito.

The mosquito we encounter today can trace its ancestry back to the era when Nüwa repaired the heavens (Nüwa was a beauty, or so it's said in *The Investiture of the Gods*. Nüwa delighted in mosquitoes, though this is not said in *The Investiture of the Gods*).

Yet the life span of a mosquito is fixed somewhere between sunup and sundown, or between two sunups and sundowns, and thus in its whole life a mosquito might only meet an average of four or five people, or twenty or thirty pigs, or one horse. This suggests that mosquitoes have established no views on good and evil.

Some people don't open windows, don't open doors, for fear that mosquitoes will enter, but in fact they are the prisoners of mosquitoes. Some people have no choice but to use public toilets on the street, and when bitten by mosquitoes, they discover that its itchiness is actually somewhat tolerable.

One of my goals in this world is to be bitten by a mosquito. They pierce their needles into my skin, they convene to cool off in my shadow, they expire in the poison of my breath.

In the depths of the night, someone half-asleep in bed slaps himself. He's not being introspective, rather he has heard the mosquito's buzz. The greater his force, the greater his success in killing mosquitoes, the sterner his sounds of self-reproach.

So what human form does the mosquito take after it dies? Someone buzzing and flitting in front of me, he must have been a mosquito in a previous life. Some girls are so skinny we call them "mosquitoes."

To protect the environment is to protect mosquitoes and others, including the god of malaria. To protect the environment, we must also accelerate our production of cooling balms. Then the mosquito can be vigorously driven from nature. Yet this has proven difficult in reality.

Bringing mosquitoes on an airplane, on a train, to foreign lands and other countries, can deepen our sensation of homesickness and strengthen our identification with the earth. Whenever a suitcase is opened, a mosquito flies out.

No one can tell the difference between a spot a mosquito has landed and a spot no mosquito has landed, just as no one can tell the difference between a spot a thief has touched and a spot no thief has touched. To scrutinize the trail of a thief is to see a dead mosquito under a microscope.

January 2003
translated by Lucas Klein

Amang (b. 1964)

Born in Hualian, on the east coast of Taiwan, Amang, the pen name of Hong Liqing, currently lives in Taipei. She published her first book of poetry, titled *on/off*, in 2003. A bilingual selection of her poetry in English translation, *Raised by Wolves: Poems and Conversations*, translated by and in collaboration with Steve Bradbury, won the 2021 PEN Award for Poetry in Translation. In addition to writing poetry, she makes documentary films and video poems.

SUPERMARKET

As for those more willing to shoulder responsibility
each is assigned
a shopping
cart.

They defend the cart
put body on the line
to bring the hunt to a finale.

Finally, humbly, take up their heavy burden and go.

ca. 1995
translated by Steve Bradbury

OH, IF ONLY ONE DAY MY MEMORY WERE GOOD

So good I wouldn't have the need to see you

might not even want to

so good that if we never meet again
I wouldn't have a single qualm

what I would have harvested that day
could well fill
a silo
enough to weather the longest
famine

what I would have reaped
would not fear the dark
would never decompose, grow stale, or sprout
(avoiding any chance of toxic offshoots)

would never run out
would never cloy

oh, if only one day my memory were good

I think I mentioned I've a wretched memory
in all these years
we met only once
had but one day together
(rounded off to the nearest whole number)

I vaguely recall your mentioning
your memory was worse than mine

if by chance you do remember everything one day
what then?

2004
translated by Steve Bradbury

ICE

Thrusting your hand down a tiger's throat
to tear out his heart
so, too, I
cut from a book a sheet of
ice

How it burns!

I round my lips
expel a plume of smoke

an alternative therapy
the witch who lives in my basement taught me
the two of us grow more and more alike
our periods now start on the very same day

I don't take a penny for rent
she has taught me a timely cure
for cursing the two gaping wounds on my face

wherein lies the soul weighing twenty-one grams, or so it was believed
the so-called window to the soul

this past month I washed them seven times
in typhoon season I must take extra care
"Lest saltwater intrusion
harm the fertile fields"

2015

translated by Steve Bradbury

Haizi (1964–1989)

Haizi, literally "Little Sea," is the pen name of Zha Haisheng, who was born in rural Huaining, Anhui. At the age of fifteen, he was admitted to the Law School at Peking University. After graduating, he taught at the Chinese University of Political Science and Law. Haizi started writing poetry in 1982. In the 1980s he traveled many times to Qinghai and Tibet in the northwest. Written at 3:00 a.m. on March 14, 1989, "Spring, Ten Haizis" was the last poem he wrote in his life. On March 26 he died by suicide in Shanhai Pass outside Beijing.

In "Motherland" Liang Mountain is in Shandong Province, famous as the fictional stronghold of outlaws against the corrupt government in the classic novel of the fourteenth century, *Water Margin*, also translated as *Outlaws of the Marsh* and *All Men Are Brothers*. Dunhuang is in Gansu, on the edge of the Gobi Desert. A major stop on the ancient Silk Road, it is best known for its nearly five hundred grottoes adorned with Buddhist statues and frescoes.

AUTUMN

Autumn is deep, in God's house eagles have gathered
In God's hometown eagles are conversing
Autumn is deep, the king is writing poetry
In this world of deepening autumn
That which should be received is not yet received
That which should be lost has been long lost

1987
translated by Michelle Yeh

MOTHERLAND (OR DREAMS AS HORSES)

I want to be the loyal son of a distant place
and the transient lover of material substance
the same as all poets whose dreams are horses
I must walk with the martyrs and scoundrels

ten thousand people want to extinguish this fire   I alone hold it high
a huge fire   just-bloomed flowers fall throughout the sacred Motherland
the same as all poets whose dreams are horses
with this fire I pass through a lifetime of boundless night

a huge fire   the language of the Motherland and the stones cobbled together
    to construct the Liang Mountain stronghold
Dunhuang dreams are supreme   in July the bones would still be cold
like snow-white firewood or hard strips of white snow   laid down on the
    mountain of the gods
the same as all poets whose dreams are horses
I launch myself into this fire   and these three are the lantern that imprison
    me   spitting forth radiance

Ten thousand people want to walk across my knife edge   to construct the
    language of the Motherland
I am fully willing for everything to begin again
The same as all poets whose dreams are horses
I am also willing to serve out my sentence

of all the gods' creations I decay most easily   with the irresistible speed
    of death
I only truly value grain   I embrace her tightly   embrace her in our
    hometown bearing and raising sons and daughters
the same as all the poets whose dreams are horses
I am also willing to bury myself atop the mountains that soar around us   to
    keep watch over this quiet homeland

facing the Yellow River I am boundlessly ashamed
my time has passed in vain   I am left with only a body of great fatigue
the same as all the poets whose dreams are horses
time passes by   not a drop remaining   a horse dies in a drop of water

a thousand years from now if I revive on the riverbanks of the Motherland
a thousand years from now I will again have China's rice paddies   and the
    Zhou Emperor's snow mountains   heavenly horses galloping
the same as all the poets whose dreams are horses
I choose the eternal pursuit

my mission   is to become a life of the sun
from alpha to omega—"sun"—incomparably glorious, incomparably brilliant
the same as all the poets whose dreams are horses
at last the gods of dusk lift me into the immortal sun

sun is my name
sun is my life
the corpses of poetry—a thousand-year kingdom and me   buried at the peak
    of the sun
riding a phoenix of five thousand years and a dragon named "horse"—I will
    inevitably be defeated
but with the sun poetry will be victorious

1987

translated by Dan Murphy

FACING THE OCEAN, SPRING WARMS FLOWERS OPEN

starting from tomorrow, become a content person
feed the horses, split wood, roam the world
starting from tomorrow, I'll concern myself with grains and vegetables
I have a home, facing the ocean, spring warms flowers open

starting from tomorrow, I'll write letters to all the relatives
to tell them of my contentedness
what that content lightning flash told me
I will tell everyone

give a warm name to every river and every mountain
strangers, I send you my blessings
I hope for you a splendid future
I hope that your lovers become family
I hope that in this dusty world you become content
I only hope to face the ocean, as spring warms and flowers open

January 13, 1989
translated by Dan Murphy

SPRING, TEN HAIZIS

spring, ten Haizis fully revive
on the brilliant landscape
mocking this savage and sorrowful Haizi
why your long, deep sleep?

spring, ten Haizis release their throating roars
encircling you and me, dancing and singing
pulling at your black hair, riding you rushing wildly away, dust swirling
your pain as the cleaving spreads over the earth

in spring, only this savage and vengeful Haizi
remains, the last one
child of the dark night, steeped in winter, losing his heart to death
unable to extract himself, in deep love with an empty, frigid village

where the grain is piled high, blocking the window
the six family members use half of it: mouths, eating, stomachs
half is for planting and reproduction
great winds blow from the east to the west, from north to south, with no
    thought for the dark night or the dawn
in the end what will your daybreak mean?

March 4, 1989
translated by Dan Murphy

Hong Hong (Hung Hung, b. 1964)

Born in Tainan in South Taiwan, Hong Hong, the pen name of Yan Hongya, received his primary education in Taoyuan. In 1977–79 he lived in the Philippines, then returned to Taipei to attend high school. In 1987 he graduated from the Taipei National University of the Arts with a major in theater. For more than four decades, Hong Hong has been active in many fields: as a poet; film script writer; theater, musical, dance, and film director; actor; fiction writer; and organizer of poetry festivals and film festivals. He cowrote the award-winning script for *A Brighter Summer Day* (1991) with the internationally acclaimed director Edward Yang (1947–2007). He won Best Director at the 1999 Festival des 3 Continents for his first film, *The Love of Three Oranges* (1998), and the Prix du Public at the same festival for his second film, *The Human Comedy* (2001). Hong Hong published his first book of poetry in 1990 and has served as the chief editor of *Modern Poetry, Now Poetry, Off the Roll* (published by Dark Eyes Ltd., which he founded in 2008), and *Performing Art* (published by Dark Eyes Performance Lab, which he founded in 2009).

A HYMN TO HUALIAN

Blessed is the Lord for bestowing on us these gifts we are so unworthy of
    receiving,
The mountains of Hualian. The azure of a summer evening at the stroke of
    seven.
Deep sleep. The broad sweep of the sea tilting out of kilter on those hairpin
Turns we take at sixty miles per hour. Love
And transgression. His injustices.
Your loveliness.

published in 1996
translated by Steve Bradbury

THE LAST SUPPER

I clench my fists to prevent
The wounds from breaking out in advance of the event

No one has the heart to speak up as you clasp your cigarette
Your fingers already forming the sign of the cross

But O there is a shaft of moonlight in my heart
Gleaming on the garden where you will rise from the dead

Each savory dish the skeptic sets before us is more delicious than the last
The love songs of the infidels outside the walls reduce me to tears

If there be a Judas among us
It must be that side of the fish not cooked to perfection

With more than our fill we grow drowsy and tired
And with that quite forget the sorrow

published in 1996
translated by Steve Bradbury

HOMEMADE BOMB

Expel Red Savages
Establish America

Expel Jews
Establish Deutschland

Expel Palestinians
Establish Israel

Expel barbarians
Establish China

Expel impurities
To extract a pure poem

Those characters out of rhyme
Those words weak in poeticity

Those corpses of languages
Those refugee camps of languages

Those guerrillas of languages
Those resistance fighters of languages

An orphan smashes a baby bottle
To make a homemade bomb

published in 2005
translated by Michelle Yeh

The world is not outside, it's here
In these movie trailers where every hour of the day
War and terror, love and laughter
Heroes and demons, celebrities and children
Flying or floating through
Prehistory or futurity
Pass before our eyes like ghostly visions
Myopic and heavy with sleep
The world is here
Inside this endless spectacle of
Formulaic teasers
No need to even buy a ticket
You can stand here and watch them for hours
And in every single one they all speak English

published in 2006
translated by Steve Bradbury

Luo Feng (Lok Fung, Natalia Chan, b. 1964)

Luo Feng, the pen name of Chen Shaohong, received her doctorate in comparative literature from the University of California, San Diego, and has taught at the Chinese University of Hong Kong. In the 1980s and 1990s, she was involved in the editing of the *Hong Kong Literature and Art* and *New Harvest Poetry Magazine* and the founding of another poetry journal, *One Ninth*. In addition to being a poet, Luo is a fiction writer, film critic, and cultural critic.

THE FLYING COFFIN

Woken by thunder at five in the morning
the first thing I want to tell you
is that all of our plans have gone wrong

Outside our building is a highway
on the highway is a flying coffin
inside the coffin are sixteen lives
all handed over to the driver
if he doesn't drink or smoke or talk on his cell phone
if it doesn't rain or turn foggy
if no dogs or old people suddenly appear on the road
I believe we will lead long and full lives
Often on these desperate escapes
I listen to the same song and hum along
each time the song rises to its highest pitch
the minibus swerves by a deadly corner
the wheels squeal
people collapse in the centrifugal force of lost love
and so I remember the thunder's warning before dawn
do we really have no way out?

On holidays the highway is one big traffic jam
like a colorful centipede with neither head nor tail
the zigzagging links at either extreme are neither the beginning nor end
along the way the police maintain or disrupt order
but there's no improving an impossible situation
When the pressure builds into indecision
should we abandon the gridlock?
When a car hits the one in front out of impatience
should it flee the scene?

The CD's music flows like before
not pausing for the weather or distance or accident
even so
the reckless minibus driver is suddenly seized by a whim
to speed through the yellow light at a critical juncture
and in an instant strikes the curb and bounces back to the railing
with the skip of the disc and cut power I realize
how hard it is to love one another
when you're at one end of the highway and I'm at the other

What we see along the way
determines which window we choose
from the overpass to the road
no direction has ever been dependable
we thought that being on the ground
would be easier than being suspended in the sky
but we didn't realize we would only get
a bird's-eye view of everything in midair
it all happened so quickly
and before there was a chance to remember details
you were saying goodbye from the opposite lane

Only waking up from the abyss of five o'clock did I remember
that our love
is a flying coffin speeding down the highway
and at any moment it could hit a dead end

June 21, 2002
translated by Eleanor Goodman

DAYS WHEN I HIDE MY CORPSE IN A BOX

This sick body curls up, fears the light
dreads sound   but likes the damp
these are the days I hide my corpse in a cardboard box
Through contracted pupils
the width of four banknotes is expanding
I see my rotting heart hardening bit by bit
turning glittering and transparent

After enduring two hundred forty-four days
I climb out of the box   and in the hypothermic cold
take a heated long-distance bus (another steel box)
from the bright daylight to the black night
in the city there are people and streetlamps,
cars drive through midair   I can see into buildings from the overpass

the swaying shadows of people   blue clamor of televisions
the far-wafting scent of cooking
turning, the bus wheels almost hit the pedestrians' heels
red and green sales signs
and fluorescent advertising jingles shout at each other
I think   Christmas must be coming
and then it's New Year   Lantern Festival   Valentine's Day
Tomb-Sweeping Day and Easter   year after year after year
how do we deal with these continuous interminable holidays?

What's tired now are these bloodshot eyes
dizzy from the flashes   unable to distinguish
the city's dense lights and groups of people
the holiday well-wishing is about to begin
how do we deal with all the prosperous commotion?
Parents take their children on and off the bus
lovers go arm in arm from the front of the bus to the back
the slow-moving elderly are least likely to be forgiven
how do we deal with such a packed jostling space?

Finally the bus passes the entrance
of the hotel from whose heights you leaped that day
the shattered steel fence has been repaired the blood stains and fresh flowers
are just pictures in the news   in this city
there are always new neon lights switching stories every day
looking out through the window at the gradually narrowing harbor
we have reason to believe   that next year
will still go on!

I can't stand these cycles of change from old to new
so in the end I decide to spend more time
hiding my corpse in a cardboard box
I give up water, hope, and light
and get along quite well with myself

November 29, 2003
translated by Eleanor Goodman

Zang Di (b. 1964)

Zang Di, the pen name of Zang Li, was born in Beijing and received his BA and PhD degrees in Chinese literature from Peking University. Since 1997 he has been teaching at his alma mater and currently holds the position of associate professor. In 1999–2000 he was a visiting scholar at the University of California, Davis. In addition to being a poet, Zang is an influential poetry critic and scholar.

SPINACH

This beautiful spinach hasn't once
hidden you in its green shirt.
You have never even worn
any green shirts at all.
You avoid this kind of image—
yet I can clearly remember
your silent flesh resembled
a seed at its apex.
Why does spinach look
beautiful? Why
do I know you will think
this question but won't ask it?
Washing spinach, I feel
its deep green quality
seems like a child I had with the plant.
So spinach answers the question
of how we can see in our lives
angels that others say don't exist.
The beauty of spinach is weak—
when we face the mere fifty square meters
of standard living space, this vivid spinach
is the weakest politics. On the surface
a bit wild, difficult to clean—
its beauty one might say

is sustained by the power of little irritations.
Yet its nutrients determine
its value, not to the left nor to the right.

October 1997
translated by Eleanor Goodman and Wang Ao

BUTTERFLY-ATTRACTING FLOWER

You aren't weakened by my blindness.
You're like a flower, but when I look carefully
you more closely resemble jade;
only your natural colors aren't meant to shine.
You are the remnants of a life,
which make me search for the greater part of my life.

You aren't frightened by my flames,
you emit a cracking sound,
like someone is extracting
a tooth from our language.
And when you bite me painfully, I know
I'm not just a toothsome piece of meat.

You use more eccentricities
to dice up my personality,
you feel that in the final result
there's an overlooked clue.
You're not only incisive in my concealment
but also incisive in our unity.

You're unequal to your uprightness,
just as I'm unequal to my experience,
and occasionally I'll stumble at your feigned turns.
I am dampened by your wetness,
but you remain unconvinced, because the ocean waves there
aren't pushed by a blue bulldozer.

You're not simplified by my ideals.
You don't burn, you have another kind of vitality.
Your outline is unbending, but it also
can dissolve into tears.
You're transparent in my vagueness,
you are an impression of the world.

You're rounded by my caress—
it is a tangent moving along a lead wire.
You don't inquire into my geometry.
You're symmetrical in my dim vision,
and so, you are basically my dizziness;
when I fetch water, you are the crystal glass on the table.

You've tried all manner
of circumspection, and one might as well say
you're tautened by the beauty of leanness.
You like to eat but aren't lazy about cooking,
your kitchen skills were mostly
learned from me, but you're more successful at it.

You also succeed over their confusion
and their mythologies. You're even
made arrogant by all their perplexity,
you refuse to take advantage of their muddied water,
though you love to catch fish with your hands.
As for their ordinary knowledge, you say, Bah!

You exceed my harvest,
just as you use your true nature
to exceed my natural lust.
You seem eternally less than my milling;
you're finer than medicinal powder;
if there is a judgment day, you're the final cure.

You're not smaller than one, but you
are still an exception. You integrate
with my height and quiver on a branch
like a nest in an autumn breeze.
It's just that you don't fly. You are good at extremes,
and it seems an extreme is also a journey.

You're prettier than not pretty enough,
and I'm amazed that you don't amaze others,
even compared to a shadow, you're a master.
You don't flower in a flowery world.
You don't lie on top of a colorful flag;
you flutter, but you don't go against the wind.

You're not a hundred meters away,
you're closer than what they call the distant,
but when I sprint there, I feel
butterflies pulling at my hind legs;
I'm furious my forelegs are just as clumsy,
so I cannot leap like a horse.

November 1999
translated by Eleanor Goodman

THE ABSOLUTE AESTHETICS ASSOCIATION

I squat down, waiting
to speak with an earthworm thin as a shoelace.
All around me is a field of knee-high canola,
and my bike sits to one side, like I have no more road to get lost on.
As an adult, everyone professes
never to have seen a talking earthworm.
The world is small enough already, yet we still
haven't found what you really want.
Mr. Earthworm, do you know
what you thirst for the most? The lines of your body

are miniscule, as though inviting us
to think of you as bait.
Yet your long slender body is perfect for dancing an underground tango.
I admire you for that.
I have more patience for you
than for my own life.
I don't mind your gender—if I invited you to be my muse,
would you care that this poem isn't the least bit dirty?

August 2005
Translated by Eleanor Goodman

ASHES PRIMER

The furnace door opens, the dead straggle behind.
A burst of rain falls in the dim light of green foliage
as though time never remembers
we could just be guests of the rain.
The skeleton waiting to cool may need
ten thousand years to turn cold;
the quickly solidifying air seems
to behave more professionally than fate;
but in breath is a newly formed
unnamed abyss that can perceive
even the most hidden pain. On the conveyor belt,
a youthful shape
like a relief sculpture of life,
and it seems there will never be anything else
in that purgatory worth exploring.
The world is too heavy, lending an unfamiliar,
broom-wielding hand, and you leave behind
your lightest self, as though it
were a ruse you fooled life with
while you reserved the final justice for me alone.
More cruel still, it seems that only after
becoming the best father

could I apprehend that falling tears,
accelerating toward a bottomless interior,
are more terrifyingly dependable
than all of our known truths.

August 12, 2017
translated by Eleanor Goodman

Xu Huizhi (b. 1966)

Xu Huizhi, the pen name of Xu Youji, is a native of Taoyuan in North Taiwan
and graduated from the Taipei University of Science and Technology, where he
majored in chemical engineering. He published his first book of poetry in 1990
and has gone on to publish four more in addition to prose and children's literature.
Xu is also an editor and publisher, having served as the chief editor for the literary supplements to the *China Times Evening Post* and the *Liberty Times* as well
as the literary magazine *Unitas Monthly*. In 2009 he cofounded Route Culture
Publishing Company and has served as its president. In recent years Xu has also
gained recognition for his calligraphy. Both his writings and calligraphy show a
deep affinity with Buddhism, which he has been studying since he was a teenager.

STRANDED HUMPBACK WHALE

The stranded humpback whale
Finally stops breathing
We circle its gigantic body
Embrace one another in awe, and weep
The nuclear power plant exploded a long time ago
In a forgotten summer of the Common Era
Now we tie knots
To mark the death of the great whale
Who strayed into the prohibited zone called Earth

June 3, 1992
translated by Michelle Yeh and Frank Stewart

FRAGRANCE

Holding a flower
You walked past my door
And vanished out of sight

Leaving behind
Only an indefinable fragrance
That has refused to leave

Oh, infinite happiness
Endless hell

March 8, 1999
translated by Michelle Yeh and Frank Stewart

THERE STANDS A DEER

The sky is ablaze with silent
Nonstop fireworks
Holding hands
We pause in our walk
Beside the vast lake
And we exchange gazes
for a long time with a deer

The deer is alone
Forlorn in the wild
Grazing on lilies

1999
translated by Michelle Yeh and Frank Stewart

MY OBSESSIVE-COMPULSIVE DISORDER

When a cool wind blows
I am a fox that has lost its way
Gazing at the sun as it sets
And the hazy moon as it rises

I keep dialing on my phone
To connect with the next life
To connect with the previous life
To connect with you in this life

Your voice
Your gray hair
Your body that in the end will grow old
The sum of my obsessive-compulsive disorder

published in 2017
translated by Michelle Yeh and Frank Stewart

Lan Lan (b. 1967)

Lan Lan, born in Shandong, began publishing at fourteen. One of the most celebrated contemporary Chinese poets, she has published nineteen poetry collections in a dozen languages worldwide, winning many awards. She has also written twelve volumes of essays and children's tales. English versions of her poems may be found online at *Pangolin House* as well as in *Canyon in the Body*, a Zephyr Press collection. In recognition of Lan Lan's deep connection to Greece, where her drama has been performed, she was awarded honorary citizenship of Chios. She has served as visiting professor at several institutions, and as poet-in-residence at Renmin University. Currently, Lan Lan lives in Beijing.

IN MY VILLAGE

In my village, time runs swift.
One flock of birds takes wing
as another lands.
Wind tells the scarf
summer's coming.

Summer comes. Quail at noon
plunge through tall grass.
In the fields, foxtail
sees the wheat breed grain.
Whoever stops to cherish this
shall cherish me.

In my village
candlelight saves its window for a serenade.
Through the fragrance of roses,
go there. All night long,
the murmuring creek
restless in moonlight.

1992
translated by Diana Shi and George O'Connell

LEARNING: THE BEAUTIFUL, THE LUSTFUL

The beautiful, the lustful—
faint graze of an ambiguous glance,
throat of a pagoda tree grove, a leaf
filigreed by insects, (sweet mole
on the thigh), and
across the blanched breast of winter, the cry
of one sparrow.

The beautiful, the lustful—
at the blue shade of the axilla, a vanished path.
Into the furrows on the brow of a woman bearing grain
sifts a secret dust.
March, the fragrance of desire, calling
from spring's cave its filament of ants.

I love your poplar body, your lips
a starry, tender sky,
the kiss of the infinite:

—the beautiful, the lustful.

1995
translated by Diana Shi and George O'Connell

TRAIN, TRAIN

Dusk ships off white day. Windows fade
from the capital to the sullen twilight of north China.

From here to here.

On this great earth, roads gash poplar groves.
Thunder follows lightning
but our mouths are safely stopped.

The train crosses fields, pages of laboring feet erased.
We tremble, speak no more
of nodding sheep, the thick smoke of brick kilns.

Wheels plunge through night. From here
to here. Imperishable stars
attend the long cortège
stretched on the rails of our courage.

Train. Train. Beyond the headlines,
we shiver through numb countryside:
this dying man, hoist by his heels,
gazing from the sky.

2006–7

translated by Diana Shi and George O'Connell

Chen Dawei (Chan Tah Wei, b. 1969)

Born in Ipoh in southwestern Malaysia, Chen went to Taiwan in 1988 to attend the National Taiwan University, where he majored in Chinese. He went on to receive his MA degree from Soochow University and his doctorate from the National Taiwan Normal University in 2000. Currently, he is a professor and chairman of the Chinese Department at the National Taipei University. Chen started writing prose in 1989 and poetry in 1990. In addition to being a creative writer, he is a literary critic and editor.

Nanyang, or "South Sea," is a Chinese term designating the states to the south of China around the South China Sea. Wong Fei Hung (Huang Feihong in Mandarin, 1847–1925), in the poem "In Nanyang," was a legendary Chinese martial artist and physician who has been the subject of numerous films and television series. In "Departing with the Crane" a *suona* is a woodwind instrument that originated in Persia and was introduced into China in the third century.

IN NANYANG

In Nanyang   a savage place where history languishes in hunger
Storybooks, born with a long tongue,   cannot even fill
Half a page
Sit idly under a tree for ten years
All you'd see are herds of elephants and macaques stumbling down the
    mountain trail

Blank   content absolutely unbearable for durian
The shaman speaks a language
That confuses the Han Chinese   gesturing toward the mountain haze
As if a thunderstorm is brawling in his movement
Horror   is Borneo where the apes never stop howling
I remember the ancient stone axe
The stone axe remembers   the wind-dried skulls of three hundred years
Still hanging in the longhouse—

No trivial matter like a jug of wine   or an opium pipe
To stake claims to the land   you need the strength of a bear's paw
And penetrating speeches
I guess   they must have ancestors
As adept as Wong Fei Hung the kung fu master
Who secretly acquired the skills of a panther chameleon
Learned to cling to tall trees like ferns
And rode on flying spores   to kiss the soil under the chieftain's feet

In Southeast Asia   a group of Chinese pioneers overlooked in textbooks
Rode their dreams like horses   kicked aside the moon and the wind
And the protective fence of the old indigenous tongue
My irrepressible poem resembles wild grass shooting up throughout the night
Devouring the garden mound in deep sleep
Or more like a wolf   its purple fangs abstracted in oil paintings
Hurriedly I unload from my backpack
Rhetorical expressions   both mandatory and spare
And hand the rainforest over to roast over a slow fire till it emits an aroma . . .

Right here   a savage place that gave the brave men
A headache
I will rebuild the clubhouse   the *dim sum* restaurant
And the street known for terrifying sword fights
Wake up, O wake up   postcolonial *Sol* slumbering in English
Give me a little light   a hint of
The texture of the passing years and months that spare no one
For I am the storyteller who is three hundred years late
With loose front teeth
Trying hard to mimic an aging hero   shooing dogs away with swear words

Hey   don't take it too seriously
Who am I to make the eloquent three-inch-long tongue rot away?
In Southeast Asia   by all means activate the molar teeth of the epic
To chew on the image cluster that is an equal mix of muscle and tendon
Set off the arrowheads of poetry   to hunt for Java mouse deer
And precious ideas that flit across your mind
Please pour cold water on yourself
Pass me the lamp   give me an ironclad applause
My historical consciousness
Will soon blend into the tawny paunch of history with the python
Follow the hawk   to scissor and sew the sky's hundred years of solitude
Listen   It's the perspiration of the brave men
Responding to the tiger roar of the hundred thousand pores of mine   in the
     mountain woods—

Don't ever doubt me or the fine tip of my brush
Don't try to force your way in   The columbarium for brave men
Has already occupied half of the territory on my desk
I must stock up on tea and crackers for another sleepless night
Easy now   Chapters of the epic will soon unfold
In Southeast Asia   where history languishes in hunger

1998
translated by Yanwing Leung

DEPARTING WITH THE CRANE

First came the brass *suona*, followed by more
Suona   the soul-snatching clarion of Impermanence
Advancing in the opposing direction, wailing   I was told
Half of the old men in town
Had mouths sealed   to strangle back inauspicious last words
Like a puff of gray smoke the old men
Had departed with the crane
I armored my fear   like a Tiger tank
And drew a line of defense against Impermanence
Untroubled   Grandpa walked out

In a sharp Western-style suit and stood at the entrance to the alley
Saying the crane was on its way to pick him up
He could hear its warm wings in the distance
In my mother's condolences book he wrote
An auspicious message
In neat handwriting and simple words
I asked him what I should write in the obituary
He asked me what I would write in my own obituary

Grandpa turned to Grandma asking her to prepare a full breakfast for the
  next life
And complained the fabric of the burial suit was too coarse
As for the rest
The rest was consigned to the records
And the three medals conferred by the king
Mother understood his last words and ordered the military brass band to play
Grandpa nodded
And departed with the crane

Leaving behind the public square the polygonal emptiness
As the flames rose I recited
The Sutra of Great Compassion uncertain if it would help
I tried hard to constrain my sorrow
I compressed it affixed a stamp to it
And gave it to the dying old shopkeeper: Would you
Take this with you when you depart with the crane would you

2011
translated by Michelle Yeh and Frank Stewart

Chen Mie (Chi Tak Chan, b. 1969)

Chen Mie is the pen name of Chen Zhide, who was born and raised in Hong Kong. He received his BA degree in Chinese from Tunghai University in Taiwan and his MA and PhD degrees from Lingnan University. He was an associate professor at the Hong Kong University of Education and currently lives in Taipei. Chen Mie was a cofounder of the poetry journal *Breathe* in 1994 and has written extensively on Hong Kong poetry and film as well as on modern Chinese literature.

"The Ruined Pier" refers to Queen's Pier in Hong Kong. In September 2006 the Legislative Council announced that Queen's Pier and the adjacent Star Ferry Terminal would be demolished to make way for land reclamation and the construction of the Central–Wan Chai bypass. Public outrage erupted because many residents saw the pier as being a part of the city's collective memory and cultural heritage. Protests, sit-ins, and hunger strikes went on well into 2017 to no avail. The pier was demolished in February 2008.

LO-FI

It's just a darkened stairway, but for believers,
music will rise up from both sides, sounds drifting
like the light bulb, so dim it seems always ready to move from its spot
Is there really a light there? The stairwell's music is full of extraneous noises
A lo-fi sound system, but no one misses fidelity

Turn the corner and you're there. My home
Is in the same location on a different floor
A barking dog in front of the dark-green metal gate
and a blue-gray human form that hasn't moved yet
nor vanished. Is someone really there?

This is my pale-blue gate
My home, reclusive as a record player
Each time, before I even drop the needle
the record plays on its own, right up to where it starts skipping
the starting-stopping lyrics reveal their deeper meaning

If there were a storm indoors
it might halt this home's advance
The book in my hands is already finished before I've opened it
The newsman is already done reporting before the news happens
The sun has already risen before I lie down, and before I even put pen to paper

the poem is already full of "I," "me," what a bore
Turn up the old amplifier a little more, and a little more
I can hear new noises each time I replay the record
In the midst of massive degradation, only a tiny bit of the original remains,
noise slowly burying the sound that once seemed like all there was

Again, the spinning record returns to the beginning
It plays a distant song, almost inaudible
These rotting old things are still newer than new in one way
Do you really want to know what will happen in the next minute,
Do you really? Then drop the worn-down needle

Play something slow. There are tapes
that start off hissing before unspooling a dozen nights, each time
waiting for the next minute, copied from a copy
Listen to the end and then get some sleep, put out the light
Wind from the blank recording stirs the blinds

July 24, 2001
translated by Brian Skerratt

COMPULSIVE-SHOPPING SYNDROME

The mall escalator rises by semitones
escalating the fervid terror in our voices. Merchandise,
crowds. The torrential flow out of each shop
slows. Life
burns its own leaves.
The flame tree standing in a display case, moves.
Dredge out all the nothing, but there is still something
In debt to the world but still chasing the world for more

The mall escalator's semitones slide down
His project has only just launched. Everywhere
everywhere there is light you can own
Round a corner and there's a carousel
On the other side, someone is spinning cloying cotton candy
Behind a curtain, they're projecting a movie, winding smoke
Harsh light illuminates roads, cars, tall buildings
A real world

Commerce dances a slow triple meter, this world
spins in a circle once and then again
In debt to the crowd, but still chasing the crowd for more
In the mall built of semitones
he is the only one who feels elated and terrified
The crowds rise and plummet along with the escalator. Everywhere
everywhere they arc lining up for a wedding, but it looks like a funeral
grand and deserted, fervid and isolated
Now it slows, solidifies
Only he returns to his own speed
Dredging out new nothings, but there is still something
In debt to the world but still chasing the world for more

July 20, 2003
translated by Brian Skerratt

THE RUINED PIER

Is it life or the world that beats with eternal patience
against our hearts' sturdy, secluded pier?
The history bared by the receding tide is a deeper scar
The high tide advances and we are made to withdraw
Who is it, leaping into the sea with a splash?
Who is visiting those lost souls in sunken ships?

Seawater freezes the flow of time. Only the ocean swimmers surge up,
swimming over from that equally surging era. In the distance, I can see
the salty wind carry them to that indistinct pier.
They are methodically changing the queen's name, replacing it with their own
The swimmer coming ashore at the pier is soaked,
but the pier is about to dry up, a bit of the harbor has evaporated,
packaged as distilled water, sold wholesale or retail

In the end, the seawater really froze the flow of time,
passing through the mall before landing at the pier.
I can only see the plaza full of bronze statues of swimmers, statues of the willing
and statues of the coerced, standing like gravestones.
A grounded boat, moored at the waterless bank.
The city withers from a self-identified desert, into an actual desert

Will the grains of sand float on the sea, to gather on the shore?
Children will shape them into sandcastles,
utopias constructed of water and sand.
What memories? What islands of collective association?
Our accumulated life of ten years—like the winners
counted down again and again on the medal podium,
like toy blocks, like history that elapses from the bottom up—
is pushed over with a mere tap.

2007
translated by Brian Skerratt

Fang Wenshan (Vincent Fang, b. 1969)

Born into a blue-collar Hakka family in Hualian, Taiwan, Fang was known for
his essays even as a schoolboy. After graduating from a vocational school, he held
a number of menial jobs while writing song lyrics. In 1999 he was discovered by
the singer, producer, and TV show host Wu Zongxian, who introduced him to
Jay Chou. The initial collaboration with Chou cemented a partnership that has
resulted in many megahits and music awards. Fang draws on classical Chinese

culture—poetry, fiction, history, even medical treatises—for inspiration for his lyrics and has almost single-handedly created the "Chinese style" in pop music, which has swept the Chinese-speaking world. Since 2013 Fang has organized an annual festival that celebrates Han culture—mainly through traditional apparel and rituals—in the ancient town Xitang, Zhejiang. With hundreds of songs to his credit, Fang is also the author of eight books, a film director, and an actor.

JASMINE ORANGE

Sparrows chitchat on the power lines outside my window
You say this sentence makes you feel like summer is here
The pencil in my hand moves back and forth on the paper
With a few lines I describe what it is that you mean to me.

You and the kitten are both eager to sample the Pacific saury
How we rediscover the taste of first love this way
The warm sunshine feels like a newly picked strawberry
But you say you can't bring yourself to eat such a feeling

Rain all night long, my love overflows like rainwater
Falling leaves in the yard pile up like my thoughts of you
A few busybodies cannot cool my passion
You appear on every page of my poems

Rain all night long, my love overflows like rainwater
Butterflies by the windowsill flutter like beautiful verses
So I keep on writing
My undying love into the last stanza
 Your belief in me is the only thing that matters

The laden ears of rice bring happiness to the season
And your cheeks are like tomatoes ripening in the field
Out of the blue you say orange jasmine is a beautiful title
But this moment all I want is to kiss your willful mouth

Rain all night long, my love overflows like rainwater
Falling leaves in the yard pile high like my thoughts of you
A few busybodies cannot cool my passion
You appear on every page of my poems

Rain all night long, my love overflows like rainwater
Butterflies by the windowsill flutter like beautiful verses
So I keep on writing
My undying love into the last stanza
Your belief in me is the only thing that matters

2004
translated by Michelle Yeh and Frank Stewart

END THE WAR: AN ELEGY FOR THE FALLEN

Light   weightless as paper
Light   scattered on the floor
Light   in the fading applause panics
She sings of   unbearable wounds
A script for the stage   puts on the last performance
And all the villagers in their seats
Watch quietly   how time has abandoned the theater
Battle fires have sullied   her gleaming teardrops
Who in the wind   is clamoring for sweets
From the beginning of the tale the dust on the lens has blocked the sunlight
Biang!

Fear imprinted on the children's faces
Wheat fields bend toward the tanks rolling by
The shape of a dandelion   drifting away
On a flight   of despair
All she sings   all she wants
Is this elegy   to put an end to war

In the wicked night sky candles burn   at the break of dawn fighting stops
An elegy sung across a thousand miles   no more famine in her hometown
Innocence stumbles   on this road
She is cut by silver grass

What is the shape   of hope in the eyes of the children
When they wake up will there be bread   and a bowl of hot soup for breakfast
Farmers have lost their land and villages to flames   now they pick up a gun at
    last
But slowly she has gotten used to letting go of resistance

What is the shape   of hope in the eyes of the children
Are there swings in the playground   candies in the pockets
Bayonets are shined by hatred   they ravage in a faraway place
But she smiles a faint smile and does not panic

Fear imprinted on the children's faces
Wheat fields bend toward the tanks rolling by
The shape of a dandelion   drifting away
On a flight   of despair
All she sings   all she wants
Is this elegy to put an end to war

2004
translated by Michelle Yeh and Frank Stewart

BLUE-AND-WHITE PORCELAIN

On the porcelain vase the brush outlines a shape in shades from dark to pale
    The painted peony reminds me of your freshly made-up face
Sandalwood scent wafts through the window, I know what is on your mind
    Halfway finished, a brush pauses over rice paper
Porcelain glaze applied to the portrait of a lady, her aura to be treasured by a
    connoisseur
    Sweetly you break into a smile like a flower bud about to open
Your beauty floats in the air
    To a place beyond my reach

The blue sky awaits the misty rain, and I am waiting for you
Ribbons of fragrance rise, a thousand miles beyond the river
On the bottom of the vase, the Han script evokes the grace of an ancient dynasty
  My signature foreshadows our encounter

The blue sky awaits the misty rain, and I am waiting for you
Gathering up the moonlight, a hazy rendering of the ending
Like the blue-and-white porcelain passed down for ages absorbed in its own
 beauty
  Your eyes are smiling

A leaping carp below blue flowers on a white background
  I imitate the Song dynasty style all the while thinking of you
You hide yourself in the secret of a thousand-year-old kiln
  Delicate like an embroidery needle falling to the floor
Outside the curtain the plantain tree flirts with the rain, the door knocker flirts
 with verdigris
  I pass through the small town south of the Yangzi to flirt with you
In the splash-ink landscape painting
  You recede into the depths of dark ink

The blue sky awaits the misty rain, and I am waiting for you
Ribbons of fragrance rise, a thousand miles beyond the river
On the bottom of the vase, the Han script evokes the grace of an ancient dynasty
  My signature foreshadows our encounter

The blue sky awaits the misty rain, and I am waiting for you
Gathering up the moonlight, a hazy rendering of the ending
Like the blue-and-white porcelain passed down for ages absorbed in its own
 beauty
  Your eyes are smiling

2007
translated by Michelle Yeh and Frank Stewart

Yinni (b. 1969)

Yinni, literally meaning "Hidden," is the pen name of Xu Guifang, who is a native of Zhanghua in Central Taiwan. She graduated from Gaoxiong Business School and for years ran a bookstore in Tamsui, a suburb of Taipei, which specialized in books in the humanities and was frequented by writers and literature lovers.

EARTH GOD AND POETRY

An Earth God shrine no bigger than a grave, hidden behind the houses that line an alleyway of stone stairs. It stands peacefully, the fragrance of pure incense rising from it, with two red candles burning year-round. On the tiny altar, sometimes offerings of chocolate candy bars, Want Want rice crackers, or fresh flowers.

Each time I take the shortcut that passes by it, the little shrine comforts me, especially as a few steps away are crowds of unruly tourists, attracted by karaoke bars and food stands that cater to them with nauseating snacks, flavorless, impossible to swallow.

Having lived near the shrine for a few years, I often stop to pay it a visit. Though I am not a religious person, I get a feeling of awe every time. For some reason, I believe the god watches over the residents, cats, and rivers in the area. I talk to the god silently from inside my heart, sometimes just a few pleasantries, but more often I sigh, "Do you know how miserable I am . . ." I have been pressuring the Earth God by pouring out my complaints, even though I have never actually worshipped nor left any offering, not even a single candy.

There were three times when I could not stop myself from asking to be granted a wish. But all three times I regretted it right away and pleaded to take my wishes back.

The first time, I prayed for the Earth God to give up the shrine's plot so that the bookstore nearby wouldn't have to close. But the moment I made the wish in my heart, I realized it was the wrong thing to do. So I quickly repealed it: "Forget it, if it's going to close, let it. Just pretend I didn't say anything."

The second time, I prayed that the Earth God make my sick kitty well again.
But the moment I made the wish, doubt arose in me: since when did I become
a supporter of longevity? So I revoked that wish right away.

The third time, I prayed for the Earth God to let me write truly good poetry.
But the moment the wish entered my mind, I felt chills run up my spine!
I knew all too well that every good poem is born out of something bad:
humiliation, rage, despair, inescapable sorrow, fierce pain, unbreakable shackles
. . . Is that what I am praying for? Oh, forget it, forget it, let it be! In the end I
realized that I was the kind of person who could not pray for anything.

The only reason that I keep praying to poetry is because it has never granted my
wish.

2010

translated by Michelle Yeh and Frank Stewart

THE EDGE OF BEAUTY

Today I noticed something
No matter what it is, the edge of anything
is beautiful

The edge of clouds
is where rolling white waves end

The edge of a mountain
is a fuzzy green ridge
meeting the blue sky

The edge of an expanse of redwood trees
is a swamp with a cast of giant, claw-waving crabs
and on the clacking edge of that
is the origin of a river
the billowing of another leaf vein

As for the edge of a waterfowl's wingspan
it is the wind

The edge of an asphalt road eroded by time
is a patch of beautiful oxalis

As for me?
I always walk along a beautiful edge
with no intention of being on the inside

May 18, 2015
translated by Michelle Yeh and Frank Stewart

Zhu Zhu (b. 1969)

Born in Yangzhou, Jiangsu, Zhu graduated in 1991 from the East China University
of Political Science and Law. In October 1998, after working in the field of law and
teaching law for several years, he resigned to devote himself to art and poetry. He
has since been working as a curator. In 1986, as a senior in high school, Zhu read
the Czech poet Jaroslav Seifert and became interested in modern poetry. While
a freshman in college, in 1987, he founded the poetry club Cold Landscape. He
published his first book of poetry in 1994. In addition to poetry, he has published
prose and books on contemporary Chinese art.

Duolun Road, formerly Darroch Road, was named after the British missionary
John Darroch. It is a historic street in Hongkou District in Shanghai. Lu Xun
lived nearby in 1927–30; the League of Leftwing Writers, which existed from
1930 to 1935, also held meetings here. Kollwitz refers to Käthe Kollwitz, a Ger-
man painter, printmaker, and sculptor of the late nineteenth and early twentieth
centuries. Beardsley refers to Aubrey Vincent Beardsley, a nineteenth-century
English illustrator and author whose ink drawings were influenced by Japanese
woodcuts. Xianglinsao, literally "Sister-in-Law Xianglin," is a tragic character in
Lu Xun's short story "Benediction." Twice widowed, she lost her little son to a
wolf and was kicked out of her home for her "sins"; she died from hunger and
cold. Lu Xun attended Sendai Medical School in Japan in 1904–6. Bruno refers

to Giordano Bruno, a sixteenth-century Italian Dominican friar, philosopher, mathematician, and poet.

In "South-of-Yangzi, a Republic" Liu Rushi was a famous seventeenth-century courtesan known for her talent in poetry and painting. She often dressed as a man and befriended some of the leading literati of her time. After the Manchus overthrew the Ming dynasty, in 1644, she remained loyal to the former regime even though her husband, Qian Qianyi, a highly respected scholar, had surrendered. After Qian's death in 1664, Liu took her own life. Zhaojun is Wang Zhaojun (ca. 51–ca. 15 BCE), a beautiful lady in the Eastern Han court who was married to the chieftain of Huns as a form of peacemaking. A *pipa* is a four-string musical instrument.

In "Duolun Road," "Tune of Backyard Flowers" is an ancient allusion to the decline of a dynasty. In "New Jersey on the Moon" *Mérimée* refers to Prosper Mérimée, a nineteenth-century French writer of the Romantic movement and a pioneer of the novella. *Delacroix* refers to Ferdinand Victor Eugène Delacroix, a French painter and the leader of the French Romantic School in the nineteenth century.

SOUTH-OF-YANGZI, A REPUBLIC

—Before the grave of Liu Rushi

I.

The tailor brings in the vermillion cloak,
which has a snow-white turned-out collar of fleece. The hatter
brings in a leather rain hat. The cobbler brings in high boots.
Out the door, a night-black horse is already saddled—

I am dressed in my Sunday best, sitting in the mirror, like
a vivacious young lady about to take the stage, in the role of Zhaojun,
the hostage who crossed the border, the bride to political copulation
who won her country a moment of breath.

Now early summer, snow and ice are buried in the cellar,
locust blossoms of bygone years have been made into honey.
This moment the city is quiet, all its gates shut tight,
only the river's rolling tide broadcasts hoof beats from the other bank.

I am dressed in my Sunday best, dressed as a literary allusion,
blending allure with parable. I want to cross the city.
I want to climb its walls. I want to ride horseback to the riverfront
to rouse our demoralized troops.

II.

I love watching those young soldiers
with their downy lips. The look in their eyes
shy yet direct, their hemming and hawing desires bob
alongside their large Adam's apples, above their blood-swelled chests.

They are far better than these holdovers around me,
these complaining ladies who pass for honorable men,
rubbing heavenly beads to tally their own loss and gain,
before the enemy, as in bed, soon pulling back from the fray.

Alas, I feel repressed,
like the long dissatisfied wife in the arms
of an old warden, who enters the walled yard on some made-up pretense
and harvests pleasures from the inmates' hungry gazes.

But deep in my heart there is
an obscure illusion that I dare not speak of,
like when the women of Boulogne eagerly waited to be conquered.
Alas, decadent life—it needs a hard thrust from the outside.

III.

At dusk I come home, by the light of a lamp with a trimmed wick
I use smart, delicate words
to rebuild the godly pagoda of humanism
on the reflection of an edifice in the water.

Once again, pride and tranquility
ripple through my heart and I believe
there is a depth that cannot be conquered. It is like
a vagina that can swallow even the most virile men.

I believe that every deep wound and every hard blow
is a passing whirlwind, and afterward
peach flowers still waver in the clear midair,
a pond reflects the vast sky, the sound of the *pipa* rumbles from deep alleys.

2010
translated by Dong Li

DUOLUN ROAD

Under a sky cold and gray like a clamshell
are rows of old redbrick buildings. By the street corner,
in front of a café that shows silent films,
a female model wears a cheongsam and poses
before a lens for the next month's cover—
often this city feels the need to return to that time.

There was a small building on the nearby block
that still looks full of smoke and coughs . . .
on a large motley table by the window, he
used a scalpel-like nib, to open
old China's chest, to check its liver and gallbladder,
its lungs, its stomach and respiratory tract—

then he washed his hands, went downstairs and accepted
the reverent gaze of his young wife and disciples;
during dinner he attacked his peers and patients,
attacked all those frail, maudlin creatures. He planned
to revive the nation's woodcut business on his own
and demanded that they produce works just like Kollwitz's . . .
(in private he liked Beardsley).

He also attacked the surrounding foreign concessions.
Lipstick-wearing neon lights engulfed country moneybags
who came to taste foreign titillations; business ladies
in cheongsam and "Tune of Backyard Flowers"
played in a jazz style were everywhere. Decibels
of amusement overshadowed Xianglin Sao's sobs,
revolutionary speeches and approaching gunshots.

Cold, stiff, his voice pointed out
every organ, every nerve, and every imminent death
of hope, stating that the entire old continent
was a burning iron house, was a
lone island beset by plagues and tsunami;
don't wake anybody up,
there's no escape . . .

he should have been glad that he had not survived
into the latter half of the century, for what awaited him
was *either shut up or go to jail*, no, even if his mouth
had been shut, he could not have escaped prison, and
together with those he never intended to forgive,
to be denounced and insulted . . . his

combative days were no more than a game,
when he realized his flaws, it would have been too late—
in the face of shared fate, apologies were of little use.
Had he survived, it would have been in the deep
of a living hell where tongues were ripped out, he would have borne
the pain of ribs being kicked, cleaned toilets with a hunchback; but

perhaps he would still never forgive anyone,
because to the very end he could not emerge from that day—
when those slides were shown during the anatomy lesson
at Sendai Medical School, from that day on, he felt himself
like Giordano Bruno thrown to death on a pyre, life's flesh destroyed,
morals flying straight up, like a vulture chasing after the rancid;
there was nothing his charred eyes could still see.

2010

translated by Dong Li

SEPTEMBER, MADRID

I.

Peaceful days, like an olive orchard
Spreading across the low hills, no
Skyscrapers, hardly a speck of pollution,
And no nouveau riche neighbors;
Shop doors stand unopened in shaded alleyways,
Guitar music accompanies a long-winded lunch.
A paean to a military campaign lies closed on the shelf,
The revolution is over, the king is still there,
Over the rooftops statues of new heroes stand in file.
Blood-thirsty instincts flare up like fireworks
Turn into hurrahs for weekend bullfights and soccer;
In the dry air under the azure sky, kisses are flung out
like sparks, and settle slowly
Onto the wide lawn as pillowy as fresh flowers.

II.

Standing in the cool shade of the crowded train station,
Suddenly I am weary of traveling and just want to stay,
Want to switch on a table lamp with a green shade
In a small apartment; shirts hanging up to dry on the balcony,
Their moisture evaporating like a manic episode; the roads I've traveled

Have become silky-white contrails in the sky.
Kindnesses can finally be collected little by little,
And exchanged with other people for basic dignity . . .
Make all things from the past cross the Atlantic to find me,
For I love the beach at low tide more than the concerns of the present.
Even if self-reproach makes me a deserter, even if my regret is like
That of a young girl who has married an old widower, to return
Would be exile.

2012
translated by Michelle Yeh and Frank Stewart

NEW JERSEY ON THE MOON

—to L.Z.

This is your tree, river, lawn,
your big house, your America.
This is your life on another planet,
you slow down the car to lead me through the foothills,
like a documentary of private life on the big screen.

Prints by the Impressionists hang on the living room wall,
your daughter's toys piled high on the floor.
When your husband commutes to Manhattan during the day
and your child to kindergarten, the streets fall silent
except for conversations between vacuum and lawn mower.
On the treadmill, like a toy train
on its oval track, you go around and around . . .

here I am surprised by a sense of strangeness,
not that you have already changed your nationality
or become someone's wife. I am
surprised that your wanderings have so soon come to an end—
the happy land of our youthful dreams
already abbreviated into a comfortable cage,

and on the thick velvet couch,
once we speak of China, your mouth curls in a smirk.

I am saddened that you have missed an epic change in time,
a myth of time upended amid reality;
every one of your years here
is a day that we have spent back home.
At twilight, I return to the hotel in Queens,
put my coat on the back of the chair. Before my eyes,
that wild girl floats by, loving
freedom more than Mérimée's Carmen, walking
among the marchers in a parade, like a goddess painted by Delacroix

. . . memory retains nothing but the kite's spool.
I know I can no longer take you home,
even blessings seem unnecessary.
No one to entrust a mission to, deep in the night,
I dream of myself one step over the Pacific,
returned to fire-bright, smoke-thick battlefields,
loading my crossbow and shooting down those toxic suns.

2014
translated by Dong Li

Jiang Hao (b. 1971)

Born in Chongqing, Sichuan, Jiang graduated from the History Department at
Southwest Normal University in 1992. He has worked as a newspaper reporter,
editor, university lecturer, and book designer in Beijing, Chengdu, Hainan, and
Ürümqi. He has been living in Hainan since 2002.

JULY 19, COMPOSED ON THE WAY
TO FIVE FINGER MOUNTAIN

1.

The car is still too slow.
The mountains shifting in the distance.

May a corner of this mountain,
a leaf of this tree, be brought to your desk.

Your clothes are covering you up again.

2.

How many towns have we driven past?
There's no need to tell this tree by the wayside.

It will send the car's exhaust to a valley far away.
The dust settles thickest on the leaves near us.

Before I arrived,
it was already standing here.

July 19, 2002
translated by Chenxin Jiang

WHAT SHAPE IS THE SEA

Every time you ask me what shape the sea is,
I should bring you two bags of seawater.
This is the shape the sea is, like a pair of eyes:
or like the shape of the sea that eyes can see.
The way you touch them, it's like you're brushing away two burning tears.
That's the shape the sea is too. Its transparency
comes from the same deeper soul.

Even if we pour both bags into one, that doesn't change
the sea's breadth. They're still fresh,
as if two anti-fish could swim out any minute.
You use its flour-like fine sand
to temper bread, and that's the shape the sea is too.
Before you can cut it open with a sail,
it's already departing like a vanishing steamship.
The pair of plastic bags left on the table
are also the shape of the sea. They're becoming flatter,
like the tide slowly receding from the beach.
When the real tide recedes,
the salt it proffers is also the shape the sea is.
You don't believe me? I should bring you a bag of water,
a bag of sand. This, too, is the shape the sea is.
You agree, disagree, but don't agree,
don't disagree? You can conduct your own repeated experiments. It's your shape
    too. But you say,
"I'm just my own shape."

October 30, 2003
translated by Chenxin Jiang

Duo Yu (b. 1973)

Duo Yu is the pen name of Gao Zhaoliang, who was born in Shan County, Shandong, and graduated from Beijing Normal University with a major in Chinese. In 2000 he was a cofounder of the Lower Body movement, which promoted explicit depictions of vulgarity and sexuality in everyday life. Currently, he lives in Tianjin.

In "Poetry and Life" the poet writes of the Ili River, which is in the Xinjiang Uighur Autonomous Region in northwestern China and southeastern Kazakhstan.

POETRY AND LIFE

In the starry sky overhead the chess pieces are now arranged
underfoot the Ili River flows day and night
the wine cups are now in disarray, we are discussing harsh reality
and the impossible future, seems there's no path
to follow, but life persists in passing year by year
and that's just fine, even despite the helplessness
after all, there's still poetry, carrying us into nothing
he says he's too busy with his livelihood and can't enter poems
not me, because I have lived so long inside poems
that I can't enter life—this is
what makes us different, but it's hard to say who's right
perhaps whatever doesn't belong to poetry is what rouses love
what isn't love fills out our lives. . . .
we're silent, the moonlight spilling over the Ili River.

2017
translated by Nick Admussen

SILENT KNOWLEDGE

At nightfall, I invite the god of wine
to sit with me before the window
to watch a netherworld of night sky rise up out of the neon
and talk through the thoughts the setting sun brings
after a moment of sweet passion
the sound of sleepy midnight piss
demonstrates that we are still in the human world
but when comparing a life among the people
to life in the world of one person
what is the difference?
I think of the clear, bottomless ideas
conceived among the chatter of the people
thanks to the billowing flags, I recognize the storm
but thanks to what silent knowledge

can I understand you—
to see you as completely unforeshadowed?
On earth's chessboard, there is killing in all directions
the starry sky is vast, leaves me unable to reply.

2017
translated by Nick Admussen

EVERYTHING IS UNDER CONSTRUCTION

I've seen the sun sink, totter, almost collapse
the dusk of an era approaching
metaphors for night visible anywhere you look
the songs of the night birds
grieving for this deaf and mute world
and the spirits of those who persevere
are still trapped in the blue glow of early morning . . .
all confidence is well on its way to ruin
truth only descends when nobody's around
you teach us
we should be like a puddle of sludge
a powerless, oh a shame-faced puddle
fermenting spiritual structures of turmoil and unrest
you teach us
to go to all our real relationships and actualize love
you can't love god once and for all
everything is under construction . . .

2017
translated by Nick Admussen

Wang Ao (b. 1976)

Born in Qingdao, Shandong, Wang Ao received his BA degree in Chinese from Peking University and went on to receive his MA degree in comparative literature from the Washington University in St. Louis and his PhD degree in Chinese literature from Yale University. He is currently associate professor in the Department of East Asian Studies at Wesleyan University. Wang started writing poetry when he was an undergraduate student. In addition to poetry, he has published Chinese translations of English poetry and Harold Bloom's *The Art of Reading Poetry*.

THE CRABS I ONCE LOVED

My first time out at sea
I was only half as tall as I am now
my uncle strapped a navy cap on my head
and dove into the water, following the fish
to Columbia, I lost him
and his guidance, and soon ran free
the flames of the sea are softer than silk
there were flashes of light, from my heart spinning in the pressure
a crab came to strike up a conversation, and he told me something
thousands of years ago, the world's crabs migrated to dry land, it was a slow
    process
they weren't in a hurry, they came and left with the tides, and only when the sea
advanced would they take a few small steps, he told me he loved me and hoped
    we could
share these air bubbles, go up on shore, onto a secret rocky wharf
smiling, I shook hands with a few thousand crabs, I wanted to be like them
grow bones outside my skin, let the sun replenish the calcium of my armor
    whenever I felt weak
we started to climb
               the back of Mount Lao was covered with a film of dark green
we set its granite veins trembling with our arms and claws

when I stood naked on the mountaintop, I saw the moon being clamped by a
    shadow
the evening dripped and they fell silent, climbing onto my body, so my blood
    delicately oozed

2001
translated by Eleanor Goodman

QUATRAIN 1

I sit in a rocking chair praising the demons of drink
they are buried somewhere deep in the air
like an empty bottle I inhale

the familiar groundwater, hoping time will quickly mineralize, bring back
    yesterday's grapes

2001
translated by Eleanor Goodman

QUATRAIN 2

Why, astrologer, when you look
into my eyes, it seems they're the world's wheels inside wheels, why

does life have regret, and quatrains have life, yet the mighty carpenter
belongs to the mighty nail; why give me a cruel answer?

2005
translated by Eleanor Goodman

QUATRAIN 3

What woke us afterward, what made us take ten or twenty years
to dry off in the wind and sun, were those few lines splintering like shark-bitten
  vertebrae

that we use to describe life and death undulating black-white like dolphins, and
  how the world
tumbles into a speck of our eyes, trusting that those calling for help control
  some small probability

2010
translated by Eleanor Goodman

QUATRAIN 4

After the disaster children lay on the ground
draped in a giant moth, we don't want to remember

how that moth plummeted to transform into sand
and suspicious powder, opening its eyes now and then to regard us

2020
translated by Eleanor Goodman

Lin Wanyu (b. 1977)

A native of Taizhong in Central Taiwan, Lin studied nutrition at Taipei Medical
University and theater at Taipei National University of the Arts. She started
writing poetry at the age of twenty and has won numerous awards. Besides poetry,
she also writes prose and song lyrics.

THE SPEED OF BLOSSOMING

I bought a bouquet of lilies
that hadn't yet opened
and gave them to you on the night you departed

"They will open in another week."
You said nothing and, neither pleased nor not-pleased
accepted my budding flowers

A week from now
in your room
the flowers will unfold with the purest, sweetest scent
and you will remember
that such pleasure
was a gift from me

(Will it be like that? Will you remember?)
When it comes to you and me
the only thing in my power
is the speed of that blossoming, nothing more

2013
translated by Michelle Yeh and Frank Stewart

UNPRINCIPLED

Deep in my heart I love two or three poems
but I cannot say their titles out loud
for fear that if I do
the poems that I don't mention will be sad
Deep in my heart I love a certain person
but I cannot proudly say his name out loud
for fear that if I do
those I have not loved will be unhappy

I have colorful sweets in my pocket I could give away
but I can't show them
because inevitably
inevitably
those who don't get sweets
would rush at my pocket
and rip my pocket to shreds
and so . . . I read my poems secretly
and I love someone in secret
and I secretly clutch the sweets in my hand
even though they are gradually
gradually melting
I possess the sweets
I am losing the sweets

2016
translated by Michelle Yeh and Frank Stewart

Ye Mimi (b. 1980)

Ye Mimi, the pen name of Lin Qiaoxiang, was born into a Hakka family in Jiayi in South Taiwan. She received her BA degree in Chinese literature, her MFA in creative writing, and her MA in Chinese literature from the National Dong Hwa University in Hualian. While in graduate school, in 2005, she also made her first film. She went on to receive another MFA degree in film, video, and new media from the Art Institute of Chicago in 2009. Ye Mimi published her first book of poetry in 2004. In addition to poetry, she has created flash fictions, short films, poetry films, and photography. She was invited to the Poetry International Festival Rotterdam in 2007 and has been a writer-in-residence in France, Taiwan, and the United States. Since 2017 she has been developing a project called Poetry Tarot Spiritual Consultation, which combines Tarot cards with original poems and photographs. She acknowledges the influence of Jane Roberts, the twentieth-century American poet, psychic, and New Age philosopher who popularized the notion of "channeling" and the belief that all creativity is a form of play.

HIS DAYS GO BY THE WAY HER YEARS

He smells like bottled root beer
her pie in the sky allays his hunger and his days go by the way her years
he is a lonely plural
her door latch is sour or sore
the au contraire of plentiful is he
(won't they help her build her tower of basil?)
she hairs his chest he heartens her sweetheart
one day every living soul will turn to soil
he ocean fleets a vessel
she mountain passes a night
Wednesday likes the rain
by rain were they woven into angelfish
eyes unfolded into riddles
yet he steals beneath her iron skin
and leaning on the chairback of time
gradually invents a kind of knock

the more he is the sun the more she is the moon

2005
translated by Steve Bradbury

THE MORE CAR THE MORE FAR

She amasses all manner of colored jars, cucumber marinade of varying vintage.
Punctually waters the flowers with Sunday's froth. In this house there is a cow,
a man and a stone for grinding ink. Often strikes a slanted line across the yard.
Now and then capers across some Cheshire cats without really meaning to.
Explosions are all one to her, even if there's barking in the pot. Likes to write
larvae-like words, larva by larva. In her belly she raises a saucer of baby debris, as
brilliant as marbles.
One day they drag a railroad track over for her, teach her how to belch black
smoke from her fontanelles.

So then she cars up. Facing the track, facing the eaves.
I am precise. I am naughty. I am gravity.
She sings.
How can we avoid being bushed?
Who is at the boundary of whom?
She sings.

As she drives by below the windowsill, her man is at the window watching her.
Hand grasping an alternating current.
He makes a long face, like a shipping container full of cinnamon gone stale.
Her cow is at the window watching her. Her inkstone is at the window watching her.
They're so perplexed their eyes ooze drops of milk of ink.
Drip drop ticktock.

Solitude is somewhat sweeter than water.
Fish are crunchier on the outside, softer in the middle than the sea.
From this day henceforth I will go forth and wilderness the wilderness.
She sang.

The more car she is the more far.

2008
translated by Steve Bradbury

TWO NIGHTS NINE SECRETS—FOR TURNING TWENTY-NINE

The pace of her escape slackens   as she continues to compose her crummy
     poetry
drinking her scalding tea   rebuffing tough subjects
eyes are Post-It notes   at times aglow at times ablack
at times they will withdraw like a flood
after all these years   she still prefers the window seat
in scenery there's sea there's snow   there are people there are timeworn streets
and gentle dromedaries on the wing

When dark clouds gather   she describes herself like this:
Fun-loving with a big carbon footprint. The hotter it gets the greater the
  stability. The colder it gets the more in bloom.
In any case she can become a lamp   a tree
an oven or a crossword puzzle
no matter what   it's simply a question of shape   she said.

She experiences some intrinsic risk-taking
her heart often switches its power source
what is dreamed of exceeds what is seen   and words, letters, characters are
  music
mostly   of course   she hides inside the body of a child

and with a child's height takes the measure of the world

2009
translated by Steve Bradbury

Zheng Xiaoqiong (b. 1980)

Born into a poor farmer's family in Nanchong, Sichuan, Zheng graduated from
Nanchong Health School and worked as a nurse at a village clinic for several
months. In 2001 she went to Dongguan, Guangdong, where she worked on an
assembly line for two years, before being promoted to the positions of clerk and
sales representative of metal hardware. Since 2007 she has become the most famous
writer of migrant workers' poetry (*dagong shige*), which is written by young men
and women who leave their homes in rural areas to work in factories under dra-
conian conditions.

   "In Middle-Aged Prostitutes" *kuai* is the Chinese equivalent of *dollar*.

TRAIN

My body contains a vast open plain, a train
travels across it, but autumn is in its deep
desolate twilight, and I follow the train's
meandering path, planting a thousand hawthorn trees in the wilderness
their white crowns and fiery fruit, permeated with humanity
and tranquility, I know fate is like an endless mountain range, rivers, fields
or a winding river, they wriggle low behind the train
the mountain ranges are covered with trees in ragged clothes, their sparse
     unreal shadows
moving with the train, one tree, two trees . . . it stops on the gray indistinct plain
I say to the trees, that is my friend, my dear one

2006
translated by Eleanor Goodman

DRAMA

She extracts a wide wilderness from her body
burying disease and ill temper, planting glimmering words
steadfast, calm, believing, setting up inside her body
a high-powered machine, it bores into time
eating through her youth and enthusiasm, and it produces
her fake fat life, this sorrow
or depression from being trapped, and it soaks her
in fabricated pain, while others imagine her life
her shabby clothes, like a tragedy
from antiquity, but really her days are ordinary though difficult
each tiny interior holds a silent soul
she writes poetry on the machinery that is Chinese, this ancient
but fictitious carrier. She places herself
at a workstation along the assembly line, employee number
replacing her name and gender, and with that machine she grinds and cuts
her heart full of love and complaint, some even think

you can find the depth of the era in these little moods
but she hides inside her thin body, using up all
of her love for herself, these landscapes, these rivers and eras
these battles, capital, scenery, to her
they mean less than a love affair, she will get used to
twelve-hour workdays, clocking in, and exhaustion
cutting out a single skinny life on the revolving machine
using Chinese to record her bloated heart and rage
more often, she stands at the window of some hardware factory
her back on her vast country, the dim dirty streetlamps
collecting her heart's loneliness with a machine

2007
translated by Eleanor Goodman

MIDDLE-AGED PROSTITUTES

Low tiled houses of the urban village gloomy humid light
filthy mildewed sewers they sit in the doorways
knitting sweaters chatting sizing up the men coming and going
their eye shadow and rouge can't hide their age
thirty or older in the chaotic urban village
they talk about their business of the flesh and their customers
thirty kuai twenty kuai occasionally a customer
who pays fifty they discuss the clothes they're holding
their patterns and colors how they'll knit something for their
parents in distant Sichuan or send the finished pieces
to a distant son their movements are agile
sometimes they'll discuss another girl working nearby who's been arrested
and fined four thousand kuai they say each month they give three hundred kuai
to an insider although this so-called protection fee
amounts to ten transactions they say
it's like being crushed ten times by a ghost although this ghost
is enormous but empty they lose out
I imagine their current lives and their former lives
and their future lives as though under the sweaters they're knitting

is a mother's heart a wife's heart and
a daughter's heart they sigh in the dark and
moan helplessly after shutting the door seen from behind they are
a bunch of mothers sitting in a doorway knitting sweaters these
middle-aged prostitutes with eyes like this country's face
just as uncertain turning everyone hazy together

2010

translated by Eleanor Goodman

Glossary

Personal names, titles of poems, and other terms are given in traditional Chinese characters if they are associated with traditional China, pre-1949 mainland China, Taiwan, Hong Kong, and Southeast Asia. Simplified characters are used for poets, titles of poems, and other terms associated with the People's Republic of China.

"Abandoned Woman, The" 棄婦
"Absolute Aesthetics Association, The" 绝对审美协会
"Accessory to the Crime" 从犯
"Adagio" 慢板
"After the Sleigh Incident" 雪橇事件之后
Ai Qing 艾青
"Aloneland" 孤獨國
Amang 阿芒
"American Women's Magazines" 美国妇女杂志
Analects, The 論語
"Andante Cantabile" 如歌的行板
"Angels" 天使
"Answer, The" 回答
Anti-Rightist Campaign 反右运动
Anti-Bourgeois Liberalization campaign 反对资产阶级自由化
Anti-Spiritual Pollution campaign 清除精神污染运动
"as for great wild goose pagoda" 有关大雁塔
"Ashes Primer" 骨灰学入门
"At the Beginning" 最初
"Atayal Tribe" 卑亞南蕃社
"Autumn" (Haizi) 秋
"Autumn" (He Qifang) 秋天
"Autumn in September" 秋九月
"Autumn Night" 秋夜

Ba Jin 巴金
"Baby Girl" 女婴

"Baby Girl in My Family, The" 我家裡的小女孩
Bai Hua 柏桦
Bai Juyi 白居易
Baihuashi 白話詩
Bai Qiu 白萩
Bamboo Hat Poetry Society 笠詩社
"Beast" 野兽
"Because of the Wind" 因為風的緣故
"Beggars" 乞求者
Bei Dao 北岛
"Benediction" 祝福
Bian Zhilin 卞之琳
"Blue and White Porcelain" 青花瓷
Blue Stars Poetry Society 藍星詩社
"Bodhisattva" 觀音
"Boer" 波兒
Breathe 呼吸
Bright Summer Day, A 牯嶺街少年殺人事件
"Butterfly-Attracting Flower" 蝶恋花
"By Chance" 偶然

"Candle Fell Asleep in Its Flame, A" 一支蠟燭在自己的光焰裡睡著了
Cao Baohua 曹葆華
Cao Cao 曹操
"Cat That Enters Through the Wall, The" 穿牆貓
Chang Yao 昌耀
Chen Dawei 陳大為
Chen Dongdong 陈东东

Chen Kehua 陳克華
Chen Jingrong 陳敬容
Chen Li 陳黎
Chen Mie 陳滅
Chen Shaohong 陳少紅
Chen Shui-bian 陳水扁
Chen Wenrui 陳文瑞
Chen Yifan 陳懿範
Chen Yingwen 陳膺文
Chen Yuhong 陳育虹
Chen Zhide 陳智德
Cheng Fangwu 成仿吾
Chiang Ching-kuo 蔣經國
Chiang Kai-shek 蔣介石
"Chicken" 雞
"Childhood" 童年
"Children of China" 中国孩子
Child's Heart Poetry Society
　赤子心诗社
"Chinese Acrobatics: A Hard Chair"
　中国杂技：硬椅子
Chuci 楚辭
ci 詞
"City in Flames" 火災的城
"Cloud Ship" 雲舟
Cold Landscape Poetry Society
　冷风景诗社
"Colonel, The" 上校
"Composition" 構成
"Compulsive-Shopping Syndrome"
　強迫性購物症
"Confession" 口供
"Conversation with Tsvetaeva"
　跟茨维塔耶娃的对话
"Crabs I once Loved, The"
　我曾经爱过的螃蟹
"Craft—after Marina Tsvetaeva"
　手艺—和茨维塔耶娃
Creation Society 創造社
Crescent Society 新月社

"Crossing the Square at Dusk"
　傍晚穿过广场
"Cry of Cranes in Bassdorf, The"
　巴茨朵夫的鹤鸣
Cui Jian 崔健
Cultural Revolution, The 文革
"Cypress Forest" 柏林

dagong shige 打工诗歌
Dai Wangshu 戴望舒
"Day Is Nearly Over, The" 白日將盡
"Dayanhe, My Wet-Nurse" 大堰河—
　我的褓姆
"Days When I Hide My Corpse in a Box"
　自我纸盒藏屍的日子
"Dead Water, The" 死水
"Declaration" 宣告
Democratic Progressive Party (DPP)
　民進黨
Deng Xiaoping 邓小平
"Departing with the Crane" 隨鶴走了
"Desolate Candy Store" 荒涼糖果店
Ding Dong 丁当
"Diva" 坤伶
"Dog Barking at the Moon" 吠月的犬
"Doves" 鸽子
"Drama" 剧
"Dream" 夢
"Dreams and Poetry" 夢與詩
Dreams or Dawns 夢或者黎明
"Drifting" 悠悠
Du Fu 杜甫
Du Heng 杜衡
"Dueling with Ruan Ji" 与阮籍对剌
Duo Duo 多多
Duo Yu 朵渔
"Duolun Road" 多伦路

"Earth God and Poetry" 土地公與詩
"Edge of Beauty, The" 美的邊緣

"Edge of the Island, The" 島嶼邊緣

"Eggs under the Red Flag" 红旗下的蛋

Edward Yang 楊德昌

"Eight Poems" 詩八首

"Electric Lock" 電鎖

"elephants of 1966" 1966年的大象

"End the War: An Elegy for the Fallen"
　　止戰之殤

Epoch Poetry Society 創世紀詩社

"Evening of My Life Has Come Too Late,
　　The" 晚年来得太晚了

"Evensong" 晚祷

"Everything Is Under Construction"
　　一切，都还在建设中

Experiments 嘗試集

"Expression" 表达

"Facing the Ocean, Spring Warms Flowers
　　Open" 面朝大海，春暖花开

"Fake Monk" 假行僧

"Family Genealogy VI: Three Generations"
　　家族第六：三代

Fang Qi 方旗

Fang Wenshan 方文山

February 28 Incident 二二八事件

Fei Ming 廢名

Feng Chengzhi 馮承植

Feng Wenbing 馮文炳

Feng Zhi 馮至

"Fiction" 小说

"Field of Fragrant Grass, A" 一片芳草

"First Emperor of the Qin Dynasty"
　　秦始皇帝

"Flying Coffin, The" 飛天棺材

"Four Rhymes of Homesickness"
　　鄉愁四韻

"Fragment" 斷章

"Fragrance" 香氣

"Froth" 泡沫

fu (rhymed prose) 賦

Gao Zhaoliang 高照亮

Genzi 根子

"Ghosts Enter the City, The" 鬼进城

"Gifts from On High" 神賜

"Giraffe" 長頸鹿

"Glass Factory" 玻璃工厂

"Goddess Peak" 神女峰

Gong Peiyu 龚佩瑜

Great Leap Forward 大跃进

Gu Cheng 顾城

Gu Gong 顾工

Gu Long 古龍

Gudianshi 古典詩

Guo Kaizhen 郭開貞

Guo Moruo 郭沫若

Haizi 海子

"Half of Me Hurts" 半个我正在疼痛

Han Dong 韩东

Han Garden 漢園集

Han Yanhui 韓延徽

Hanging Coffin 悬棺

"Have No Doubt" 請莫懷疑

He Furen 何福仁

He Jinrong 何錦榮

He Qifang 何其芳

He Yongfang 何永芳

"Heavenly Dog" 天狗

"His Days Go by the Way Her Years"
　　他度日她的如年

"Homemade Bomb" 土製炸彈

"Homesickness" 鄉愁

Hong Hong 鴻鴻

Hong Liqing 洪麗卿

"Hope" 希望

"Horse in the Rain" 雨中的马

"How Can I Not Miss Her"
　　教我如何不想她

Hu Lanlan 胡兰兰

Hu Shi 胡適

Hu Yaobang 胡耀邦
Hu Yunshang 胡雲裳
Huang Xiang 黃翔
Huang Zheyan 黃哲彥
Human Comedy, The 人間喜劇
"Human Work" 人类的工作
"Humans: Uniformity" 人：千篇一律
Hunter Culture 獵人文化
"Husband-Gazing Rock" 望夫石
"Hymn to Hualian, A" 花蓮讚美詩

"I" 我
"I am ugly, but I am tender"
    我很醜可是我很溫柔
"I Run My Mangled Palm"
    我用我殘損的手掌
"I Sing for Body" 我歌頌肉體
"I Think" 我思想
"Ice" 冰
"If a War Is Raging Far Away"
    如果遠方有戰爭
"Improvised by Xiao Hong's Tomb"
    蕭紅墓畔口占
"In My Village" 在我的村庄
"In Nanyang" 在南洋
"In the Mirror" 镜中
"In the Qin Dynasty" 在清朝
Indigenous Post 原報
"Inside White Paper" 白纸的内部
"Island" 岛

"Jasmine Orange" 七里香
Ji Zha 季札
Ji Xian 紀弦
Jia Zhangke 贾樟柯
Jiang Haicheng 蔣海澄
Jiang Hao 蔣浩
Jiang He 江河
Jiang Shiwei 姜世伟
Jiaya 假牙

Jing Ke 荊軻
Jiushi 舊詩
"Jizi of Yanling Hangs Up His Sword"
    延陵季子掛劍
"Joy" 歡樂
jueju 絕句
"July 19, Composed on the way to Five
    Finger Mountain" 七月十九日赴五指
    山途中作

kuai 块
Kuomintang (KMT) 國民黨

Lan Lan 蓝蓝
"Landscape above Zero Degrees, The"
    零度上的风景
Lang Lang 郎朗
"Last Emperor Li" 李后主
"Last Supper, The" 最後的晚餐
League of Leftwing Writers 中國左翼作
    家聯盟
"Learning: The Beautiful, the Lustful"
    学习：那美和情欲的
Lee Teng-hui 李登輝
"Let the Wind Recite" 讓風朗誦
Li Bai 李白
Li Gedi 李格弟
Li Gongpu 李公樸
Li Guangtian 李廣田
Li Jinfa 李金髮
Li Shangyin 李商隱
Li Shizheng 栗世征
Li Shuliang 李淑良
Li Yu 李煜
Liang Bingjun 梁秉鈞
Liang Qichao 梁啟超
"Liang Shanbo and Zhu Yingtai"
    梁山伯与祝英台
Liao Xianhao 廖咸浩

"Rivers and Mountains" 江山
"Roiling Red Dust" 滾滾紅塵
"Round Jewel Box, The" 圓寶盒
Ruan Ji 阮籍
Ruan Wengzhong 阮翁仲
"Ruined Pier, The" 廢墟碼頭

"Salt" 鹽
"Scenery" 風景
"Sea Melody" 海韻
"Second Farewell to Cambridge" 再別康橋
"Seeing a Friend Off in the Mountains"
　　山中送別
"Self-Portrait" 自画像
"Sent from London" 寄自倫敦
"September, Madrid" 九月，马德里
Seven Sages of the Bamboo Grove
　　竹林七賢
Shang Qin 商禽
Shangguan Ding 上官鼎
"Shanghai Impressions" 上海印象
"She and the Earth" 她和土地
shi 詩
Shijing 詩經
Shisanbai 詩三百
Shi Zhecun 施蟄存
Shu Ting 舒婷
"Sick Ship" 病船
"side of me that is tender, the" 溫柔的部分
"Silent Knowledge" 寂静的知识
"Skies of Taipei, The" 台北的天空
"Slowness of the Past" 从前慢
"Snake" 蛇
"Snow" 雪
"Snow Is Falling on the Land of China"
　　雪落在中國的土地上
"Solo" 独唱
"Song of Everlasting Sorrow" 長恨歌
"Songs of Saigon" 西貢之歌
"Sonnets" 十四行

"sound of falling, the" 坠落的声音
"Source of Loneliness, The" 寂寞所自來
"South of Yangzi, a republic" 江南共和国
"Speed of Flowers Blooming, The"
　　花開的速度
"Spinach" 菠菜
"Spring" 春
"Spring 1985" 1985年春
"Spring of the Logic-Crazed"
　　邏輯病者的春天
"Spring, Ten Haizis" 春天，十个海子
"Stargazing on Haergai" 在哈尔盖仰望
　　星空
"Stranded Humpback Whale" 擱淺的鯨魚
"Strange Tale of Nanjing Street, A"
　　南京街誌異
Strange Tales from the Make-Do Studio
　　聊齋誌異
"Strawberry" 草莓
"Street Corner" 街頭
"Submarine's Lament, The"
　　潛水艇的悲伤
"Such a Man" 斯人
"Summer is still far away" 夏天还很远
"Summoning the Recluse" 招隱士
Sun Pu 孙璞
Sun Weimin 孫維民
Sun Yat-sen 孫逸仙
"Sunflower in the Sun" 阳光下的向日葵
suona 嗩吶
Survivors 幸存者

"Tale (in the meter of *Metamorphosis II* by
　　Philip Glass)" 故事（用韻Philip Glass,
　　Metamorphosis II）
"Tales no. 14: Reset to Zero"
　　本事之拾肆：歸零
Tang Xiaodu 唐晓渡
"Tango for the Jealous" 給嫉妒者的探戈
Tao Yuanming 陶淵明

Xiaoyuan Minge yundong 校園民歌運動
Xie Ye 谢烨
Xin Di 辛笛
Xing Tianzheng 邢天正
Xinhai Revolution 辛亥革命
Xinshi 新詩
Xu Guifang 許桂芳
Xu Huizhi 許悔之
Xu Jingya 徐敬亚
Xu Youji 許有吉
Xu Zhimo 徐志摩

Ya Xian 瘂弦
Yan Hongya 閻鴻亞
Yang Lian 杨炼
Yang Mu 楊牧
Yang Xianqing 楊憲卿
Yang Yuhuan 楊玉環
Yang Ze 楊澤
Ye Mimi 葉覓覓
"Yelü Abaoji" 耶律阿保機
Yesi 也斯
Ying Peian 英培安
Yinni 隱匿
"Young Revolutionary" 革命青年
Yu Dafu 郁達夫
Yu Guangzhong 余光中
Yu Jian 于坚
Yu Luoke 遇罗克
Yuan Shikai 袁世凱
Yuefu 樂府
Yuen Ren Chao 趙元任

Zang Di 臧棣
Zang Li 臧力
Zha Haisheng 查海生
Zha Liangzheng 查良錚
Zhai Yongming 翟永明
Zhang Fenling 張芬齡
Zhang Liang 張良
Zhang Mo 張默
Zhang Shuguang 张曙光
Zhang Yan 張彥
Zhang Zao 张枣
Zhao Chuan 趙傳
Zhao Zhenkai 赵振开
Zheng Chouyu 鄭愁予
Zheng Min 鄭敏
Zheng Wentao 鄭文韜
Zheng Xiaoqiong 郑小琼
Zhong Dingwen 鍾鼎文
Zhong Ming 钟鸣
Zhongguo feng 中國風
Zhou Mengdie 周夢蝶
Zhou Qishu 周起述
Zhou Shuren 周樹人
Zhou Yunpeng 周云鹏
Zhou Zuoren 周作人
Zhu Zhu 朱朱
Zhuang Zhou 莊周
Zilu 子路
Zixia 子夏
Zuo Ci 左慈

Translators

NICK ADMUSSEN is associate professor of Chinese literature and culture at Cornell University. He holds an MFA degree from Washington University in St. Louis and a doctorate in East Asian Studies from Princeton University. He is the author of *Recite and Refuse: Contemporary Chinese Prose Poetry* (2016) and the translator of *Floral Mutter* by Ya Shi (2020).

JOSEPH R. ALLEN (周文龍) is professor emeritus of Chinese literature and cultural studies and founding chair of the Department of Asian Languages and Literatures at the University of Minnesota, Twin Cities. His literary research ranges from early classical lyrics to contemporary poetry and poetics, including *Sea of Dreams: The Selected Writings of Gu Cheng* (2005). Currently, he is working on the history of colonial photography in Taiwan and an annotated translation of the *Shijing* (*Classic of Poetry*, or *Book of Songs*).

SHIU-PANG ALMBERG received her BA degree in English from the University of Hong Kong and her doctorate in Sinology from Stockholm University. She is a prolific translator in three languages: Chinese, English, and Swedish.

WANG AO (王敖) is a poet, scholar, literary critic, and translator who received his BA degree in Chinese from Peking University, his MA degree from Washington University in St. Louis, and his doctorate from Yale University. He is currently associate professor at Wesleyan University.

JOHN BALCOM (陶忘機), professor emeritus at the Middlebury Institute of International Studies, is a prolific translator of poetry, fiction, and nonfiction from Taiwan. His recent publications are *My Village: Selected Poems of Wu Sheng, 1972–2014* (2020) and *The All-Seeing Eye: Collected Poems by Shang Qin* (2021).

STEVE BRADBURY is an artist and writer who translates the work of contemporary Chinese-language poets. His most recent book-length translation, Amang's *Raised by Wolves: Poems and Conversations* (2020), won the 2021 PEN America Poetry Translation Prize.

COLIN BRAMWELL is a poet, performer, and translator from the north of Scotland. He is currently studying for his doctorate at the University of St Andrews.

FEN-LING CHANG (張芬齡) received her BA degree in English from the National Taiwan Normal University and taught in Hualian and Taipei before she retired. She is a literary critic, prose writer, and translator of Chinese and world poetry. Often in collaboration with her husband, the poet Chen Li, she has translated the work of Pablo Neruda (1904–73), Sylvia Plath (1932–63), and Wisława Szymborska (1923–2012), among others.

EUGENE CHEN EOYANG (歐陽楨) (1939–2021) was a renowned scholar in comparative literature and translation studies. He was professor emeritus of humanities at Lingnan University in Hong Kong and professor emeritus of comparative literature and of East Asian languages and cultures at Indiana University, Bloomington.

CLAYTON ESHLEMAN (1935–2021) was an American poet, translator, and editor. Winner of the National Book Award for Translation, a Guggenheim Fellowship, and two Landon Translation prizes from the Academy of American Poets, he was noted in particular for his translations of César Vallejo and for his studies of cave painting and the Paleolithic imagination.

JENNIFER FEELEY (費正華) is the translator of *Not Written Words: Selected Poetry of Xi Xi* (2016), the *White Fox* series by Chen Jiatong (2020, 2021), *Mourning a Breast* by Xi Xi (forthcoming), and *Tongueless* by Lau Yeewa (forthcoming). She is the recipient of the 2017 Lucien Stryk Asian Translation Prize and a 2019 National Endowment for the Arts Literature Translation Fellowship.

ELEANOR GOODMAN (顧愛玲) is the author of the poetry collection *Nine Dragon Island* (2016) and the translator of five books from Chinese, the most recent being *In the Roar of the Machine: Selected Poems by Zheng Xiaoqiong* (2022). She is a Research Associate at the Harvard University Fairbank Center.

LLOYD HAFT (漢樂逸) grew up in the United States but has resided in the Netherlands since 1968. From 1973 to 2004 he taught Chinese language and literature at Leiden University. Since retirement, he has spent increasing time in Taiwan. His publications include *The Chinese Sonnet: Meanings of a Form* (2000) and *Zhou Mengdie: 41 Poems* (2022). He has also published eleven volumes of original poetry, including a Dutch free verse adaptation of the Psalms.

BRIAN HOLTON (霍布恩) translates poetry and prose from modern and classical Chinese into English and Scots. He has published many books of Yang Lian's work, including *Anniversary Snow* (2019), winner of the inaugural Sarah Maguire

Poetry Translation Prize in 2021. His collections of classical poems in Scots include *Staunin Ma Lane* (2016), *Hard Roads and Cauld Hairst Winds: Li Bai and Du Fu in Scots* (2021), and *Aa Cled Wi Clouds She Cam* (2022).

MAY HUANG (黃鴻霙) is a writer and translator from Hong Kong and Taiwan. Her translations of Chinese literature have appeared in *Asymptote, Circumference, The Common, World Literature Today*, and elsewhere. She graduated from the University of Chicago in 2019 and is the recipient of a 2022 PEN/Heim Translation Grant.

LUO HUI (羅輝) received his doctorate from the University of Toronto and now teaches at Victoria University of Wellington in New Zealand. His translations of Chinese poetry have appeared in journals and anthologies in many parts of the world.

CHENXIN JIANG (江晨欣) translates from Chinese, German, and Italian. Recent translations include *Tears of Salt: A Doctor's Story* by Pietro Bartolo and Lidia Tilotta (2018), which was shortlisted for the 2019 Italian Prose in Translation Award, and *The Cowshed: Memories of the Chinese Cultural Revolution* by Ji Xianlin (2016), which won the PEN/Heim Award. She also serves on the board of the American Literary Translators Association.

NICK KALDIS is the author of *The Chinese Prose Poem: A Study of Lu Xun's Wild Grass* (2014) and "Aesthetic Cognition and the Subject of Discourse in Lu Xun's Modern-Style Fiction," in *May Fourth as Methods: New Approaches to Chinese Modernity*, edited by Carlos Yu Kai Lin (2020). He is director of Chinese studies at Binghamton University, New York.

LUCAS KLEIN (柯夏智) is a father, writer, and translator as well as associate professor of Chinese at Arizona State University. With a doctorate from Yale, he is executive editor of the Hsu-Tang Library of Classical Chinese Literature (Oxford), author of *The Organization of Distance* (2018), coeditor of *Chinese Poetry and Translation* (2019), and translator of Mang Ke (2018), Li Shangyin (2018), Duo Duo (2021), and Xi Chuan (2012, 2022).

YANWING LEUNG (梁欣榮), poet and translator, was chair of the Department of Foreign Languages and Literatures and director of the Graduate Institute of Translation at the National Taiwan University before he retired in 2018. He is the chief editor of the *Taipei Chinese PEN Quarterly* and author of *Poems Inspired by* The Rubaiyat (2013) and *The Forgotten* Rubaiyat: *A Verse Interpretation in Chinese*

(2015). He has also translated two books of poems by the Hong Kong poet Xiu Shi, *Lonely as My Moggy* (2016) and *A Book of Depression / Cartea Deprimării* (2021).

DONG LI (李棟) is a multilingual writer who translates from Chinese, English, French, and German. He is the English translator of Zhu Zhu (2018) and Song Lin (2021); the Chinese translator of Forrest Gander (2021, 2022) and Ann Weber (2022); and the German co-translator (with Lea Schneider) of Zang Di (2019). His debut collection of English poetry is *The Orange Tree* (2023).

WEN-CHI LI (利文淇) is a poet, translator, and scholar of Sinophone literature. He received his MSc by research degree in Chinese studies and MSc degree in general and comparative literature from the University of Edinburgh, and his doctorate from the University of Zurich. Currently, he is a postdoctoral fellow at the University of Edinburgh.

YANTING-LEAH LI (連汀) is currently pursuing a doctorate in modern and contemporary Chinese poetry at Cornell University.

ANDREA LINGENFELTER (凌靜怡) is the translator of *The Changing Room: Selected Poetry of Zhai Yongming* (2011), a California Book Award winner; *The Kite Family* by Hon Lai-chu (2015), awarded a National Endowment for the Arts Translation Fellowship; *Farewell My Concubine* (1994) by Lilian Lee; *Candy* (2003) by Mian; and *Ghosts, City, Sea* (2021), a collection of poems by Wang Yin. She teaches literary translation as well as film and fiction of the Asia Pacific at the University of San Francisco.

CHRISTOPHER LUPKE (陸敬思) received his doctorate from Cornell University and is currently professor of Chinese cultural studies at the University of Alberta, where he has served as chair of East Asian Studies. His English translation of *A History of Taiwan Literature* by Ye Shitao (2020) won the MLA Aldo and Jeanne Scaglione Prize for a Translation of a Scholarly Study of Literature. His most recent publication is a coedited volume with Thomas Moran, *Dictionary of Literary Biography: Chinese Poets since 1949* (2021).

DENIS MAIR (梅丹理) is an American poet and translator. His book of poems, *Man Cut in Wood*, was published in 2003. His numerous translations of modern Chinese poetry have appeared in *Frontier Taiwan: An Anthology of Modern Chinese Poetry, Chicago Review, Literary Review, Trafika, Kritya, Melic Review, Poetry Sky, Point No Point, Paper Republic*, and other journals. He holds an MA degree from Ohio State University and has taught Chinese at the University of Pennsylvania and Whitman College.

BONNIE S. MCDOUGALL (杜博妮) is honorary professor at the University of Sydney and professor emerita at the University of Edinburgh. She has written extensively on modern Chinese literature and has translated poetry, fiction, drama, letters, essays, and film scripts by many authors. Recent publications include *Love-Letters and Privacy in Modern China: The Intimate Lives of Lu Xun and Xu Guangping* (2002); *Fictional Authors, Imaginary Audiences: Modern Chinese Literature in the Twentieth Century* (2004); and *Translation Zones in Modern China: Authoritarian Command versus Gift Exchange* (2011).

DAN MURPHY (慕浩然) is the executive director of the Mossavar-Rahmani Center for Business and Government at the Harvard University Kennedy School. He traveled to China in 1999 and experienced Haizi's poetry soon after that first visit.

GEORGE O'CONNELL (乔直), American poet, translator, and professor of creative writing and literature in the United States, China, and Taiwan, served as Fulbright Scholar at Peking University and the National Taiwan University. Among his US honors are the Pablo Neruda Prize for Poetry and two NEA Literature Translation Fellowships. He also received two Hong Kong Arts Development Council awards. With Diana Shi he founded *Pangolin House*, the international journal of Chinese and English-language poetry and art. Their bilingual anthology, *Crossing the Harbor: Ten Contemporary Hong Kong Poets* (2017), was followed by *Passages: Thirteen Contemporary Taiwan Poets* (2022).

MIKE O'CONNOR (1944–2021), a native of the Olympic Peninsula in Washington State, was an award-winning poet, writer, and translator of classical poetry, modern poetry, and fiction from China and Taiwan. Beginning in the 1970s, he engaged in farming and forestry, followed by a journalism career in Asia.

TERESA SHEN (沈鄧可婷) is an editor, writer, and translator based in Hong Kong. She studied English and comparative literature at the University of Hong Kong. Apart from a short time teaching English and working as an English editor, she has held a number of management positions in the chemical and luxury goods industries. For the past decade, she has returned to her first love, writing, and started an affair with ceramics.

DIANA SHI (史春波) translates Chinese-language and contemporary American poetry. With George O'Connell, she edited and translated the 2008 *Atlanta Review* China Issue; *Darkening Mirror: New & Selected Poems* by Wang Jiaxin (2016), a finalist for the American Literary Translators Association Lucien Stryk Prize; *Crossing the Harbor: Ten Contemporary Hong Kong Poets* (2017); and *Passages: Thirteen Contemporary Taiwan Poets* (2022). In 2014 and 2022 she was the co-recipient of US National Endowment for the Arts Literature Fellowships in Translation, and she has also been awarded grants from the Hong Kong Arts Development Council and Taiwan's National Culture and Arts Foundation.

BRIAN SKERRATT (施開揚) is assistant professor at the Graduate Institute of Taiwan Literature and International Cultural Studies at the National Chung Hsing University in Taiwan. He was a Fulbright senior scholar at the National Chengchi University and a postdoctoral researcher at the Institute of Chinese Literature and Philosophy at Academia Sinica. He received his doctorate from Harvard University with a specialization in modern poetry in Chinese. His translations have appeared in *Taiwan Literature: English Translation Series* and the *Taipei Chinese PEN*, among others.

LAWRENCE R. SMITH is a novelist, poet, magazine editor and publisher, and translator from Italian and Chinese. He has taught at the University of California, Berkeley; Eastern Michigan University; University of Rome; University of Hawai'i; California State University, San Bernardino; and Hong Kong University of Science and Technology.

JOSH STENBERG (石峻山) is senior lecturer in Chinese Studies at the University of Sydney. He is the author of *Minority Stages: Sino-Indonesian Performance and Public Display* (2019) and *Liyuanxi—Chinese "Pear Garden Theater"* (2023) as well as the editor of *Irina's Hat: New Short Stories from China* (2013) and *Kunqu Masters on Chinese Theatrical Performance* (2022).

FRANK STEWART is a poet, editor, and translator. His books include *The Poem behind the Poem: Translating Asian Poetry into English* (2004). His Chinese translations have appeared in numerous journals and books, and his honors include the Whiting Writers Award. His fifth book of poetry is *By All Means* (2021). Professor emeritus of English at the University of Hawai'i, he is the founder and editor of *Mānoa: A Pacific Journal of International Writing*.

WEIMIN SUN (孫維民) received his doctorate in English literature from the National Cheng Kung University in Taiwan. He has taught at various colleges for many years and recently retired from the Far East University of Science and Technology in Tainan, Taiwan.

ARTHUR SZE (施家彰) is the author of eleven books of poetry, including *Sight Lines* (2019), winner of the National Book Award, and *The Glass Constellation: New and Collected Poems* (2021). A fellow of the American Academy of Arts and Sciences, he is professor emeritus of creative writing at the Institute of American Indian Arts and was the first Poet Laureate of Santa Fe, New Mexico, where he lives. His translation of classical and modern Chinese poetry has been collected in *The Silk Dragon: Translations from the Chinese* (2001).

RANDY TRUMBULL holds a doctorate in Chinese Literature from Stanford University and an MFA degree in screenwriting from the University of California, Los Angeles. While pursuing his own creative projects, he has partnered with Chinese journalist Yuan Ling to translate Yuan's award-winning work of literary nonfiction, *Silent Children* (2019). Randy and his wife split their time between Michigan and New Mexico.

CHEN-CHEN TSENG (曾珍珍) (1954–2017) was an award-winning translator of Toni Morrison's *The Bluest Eye* and Elizabeth Bishop's poetry. She graduated from the National Taiwan University and went on to receive her doctorate in Comparative Literature from the University of Washington. For years she taught at the National Dong Hwa University in Hualian, before her untimely death.

JON EUGENE VON KOWALLIS (寇志明) studied at Columbia under C. T. Hsia as an undergraduate, at Hawaiʻi under Lo Chin-t'ang for his MA degree, at Beida under Sun Yushi, and at the University of California, Berkeley, under Cyril Birch for his doctorate. Author of *The Lyrical Lu Xun: A Study of His Classical-Style verse* and *The Subtle Revolution: Poets of the "Old Schools" during Late Qing and Early Republican China*, he teaches at the University of New South Wales in Sydney, serves as president of the Australian Society for Asian Humanities, and has been elected Fellow of the Australian Academy of the Humanities.

C. H. WANG, or Ching-hsien Wang (王靖獻) (1940–2020), received his doctorate in comparative literature from the University of California, Berkeley, and for years taught at the University of Washington in Seattle. A scholar of classical

Chinese poetry, from *The Book of Songs* to Tang poetry, he was also a prolific poet, essay writer, translator, and editor under the pen name Yang Mu.

AUSTIN WOERNER has translated the novel *The Invisible Valley* (2018) by Su Wei and two volumes of poetry, *Doubled Shadows: Selected Poetry of Ouyang Jianghe* (2012) and Ouyang Jianghe's book-length poem *Phoenix* (2015). His work has appeared in the *Asian American Literary Review*, *New York Times Magazine*, *Poetry*, and elsewhere. He currently teaches creative writing at Duke Kunshan University in Jiangsu, China.

MICHELLE YEH (奚密) received her BA degree in foreign languages and literatures from the National Taiwan University and her doctorate in comparative literature from the University of Southern California. She has been a visiting professor at Harvard, Columbia, Peking, and Nanjing Universities and is Distinguished Professor of Chinese at the University of California, Davis. She is a scholar, translator, editor, and prose writer whose interests range from classical and modern Chinese poetry to East-West poetics, international avant-garde poetry, and aromatics.

YI ZHENG (鄭怡) is associate professor (reader) of Chinese and comparative literature at the University of New South Wales. Her major publications include *From Burke and Wordsworth to the Modern Sublime in Chinese Literature* (2011), *Contemporary Chinese Print Media: Cultivating Middleclass Taste* (2013), and "1911 in Chengdu: A Novel History," *boundary 2* (2020).

Index

www.ingramcontent.com/pod-product-compliance
Lightning Source LLC
Chambersburg PA
CBHW030900270326
41929CB00008B/503